Serial Killers

True Crime Anthology 2015
Volume II

By True Crime Writers

Katherine Ramsland
Kelly Banaski
Michael Newton
Peter Vronsky
RJ Parker
Sylvia Perrini

Serial Killers

True Crime Anthology 2015
Volume II

By True Crime Writers

Katherine Ramsland
Kelly Banaski
Michael Newton
Peter Vronsky
RJ Parker
Sylvia Perrini

Copyright and Published by
RJ Parker Publishing, Inc.
United States of America

ISBN-13: 978-1500505165
ISBN-10: 1500505161

Contents

Acknowledgements

A special thank you to our beta readers and loyal fans:

Andrea Strickland Carver

Ron Steed

JoAnn Arden M. Brown

Mary Daniels

Kipp Poe Speicher

Lori Smith

Jennifer Thomas

Lori Bennett

Patricia Engebretsen-Lenckus

Cheyenne Cavell

Rita Rean

Robyn MacEachern

Thank you for purchasing the second annual *SERIAL KILLERS TRUE CRIME ANTHOLOGY, 2015 Vol. II*. Please take a moment after reading this book to write a brief review. Your consideration would be much appreciated. Thanks again for your support.

Michael Newton

Sylvia Perrini

RJ Parker

Peter Vronsky

Kelly Banaski

Katherine Ramsland

Introduction

Welcome to the second volume of the annual *Serial Killers True Crime Anthology* collecting the best of true crime writing on serial killers over the year. From the Bible with its accounts of sin and murder and justice and punishment (for what is 'true crime' if not that?), to Shakespeare's plays, to the 19th century British 'penny dreadful' (also known as penny horrible, penny awful, and penny blood) printed on pulp paper and available for just a penny, to cinema, true detective magazines and prime-time television, true crime has always been a staple of our popular culture from then until now. And serial killers, since Jack the Ripper in 1888, have been the 'aristocrat' superstars of true crime accounts, our modern day monsters that universally fascinate and horrify us. In fact, probably our old time beliefs in vampires, werewolves, ogres and ghouls, were the result of real human serial killers, who sometimes perpetrate acts more monstrous than those mythological creatures. For the second year, **Serial Killers True Crime Anthology** brings together an 'A-Team' of the best authors writing on serial homicide.

While there are thousands of published and self-published true crime accounts of crime and murder, serial homicide is the Formula 1 of true crime writing. It takes the best of writing skills to effectively steer a reader through the turns and twists of the narrative complexity of serial homicide investigations and the depths of the twisted psychopathologies of the monsters that perpetrate them.

The best are the best because they are consistent and mastered their craft, and several of these authors who appeared in **Volume 1** of the anthology return this year to Volume 2 with new stories. Newly joining our group of master authors this year, is veteran true crime superstar author and forensic psychologist Katherine Ramsland, who has written 47 books and over a 1,000 articles on serial killers, CSI, vampires, forensic science, mass murder, sex offenders and ghosts.

Joining us also is this year's winner of best up-and-coming true crime writing contest held annually by **RJ Parker Publishing** in its commitment to give a promising new writer on serial murder a break in a very difficult field to break into, by offering an opportunity to showcase their writing in a volume with works by well-known established writers (and be well paid for it too.) This year we introduce Kelly Banaski, whose story was chosen from hundreds of excellent submissions received by RJ Parker Publishing from authors hoping of reaching the kind of readership that the established and well known authors in the anthology get. It's a small way by us all to 'pay it forward' and give a new promising author a chance to grow and find their readership. For those many excellent writers who did not make the cut for this year's anthology, we say, do not give up. Try, and try again. We are inviting submissions for next year's Volume 3 of the *Serial Killers True Crime Anthology*.

This is what we have lined up for you in ***2015 Serial Killers True Crime Anthology Volume 2***:

- Peter Vronsky in the chilling story "Zebra! The *Hunting Humans* 'Ninja' Truck Driver Serial Killer" describes the carnage perpetrated in 2007 by Adam Leroy Lane, a long haul truck driving serial killer who, after repeatedly watching in his truck cab a serial killer DVD movie he was obsessed with, forayed out in the night from interstate highway truck-stops dressed in ninja black to re-enact the movie scenes by killing and mutilating unsuspecting women in their homes until he was captured by a fifteen-year-old girl and her parents when he attempted to kill her as she slept in her bedroom.

- RJ Parker in "Demons" introduces us to the little known story of Canada's serial killer Michael Wayne McGray who murdered men, women and children indiscriminately and whom even prison could not stop from continuing his killing. In the "Grim Sleeper" Parker describes the brutal crimes of Lonnie Franklin, Jr. who over a 23-year killing career, took a fourteen-year hiatus (thus his nickname) before resuming his murders of women in Los Angeles.

- Katherine Ramsland in "The Babysitter" brings us up to date on the still unsolved, horrific 1976 mutilation child murders in Detroit that inspired Bill Connington's one-man Broadway play and Joyce Carol Oates 1995 novella *Zombie*. In "Really! The Other Guy Did It." Ramsland explores the bizarre case of serial killer Douglas Perry who after killing several women underwent a transsexual change into a woman, Donna Perry, who when apprehended, claimed the murders were perpetrated by his former male self who no longer existed. Ramsland asks, "Is guilt in the body or the soul?"

- Michael Newton in "Bad Medicine" and "Angel of Death" describes two serial killers where we least expect them: health care workers. Dr. Harold Shipman, who murdered 250 victims in Britain and might be history's most prolific serial killer, and the smiling mild mannered Ohio medical orderly 'Angel of Death,' Donald Harvey, who confessed to murdering 87 helpless patients, stating, "So I played God."

7

- Sylvia Perrini, Britain's true crime chronicler of female serial killers, revisits the notorious case of Rosemary West who teamed up with her husband Fred in the rape, torture and murder of ten young women in their rooming house, including her own daughter in "The House of Horrors." In "The Mum Who Killed for Kicks," Perrini looks at the recent case of Joanne Dennehy, a mother of a thirteen-year-old who inexplicably went on a thrill kill serial killing spree in which she tortured and murdered three men with a knife and attempted to kill two others.
- Kelly Banaski, a newcomer to true crime writing, brings us "Stripped of his medals and female panties," the strange case of a Canadian air force base commander, a colonel who piloted senior government officials and even the Queen of England, who suddenly began to commit a series of panty fetish burglaries that eventually escalated to horrific rape-torture murders of women.

Enjoy and be horrified!

Chapter 1: The Babysitter
by Katherine Ramsland

Pelting rain on the roof outside fed an edgy mood in the intimate space at 410 W. 42nd Street on Manhattan's Theatre Row. I'd been invited to watch Bill Connington in his one-man, one-act play, "Zombie," which he'd adapted from Joyce Carol Oates's 1995 novella by the same name. She, in turn, had based her work partly from the life and crimes of cannibalistic serial killer, Jeffrey Dahmer. But another series of murders had also inspired her, which layered the Dahmer portrait with something just as creepy. Oates's attempt to capture *this* killer's point of view reveals a mind that remains an enigma to investigators today.

Oates has stated that "the serial killer has come to seem the very emblem of evil" and she's tackled the subject on several occasions. During the 1960s, she penned a short story, "Where Are You Going, Where Have You Been?" based on Charles Schmid, "The Pied Piper of Tucson." A strange character that stuffed his cowboy boots with rags and tin cans, Schmid nevertheless managed to charm three teenage girls into becoming his victims. Oates wrote from the point of view of one of the girls, as the slick killer seduced his way into her house.

A psychological realist, Oates examines those urges toward violence, madness, and self-annihilation that occur during the struggle to become a fully realized self. "I feel that my own place is to dramatize the nightmares of my times," she told me, "and hopefully to show how some individuals find a way out."

The other "nightmare of our time," the one that partially inspired *Zombie*, was the series of mutilation murders of boys and girls in 1976 in the suburbs of Detroit, Michigan, where Oates had briefly resided. Journalists dubbed this man "The Babysitter." It's a twisted tale of suspicion and fear, which still generates leads. Between this series of bizarre assaults and Dahmer's grotesque revelations in 1991, Oates found her dark plot.

"Quentin P" tells the sinister narrative. He's a paroled sex offender who seeks to enslave a beautiful boy. He needs a zombie that will obey his every wish and fulfill his every desire, but each "experiment" ends in failure: The boys all die in some terrible manner, often while raped, but Quentin has little regard for the pain and terror they experience. He discards them to look for the next potential candidate. For Oates, this tale was an extended meditation on the darkest of evils.

When asked what it was like to put herself so deeply into the perspective of such a deranged person as Quentin P., she said, "I was trying to do two things. One was to give voice to a person who operated on the level of instinct, who's led by his fantasies. Quentin has impressions that are almost visceral ideas, but they're not articulated." Yet she also used this character to mirror specific dehumanizing preoccupations of society, "like the lobotomies of the forties and fifties, an experiment that men performed on helpless women. Quentin's experiments are like this. He's part of the culture that does this, but the culture would say he's a monster."

In the play, *Zombie*, Connington delivered an authentic sense of the bland, self-obsessed loner devising his diabolical plans of abuse and torment. "This is a guy," Connington said, "who doesn't realize that other people have thoughts that are separate from him. A lot of the time, he doesn't mean to be mean, he's just totally oblivious."

When Quentin P. fails – kills a boy rather than creating his zombie – you know it: his rage flashes hot, filling the small theater with his driving desire and unfair blame against others. Yet the play's quiet moments are the most disturbing, because in these compressed psychological spaces lie Quentin P's true perversities. The hour-long monologue about child rape and murder is intense, from start to finish. That's what a tale about the serial assault and murder of children should be. But this one, which relies on child-size mannequins as props, is stranger than most.

Which brings me to the actual story. This "nightmare of our time" is much more complicated than anything Oates dreamed up, and because it's unsolved, it's still revisited by locals with an intense desire to identify and analyze the man they called "The Babysitter."

The First Victim

Not many true crime writers have included details about the Oakland County Child Killer (OCCK), a.k.a., "The Babysitter," in their compendiums. One must carefully select items on the internet to learn about it, or look in the archives of newspapers based in or near Detroit. Here and there, you'll find it mentioned, as I did when I interviewed Detective Robert Keppel, who told me that he'd once had a discussion with the lead detective and offered some advice on the case. Yet even he does not have some of the facts right.

Keppel is best known for the central role he played in the investigation in Washington State of murders committed by Ted Bundy. When Bundy finally unloaded a stunning confession to thirty murders across half a dozen states, Keppel was there to record it. Later, Keppel wrote *The River Man*, about his involvement with the Green River serial killer. When Keppel writes a book, he likes to pull in cases from all over to make his points. In *The River Man*, he discusses the Oakland

11

County Child Murders.

It's important to know that, just prior to these incidents, a young man named John Norman Collins had been arrested in 1969 in Ypsilanti, southwest of Detroit. He was tried for the murder of a college coed, Karen Sue Beineman. Although convicted of just her murder, he was suspected in the deaths of six other college-age females in the Ann Arbor-Ypsilanti area from 1967-69. Also, in 1975, a hospital in Ann Arbor, also close to Detroit, harbored a healthcare serial killer who was never identified. Thus, in the general Detroit area, residents had been subjected to these terrifying news stories for several years before the Babysitter snatched his first victim.

To this point, the 1970s seemed to be *the* decade of serial murder. When a homely Boston Strangler mesmerized audiences as a figure of power in a 1968 movie starring Tony Curtis, it set the stage for serial killer celebrity. The early-to-mid 1970s brought us headlining names that still resonate: Ted Bundy, Ed Kemper, the Son of Sam, BTK, Juan Corona, the Candy Man. This decade also spawned focused research on psychopaths, as well as the emergence of an elite FBI unit, the Behavioral Science Unit (later renamed the Behavioral Analysis Unit, or BAU).

Keppel learned about the child murders from Captain Robert Robertson. The first one was Mark Stebbins, who was twelve years old.

He left the American Legion Hall in Ferndale, Michigan, just after noon on a cold day in 1976. It was Sunday, February 15, he was bored, and he wanted to go home to watch a movie on TV. He talked with his mother, Ruth, who was working there, and she watched him walk out the door.

But Mark didn't show up at home. He didn't get to see the movie. He seemed to have vanished somewhere along the

12

three-block stretch between the American Legion Hall at 9 Mile and Livernois Roads and his home. By 10 p.m. that night, Mark's frantic mother had called the police. It had been dark out for hours. She knew that he wouldn't be outside playing. She'd learned that he hadn't stopped off at any of his friends' houses and she couldn't think where else he could be. It was completely unlike him to not show up. She was certain something was wrong. Ferndale, about 12 miles northwest of Detroit, was considered a safe area, but she just knew that something had happened to Mark.

Officers asked for a description. Mark, she said, was four-foot-eight and weighed in around 100 pounds. He'd been dressed that day in blue jeans, a hooded parka, red sweatshirt, and rubber boots. He was blonde and blue-eyed. Please, could they just find him!

A search was launched by car and foot along the route they believed Mark had taken to get home. Then they went down each side street. People were asked if they had seen the boy. By the time morning arrived, everyone believed the worst: Mark had been snatched.

His family agonized throughout the next day, and the next. They called everyone they knew again, just to make sure. Their friends and relatives knew to call if they heard from Mark, but Ruth could not just sit still. She drove around the area, looking for her boy. It seemed impossible that he could have just vanished. Not in the middle of the day, not on a Sunday. Someone would have seen something!

Every moment carried hope for Ruth that she'd spot him, or he'd call, or someone would bring him home. She set a place for him at dinner each evening, praying for a miracle. During the darkest hours of the night, Ruth lay awake, wondering what was happening to her boy. Was he scared? Was he hurt? Was he begging for her? The image of him bound and terrified in some stranger's house haunted her.

Around 11:45 on the morning of February 19, a businessman walked from his office in Southfield, about five and a half miles from Ferndale, to a nearby mall to visit the drugstore. He crossed through a parking lot and spotted a strange object. It looked like a small figure lying down on the ground in a fetal position, but it was far too cold for anyone to be doing such a thing, even in play. He went over to look.

The figure resembled a mannequin. It was dressed in jeans, a red sweatshirt, and blue parka. The hood was pulled up as if to prevent his face from touching the ground. The man thought that one of the store employees must have dropped it out of a truck. But then he realized he was looking at a real boy. The child lay so still it was clear he must be unconscious. Perhaps he was ill. Or dead. The man ran to find a phone to call the police. They arrived and took the small body to the morgue.

It seemed clear that this boy had to be the missing Mark Stebbins. His physical appearance fit Ruth's description and he was wearing the clothing she'd recalled. Hardly able to walk, Ruth went in to see the body and tearfully confirmed that this was her son. So, the worst was now known to be true. Someone had abducted and killed him. Ruth could only hope that the news couldn't get worse.

An autopsy found lacerations on the back of his head, but the cause of death was asphyxiation. Mark had been smothered. From bruises on his wrists, it appeared that he'd been bound in some manner, and this suggested he'd been held captive. His body was fresh, but it was cold out and the freezing temperatures could have preserved it for several days. Time since death was difficult to determine, but the coroner estimated that Mark had been dead about eight hours. Strangely, he appeared to have been bathed and his clothing washed and ironed before he was unceremoniously dumped. This could have been done to remove evidence, but it seemed more meticulous than necessary. This suggested that the offender might have been familiar with Mark and felt ashamed about the treatment, so he'd wanted to at least care for the body.

With grim expectation, the pathologist looked for evidence of sexual assault and found it. Mark had been sodomized with an object. The police knew they would be looking for a pedophile or child pornographer. There was a market for photos like this.

The question was, how long had the body been in the parking lot? Officers went through the mall to ask employees and customers whether they had noticed anything. They found a man who stated that he had walked his dog around 9:30 AM very close to that spot and he hadn't seen anything there. This indicated several things.

First, the person who'd dumped the boy in such a public place at a time when people were out and about was careless, oblivious or supremely confident. Second, this person had kept Mark for over three days. Given the state of his body, it appeared that he'd been alive for at least part of this time. People shuddered when they thought of what this small boy had endured. And they were angry.

Mark's funeral was well attended. Ruth Stebbins knew most, but not all of them. She was aware that Mark's death had touched the entire community. She didn't mind them attending to share her grief. Many cards were received. The police looked through them, just in case the perpetrator had felt remorse and sent a card that might contain a clue as to his identity. They didn't find one.

But then someone who visited the spot where Mark's body had been dumped saw one of the cards handed out at the funeral home. It lay directly on the spot. Chillingly, it seemed that Mark's killer had at least visited the funeral home, if not attended the service. But there was no surveillance tape to assist police with scanning the visitors. If this man hadn't signed in, there was no way to find him. His taunting symbolic message remained as mysterious as his identity.

Another Body

The spring and summer passed with no progress in the investigation. No one had seen Mark get into a car or walk off with someone. Nothing found on his clothing provided clues, although there were some hair strands that he might have picked up anywhere. These were collected for comparisons, should a suspect develop. It was frustrating for all parties involved. The police wanted to solve this case and bring the perpetrator to justice, and Ruth Stebbins wanted to know what had happened to her boy. It was difficult to accept that she couldn't get an answer.

Winter turned bitterly cold and most people stayed inside. On January 2, 1977, Kristine Mihelich went out during the mid-afternoon to visit a 7-Eleven store in the Detroit suburb of Berkley. Hours passed but she did not return home. Her mother called around, but no one had seen her. By 6 PM, a report was filed with the police. There were no Amber Alert mechanisms in place, but by the next day, all area police departments had been alerted to the ten-year-old's disappearance. Photographs of Kristine were distributed. A clerk at the 7-Eleven on Twelve Mile Road recalled a small girl who'd resembled Kristine. She'd purchased a movie magazine, but he hadn't seen her leave, nor had seen anyone with her. As the last person to see her, he was no help.

16

TV and radio stations broadcast an alert for people to call in if they'd seen Kristine in the area. The family raised money among friends and neighbors to pay a ransom, should someone demand it. Tips came in, but none led anywhere. Then a call came in from a young girl, asking for help. She said she was Kristine. Police traced the call and found a prankster: a 14-year-old girl thought it would be fun to pretend to be the missing girl. It was a disheartening moment.

Agonizing days of waiting turned into a week, and then two. Seemingly promising leads dried up. It seemed that Kristine might have been abducted and taken from the area. Then, on January 21, a mailman walked along a dead-end road in Franklin Village. He placed mail in several boxes and then stopped in his tracks. There in plain view, in a snow-filled ditch, was the body of a young girl, face-up with her arms folded over her chest. She wore the same clothes as the missing girl described in the papers. He figured he'd probably found Kristine, and notified the police.

It was Kristine. Her body was partially frozen and the best determination indicated that she'd been lying in this place for about a day, but no longer. The cause of death, as with Mark Stebbins, was asphyxiation; she'd been smothered. There was an indentation from a car's bumper in the snow bank near her body, and someone snapped a photograph. Car manufacturers identified it as the bumper of a Pontiac LeMans or Buick Skylark.

Whether she had been sexually assaulted was a subject of some confusion. The physician who performed the autopsy found no evidence of violation but said he found sperm in the girl's vagina and rectum. Lab technicians at the state police crime lab failed to see any sperm on the slides he sent over. They believed he'd made a mistake. In later years, the accepted version of events indicated no sexual assault.

However, there were clues from Kristine's clothing that suggested she'd been undressed and redressed. Her parents said that she usually tied her blouse in back, but it was now tied in front. One fashion that Kristine hated was pants tucked inside boots, but this was how she was found.

Her clothes were clean, although she'd been away and apparently alive for two weeks. This suggested that her captor had done her laundry. Since she was not thin or haggard, Kristine seemed to have eaten well. There were similarities with the abduction and murder of Mark Stebbins, also from Oakland County, except that Kristine was a girl. Ordinarily, pedophiles have specific gender choices.

Police now wondered if there had been a third victim that they hadn't included. Just two weeks before Kristine's abduction, on December 22, another girl from Oakland County had been killed.

Who's Killing the Children?

Jill Robinson had angry words with her mother, Karol, that evening in their home in Royal Oak. Her mother had asked her to bake some biscuits for dinner and she'd said no. Karol said she was being stubborn and needed to make a contribution to the family or hit the road. She hadn't meant this literally, but Jill decided it was time to go. She made preparations to run away. She put a blanket, clothes and toiletries into a small denim backpack. Somewhat scared to go out into the cold on her own, she was nevertheless too angry to stay. "Get out!" the mother had shouted at her, so she would do just that! She put on her orange jacket and blue cap. Getting on her bicycle, she rode into the night.

Someone saw her on Gardenia Avenue, riding alone. It seemed absurd for a child to be out on a bike on a winter night, but no one stopped her to ask her what she was doing. She got as far as Main Street, where her bike was found the next day, leaning against a tree behind a store. But Jill was gone.

Karol, now repentant, contacted the police. She admitted to the argument, so they dismissed her daughter as a runaway. Kids this age who were angry with their parents took off all the time. They suggested that Karol wait until the end of the week. The girl would be back by Christmas, they believed. What kid wouldn't show up to open gifts?

But Jill didn't come back at the end of the week. She missed Christmas entirely. Her gifts lay unopened under the tree. Her family returned to the police to try to get something done.

But they were too late. On December 26, Jill's body was found on a shoulder along Interstate 75, north of Sixteen Mile Road in Troy, Michigan. This location was fifteen miles from the area where her bike had been abandoned. At the scene, Jill's killer had used a 12-gauge shotgun, aiming it at her face as she lay on the ground and blowing off the top part of her skull. It was high-risk behavior, because the Troy Police Department was nearby. Yet, no one heard it.

Because Jill had been shot, because she was female, and because there was no sign of sexual trauma, detectives had not linked her murder with Mark Stebbins's abduction and death. With the murder of Kristine, they re-examined their position, especially because there was one odd item: Jill's clothing appeared to have been laundered. It also appeared that she'd been bathed recently. From the time that had elapsed between her disappearance and murder, it seemed evident that she'd been kept alive for a while.

Now that they had three child murders in less than a year, with some significant similarities, local law enforcement had to face the possibility that they had a serial killer in their midst with a preference for children. Their victims were 10 – 12 years old, and apparently the gender did not matter to this particular offender. They theorized that perhaps he had tried to smother Jill and had believed her to be dead as he drove her to the dumpsite. When she woke up as he laid her on the ground, she'd struggled so he'd shot her. However, they couldn't tell for sure if this interpretation was correct.

Journalists came up with a moniker: "The Babysitter," due to the apparent care he seemed to take with each child, although police continued to use the more formal label, the Oakland County Child Killer (OCCK). Parents began to watch their children more carefully, clogging school grounds to drop them off and pick them up, and forbidding them from going off alone. Formerly safe areas were now viewed as potential predatory playgrounds.

Task Force

Homicide detectives from several jurisdictions met with county and state officials. They needed a task force. Residents were demanding action. Whoever this person was, they wanted him caught. They weren't about to go through what citizens in Ann Arbor, less than an hour away, had endured during the "Coed Killings" a few years before. How could there be another such monster in the area so soon?

A computer had been used for the Boston Strangler homicides over a decade earlier, so the decision was made to organize leads and suspects via computer for this investigation. They had to find someone who knew about digital technology and could get them access to a mainframe. Desktops and laptops were not yet invented.

Having two victims so close in time gave this task force

a sense of urgency. This perpetrator apparently felt immune, since he'd gotten away with at least three known murders and was dumping his victims where they – and he – could easily be seen.

But he had his own agenda. Despite plenty of news reports about the impressive task force, he grabbed his next opportunity in the middle of March.

Timothy King was a slender, freckled, redheaded eleven-year-old. He'd borrowed some spare change from his sister to buy some candy, then put on his red hockey jacket, and got on his skateboard. It was around 8 PM. He was headed toward a store on Maple Road. He reportedly told his sister to leave the front door ajar so he could get back in, because she was going out soon. (However, who would leave the door standing open during the winter?) He arrived at the Birmingham store, bought the candy, and exited through the back door into a parking lot that the store shared with a grocery chain. Apparently, someone was out there, watching for a kid alone.

When Tim's parents came home an hour later, they found the door open about 18 inches and the house empty. Tim's sister had gone out with friends. His older brother was still out as well. Alarmed, they called around to Tim's friends, but no one had seen him. They drove around the neighborhood. Tim had seemingly vanished. His home was about six miles from where the third victim, Jill, had also disappeared.

When Tim's family reported him missing, police reacted at once. This might be their chance. They wanted to catch this creep before he could murder another child. Aware that the killer generally held on to his victim for a few days, they believed they had some time.

They conducted a house-to-house search and set up

roadblocks. A witness who'd been in the parking lot had some information: around 8:30 PM, she'd seen a boy in a red nylon jacket emblazoned with sports emblems. He'd been talking to a man who'd been standing next to a dark blue compact car that had looked to her like an AMC Gremlin. It bore a white racing stripe on the side door. The man had thick sideburns, bushy hair, and was between 25 and 35. He was a dark-complected Caucasian. She described what she could remember for a police sketch artist.

However, Tim's brother, who'd gone out that night after he got home at 10 PM, said the Gremlin remained parked in that lot while they were searching for Tim. He'd gotten a good look at it and knew that this wasn't the car they were looking for. He told this to police, but said they ignored him. Tim's parents suspected that their son had been taken from their home, since the door had been open. Perhaps his abductor had followed him there.

No other leads turned up and no blue Gremlin surfaced on the roads. The task force began to contact owners of this type of car who lived in the area. But this, in itself, was quite a task.

Tim's mother, Marion King, wrote an open letter to the kidnapper, which appeared in the local paper, *The Detroit News*. She begged this person to please release her son unharmed. She also promised to give Tim his favorite meal when she saw him next: Kentucky Fried Chicken.

Apparently, the Babysitter didn't care about a mother's grief. Six days after Tim had disappeared, his body was found. A couple of adolescents spotted the body in a ditch off Gill Road in Livonia. His skateboard had been placed nearby (some accounts say next to him, others say ten feet away). He wore his red hockey jacket. The body was still warm. The cause of death was determined to be asphyxiation by smothering, but the autopsy also turned up a shocking surprise. In Tim's stomach were the remains of his last meal: fried chicken. One report stated that it bore the spice blend of Kentucky Fried Chicken.

Clearly, it seemed, the babysitter read the newspaper. Apparently, he enjoyed following coverage of the abductions and body discoveries. It was unclear whether giving Tim his favorite meal had been part of his twisted benevolence or a nasty taunt at the cops. Once again, he'd kept the boy alive and captive for a while, as Tim had been killed just six to eight hours before his body was found. He'd been bound at the wrists and had also been bathed. In fact, he'd been thoroughly scrubbed, including under his fingernails. There was also evidence of sexual assault with an object.

Linkage Analysis

Aside from similarities that were evident in the treatment of the victims, other factors indicated that all four had been grabbed, held, and killed by the same perpetrator, whether an individual or a gang. The victims were similar ages and each had been alone when grabbed. Two had been kidnapped during the winter on a Sunday afternoon, the other two on a Wednesday. All had been kept for some period before being killed. Their bodies had been placed in areas where they would be quickly found. Three had been smothered. A few hair strands were found on three of them (some reports state that dog hairs were found on all of them), but the state of analysis at the time could do little with this potential evidence unless they had a suspect for comparison.

In January of 1977, Christopher Busch, Gregory Greene, and Douglas Bennett were arrested. Greene had an extensive rap sheet including serving time in a mental hospital for almost killing a boy during a sexual assault, and Busch had two previous convictions for assaulting boys. They were charged with using physical force to make boys commit sexual acts during pornography sessions. Greene and Bennett were convicted and Greene received a life sentence, while Bennett got a short sentence that allowed for quick parole. Busch was released. Greene claimed that Busch had killed Mark Stebbins, which Busch denied. He did admit that he and Greene had fantasized together about abducting little boys, tying them up, and sexually assaulting them. Both men passed polygraphs. The following year, Busch committed suicide.

It was also important to look at other child murders in the area that might not seem related. It's a myth that serial killers always follow the same pattern. For all they knew, Mark Stebbins was not the first, and Oakland County might not be the only location. John Norman Collins, for example, was suspected in a death out in California, as well as those in the Ann Arbor-Ypsilanti area.

Keppel included three other potential victims in his account, about which Robertson had told him. Two months before Mark Stebbins, Cynthia Cadieux was abducted from Roseville and killed. Her nude body was found a day after she'd disappeared along the roadside in Bloomfield Township. She was 16, and the cause of death was bludgeoning, which had fractured her skull. She'd also been sexually assaulted. Little about this victim resembled the four attributed to the babysitter, aside from geographic area and timeframe.

A fourteen-year-old, Sheila Srock, was babysitting in an affluent neighborhood north of Detroit on January 19, 1976. A man shoveling snow from his roof on a house nearby saw a man assault and sodomize the girl before shooting her. The witness described a thin, white male nearly six feet tall in his late teens or early twenties. He ransacked the home and made off with a revolver, jewelry, and other portable items of value. He looked nothing like the man described by the witness who'd seen Tim King in the parking lot before he vanished. This killer also seemed to be from the neighborhood, as he mingled with the crowd that formed after police arrived before driving off. (Later, Oliver Rhodes Andrews confessed to, and was convicted of the murder of Srock. He'd been a burglar in the area and had grabbed an opportunity.)

Although a third victim, Jane Allen, was only 14, she liked to hitchhike. The only child to be abducted during the summer, Jane was last seen on August 7, 1976. If she was in the series, this reduced the ten months between Mark Stebbins' murder in March and Jill Robinson's in December to five months between Mark and Jane, and five months between Jane and Jill. Jane had left her home in Royal Oak to see her boyfriend in Auburn, Michigan. She arrived, but when she left him, someone grabbed her. Four days later, her body turned up in the Miami River in Ohio. Her hands had been bound with a piece of a white t-shirt. She, too, seemed an unlikely link to the Babysitter.

The FBI got involved. Years later, one of its experts on sex crimes and cults, Kenneth Lanning, said he believed that the girls were not taken by the same offender who took the boys. His experience told him they were looking for at least two, if not three, killers. He seemed not to have considered the possibility of a child pornography ring, which would account for holding the children for several days, keeping them fed and clean, and taking both boys and girls.

A resident of Troy, Doug Wilson, told the FBI that he'd seen Tim King on his skateboard that evening, and he'd been talking to a young man who appeared to be associated with a Pontiac Lemans. Inside this car was an older man. Just over a year later, when John Wayne Gacy was apprehended for his

25

abduction and murder of 33 young men, Wilson said that Gacy resembled the man he'd seen in the car. Gacy had been in Michigan during this time, but boys this young were not his known preference. Nor had he ever grabbed girls. Despite news reports that Gacy used an accomplice to bring him his victims, he actually went out to get them himself.

The task force was disbanded in 1978 without solving the case. However, it would be revisited from time to time, especially when with new developments or technologies to try. Not long ago, there were several intriguing items to pursue.

Suspects

During the course of the investigation and through the successive decades, several people have been identified as possible suspects.

Shortly after Tim King's body was found, a psychiatrist in Detroit who consulted for the task force, Dr. Bruce Danto, received a letter from someone who called himself "Allen." This correspondent claimed that he was a slave in a sadomasochistic relationship with his roommate, Frank, whom he was certain was the Babysitter. Allen had been on several road trips with Frank, looking for boys to rape, although he'd never seen Frank actually kidnap anyone or kill anyone. He said that Frank drove a Gremlin, which he'd recently gotten rid of (no details as to how or where). Apparently, Frank had served in Vietnam and had killed children there, Allen explained, which had greatly disturbed him. Thus, he was punishing wealthy American citizens in "nice" Detroit suburbs for sending him to war.

Allen needed to talk. He was uncertain what to do and was afraid he was losing his mind. He asked Dr. Danto to respond in code, in the Sunday *Free Press*, with the phrase, "weather bureau says trees to bloom in three weeks."

From the remorseful and seemingly suicidal tone of the letter, Danto believed it was genuine, so he followed the instructions, posted a phone number, and made himself available. Allen called him and asked him to persuade the governor to grant him immunity from prosecution in exchange for photographic evidence against Frank. Danto agreed to help and they arranged a meeting at a bar near Palmer Woods, the Pony Cart Bar. However, Allen failed to show up for the designated appointment. Danto never heard from him again, and this seemingly promising lead dried up. For all anyone knew, it had just been a prank. Or, Frank had discovered it and intimidated or killed Allen. Or, Allen just lost his nerve. It would be decades before someone would revisit this angle.

Another suspect, the aforementioned Chris Busch, committed suicide in 1978 by shooting himself in the face. He was the son of Harold Busch, a high level executive at General Motors who lived in Bloomfield Township. Chris had driven a blue Chevy Vega with a white stripe along the side (although it's difficult to believe that a witness would mistake a Vega for a Gremlin, despite their compact size). In Busch's home was an array of possible evidence: a sketch of the head of a screaming boy wearing a parka hood that closely resembled Mark Stebbins, shotgun shells found that might have been linked to Jill Robinson's death scene, ligature ropes, and the fact that his family owned a white Welsh terrier. Some news agencies reported that the ropes bore dried blood, but recent reports in 2012 indicate that this was media hype. No blood, hair strands, or foreign fibers were found on the ropes.

Just after the Stebbins abduction, Busch was arrested for possession of child pornography, and was part of a group of pedophiles who'd been assaulting boys. Among their victims was James Gunnels, who continued to hang out with Busch.

He's now a suspect, too.

Gunnels was involved in a number of property crimes and there is some suspicion that Busch might have used him to lure younger boys. Gunnels was 16 at the time of the OCCK murders. Just three years earlier, "Candyman" Dean Corll had been shot and killed in Houston, Texas, by an adolescent boy he'd used to bring him boys for rape and murder. It wasn't a stretch to believe that Busch and Gunnels had worked together for a similar purpose, with Busch a dominant partner over the weaker Gunnels.

Police did believe that the OCCK was not acting alone. On March 19, while Tim King might still have been alive, a woman who knew that Busch was a sex offender called police to report that she'd seen him with several boys near his family's cottage on Ess Lake. Apparently, the police did not pay attention to this report. Tim King's body was found shortly thereafter.

In 2005, nearly three decades after the murders, Detective Sergeants David Robertson and Garry Gray began going through the files once again. (Robertson's father was the original task force commander, the one who'd spoken with Robert Keppel.) They put out a public appeal for tips. Cold cases, they knew, are often solved by someone remembering something that he or she had never revealed before, or by someone once in a relationship who was no longer afraid to tell what he or she knew. Robertson and Gray were heartened by the capture after 30 years of Dennis Rader, the infamous "BTK Killer" in Kansas. He'd been caught with computer technology and DNA analysis.

By this time, the OCCK files contained nearly 100,000 names and 20,000 tips. They received even more. Gray and

Robertson intended to review each and every interview and each piece of evidence – especially those that might be addressed with new technology.

"The Oakland County Child Killer is one of the most notorious and horrific criminals in the state's history," said Gray. "What we are doing today is not re-opening a cold case, but creating a renewed focus for an ongoing investigation which will continue until the truth is discovered."

In 2007, the focus turned to a man named Ted Lamborgine. A retired autoworker who'd lived in Royal Oak at the time of the murders; he'd been implicated in a child pornography ring. He had pleaded guilty to sexually assaulting young boys in order to avoid a plea deal that required him to take a polygraph. The family of Mark Stebbins filed a wrongful death lawsuit against him. However, Lamborgine has never been charged with Mark's abduction or murder.

In July 2012, news outlets announced a potential DNA link. The FBI DNA Unit at Quantico, VA, had tested some strands of hair picked off the bodies of Mark Stebbins, Kristine Mihelich and Timothy King. Using mitochondrial analysis, they established a link between the boys, because the hair strands on them appeared to have come from the same person.

"This is the first piece of evidence that actually links any of the victims together," said Oakland County Prosecutor Jessica Cooper. "It was always believed that these two killings were linked to the same person. However, that was an assumption based on the similarities in the crime."

Cooper also made a statement at this time that she did not believe that all four murders were linked. She also said that only one of the victims had been thoroughly scrubbed, and it was not with Phisohex, as reported on several websites.

DNA tests indicated that white dog hair found on all four victims was from the same dog, but no dog was identified for matching. The lab also tested hair recovered from a Pontiac Bonneville that had belonged to Archibald Sloan, a person of interest from the 70s who been arrested for sexual assault. Mitochondrial DNA (mtDNA) analysis of Sloan's hair failed to match the hair on the boys and in the car. The only hope was to find someone who might have borrowed the car, and apparently several of Sloan's associates did.

The hairs were also not a match to Busch, Gunnels, Lamborgine, or any other named suspect. However, there was a match between Gunnels and a hair found on Kristine Mihelich. Gunnels protested that he had no knowledge of this girl. The Michigan State Police reports show that Gunnels told inconsistent stories. Yet he said something enigmatic to his sister: "I wasn't there when it happened." He apparently knows *something*. He flunked a polygraph on questions about Kristine. Yet he was not charged, because the DNA link was weak and degraded, and the strand of hair was no longer available for further testing.

In August 2013, news agencies reported an unexpected new lead. Car parts from a white-striped blue AMC Gremlin were recovered during the excavation for new homes in Grand Blanc Township. The area had once been farmland, and it was surmised that the killer, who knew his car had been identified, might have scrapped and buried it. As of this writing, the lead has not yet produced a significant development.

Also in 2013, Tim King's father, Barry, and sister, Cathy, produced a six-hour video, "Decades of Deceit," that outlines the law enforcement failures and missed chances to solve the murder. Barry King explains the leads that he and his team have uncovered. He believes that Christopher Busch is the best suspect and King questions why Busch and Gunnels are no longer a focus of the case. (There was no evidence recovered from the ropes in Busch's home that linked him to

30

any victim.)

What about "Bob"?

An odd figure also emerged in 2005. He uses the generic alias, "Bob," to communicate. He had an acquaintance in 1977 with whom he had several conversations that made him suspicious. He gave an interview in 2010 to Oakland County investigators, describing the places they visited where his friend claimed satanic ceremonies had been performed using children. "Bob" believed that the abductions and murders were related to pagan holidays and Wiccan rituals. He believed that information from the "Allen" letter to Dr. Danto would confirm his suspicions and he asked to be allowed to see it. His request was denied.

Bob told relatives of the victims that he was a member of a crew of eight investigators and said he could identify the perpetrator, but he would not reveal his specific affiliation. He refused to release the results of his investigations, because he did not trust the official law enforcement team.

In 2012, Bob used a cellphone to present his discoveries to a group of Detroit journalists. He reiterated his theory about Wiccan rites that used child sacrifice and said that there were as many as sixteen victims. This was based on a 7-year investigation involving 10,000 hours of his time. He told the Detroit Free Press that at least five people were involved and four are still alive and could be arrested. However, he would not identify a single one. He's awaiting the Justice Department to take up the investigation, because Michigan authorities can't do the job.

Few have taken him seriously, except the family of Kristine Mihelich, who filed a $100 million lawsuit based on information from Bob's report. Kristine's mother admitted that, while she'd spoken on the phone with Bob dozens of times, she'd never met him. Neither had her attorney. Bob has not been heard from since 2012.

The OCCK Case Today

The relatives of the four victims continue to feel frustrated over what they believe are significant leads that have not been given legal weight. Tim King's father has posted quite a lot of documents on the internet, apparently with the hope of persuading someone that Busch and Gunnels should be a top priority. Busch is dead, but Gunnels remains free.

Yet it's difficult to make a case with so little physical and circumstantial evidence. By some reports, there was also fiber evidence from carpeting, but this is class evidence at best, which means it will not pinpoint a specific carpet in a home or car as its source. The best evidence (hair) was used up in testing, so something new would have to emerge, such as DNA from the excavated Gremlin (if indeed a Gremlin was even the right car) or something from one or more of the victims turning up in a suspect's possession. For now, the identity of the Babysitter, or the OCCK, remains unknown.

Chapter 2: Michael Wayne McGray
"Demons"
by RJ Parker

We have been killing for thousands of years—in wars and battles, over personal enmities, in fits of rage and anger, terrorism and whatnot—the act of killing is perhaps one of the most commonly repeated acts throughout the course of history. However, killing somebody because they wanted to banish their own 'demons' is obviously not a good explanation. It borders on insanity and dementia, yet this is how it is for some.

Many serial killers that have been caught and interviewed have stated that the feeling of satisfaction or pleasure that they got from the act of killing was the reason for which they continued killing. Some claim that the fit of anger that it drives them into is what brings them satisfaction. However, despite their horrific actions, there are very few serial killers that actually claim to feel any sort of regret or guilt.

In fact, a large majority of the serial killers that are apprehended and put in prison often have to serve a life term. In some countries, such as Ecuador, a life term primarily entails a period of 20 years, which, as you might expect, is not exactly a fair treatment for taking so many lives. In Canada, a life sentence is 25 years, whether you killed 3 or 33 people.

If you were to read through police history, you would find that that there have been all sorts of killers. There have been those who merely kill for the fun of it. Then there are those who kill and keep the remains as a sort of trophy for their actions. There are those who like to terrorize and torture their victims before killing them. There is virtually no limit to the type of killers that you can find by running a simple search through a police database. There are even such people who first kill and then eat the dead bodies.

Throughout the annals of history, you can read instances of some of the most horrific crimes committed by man. As mentioned, these men have very little to no remorse for what they are doing. If you were to look at their faces, seldom would you find them looking disheveled or worried. These are people who accept their fate and don't consider for a moment that they are doing something wrong. The horrific nature of their actions does not dawn upon them, even after they have been found, captured, and convicted. Almost all serial killers that have been caught throughout the course of history have exhibited sociopathic behavior. These people also try to avoid meeting with others, and moving about in public places. Instead, most of the serial killers search for their prey from the shadows. They seek opportunities where their victims might be found alone before attacking.

The perception that most people have of the people of Canada is that they are peaceful people who love helping others and sharing happiness. And, for most part, they are right. The people of Canada are a joy to be with, or at least, most of them. They'll help strangers and are wiling to go the extra mile for people they care about. They are extremely apologetic if something goes wrong, and try their best to make up for anything as best as they can. Yet, no country can be regarded as a perfect country. There are flaws in each and every one of us, and this case is no different. What you are about to read is the heinous story of a man who single-handedly decided the fate of more than 18 individuals.

This is the story of Michael Wayne McGray, who is regarded as the worst serial killer in the history of Canada, and even when he had been jailed, his killing did not stop.

***

Michael Wayne McGray was born in Collingwood, Ontario. However, he was primarily raised in Argyle, Nova Scotia. Many serial killers often claim that the treatment they received in the early years of their childhood left a profound impact upon them, ultimately driving them to such actions. Michael's childhood was not any different. McGray's father was a longtime alcoholic and would beat his son regularly over very petty things. It was not very long before Michael was shunted from one group home and moved to the next. In the meantime, he also moved between reform schools before eventually settling into a school for boys in Shelbourne, Nova Scotia. In his later trials, Michael stated that he had been sexually and physically abused numerous times in this school. Often times, when he was unable to vent out his anger, Michael stated that he would resort to killing animals and getting into unnecessary fights at his school. According to him, it was like a "hunger." A hunger that would one day grow so big that not even murder could satiate it.

In court documents, he revealed numerous instances where he had been singled out for abuse. McGray stated that once he was walking home from school when four boys jumped him. These boys first harassed him into opening his bag, and when McGray tried to resist, they beat him and tore off his pants. Then he was sexually assaulted. McGray also stated that because of his notorious nature, very few people were actually willing to listen and help him. His anger continued to grow within. At this point, it is worth noting that Michael Wayne was still in his early teenage years. Having nowhere else to channel all the hatred growing inside him, he began killing animals.

In a private interview, Michael later stated that he had gone about killing ducks and other birds that he was able to come across. He'd kill in silence, of course, but stated that with the passage of time, his methods became more elaborate. In the beginning, he would kill only using his bare hands, but when one of the ducks that he was trying to kill managed to escape his grasp and hurt his hand in the process, Michael realized that he needed to use a more effective weapon. It was in the school kitchen that he first came across a chopping knife with a sharpened blade, which he promptly stole. Eager to try out his new prized possession, he ventured out and killed several animals over the course of the next few days.

Soon he grew tired of killing animals. After all, he had become good at it. It wasn't difficult to slit a throat using a knife. Was it time for a bigger challenge now? And that was when he was decided to kill for pleasure.

McGray's murder spree lasted for more than 14 years before he was finally arrested. During that period, he had taken the lives of many people and all through this period, the Royal Canadian Mounted Police could not make heads or tails of what was happening.

His first victim, Elizabeth Gail Tucker, was just 17 years old. One day in 1985, he stumbled across her as she hitchhiked her way to a fishing plant where she had gotten a job. Not even in her wildest dreams could she have imagined that she would end up losing her life in a horrific manner, falling prey to the whims of a monster. Michael began chatting up with Elizabeth as she walked along the road looking for a ride. As soon as he found a secluded spot with her, he kidnapped her and took her away from the roadside. Then, he stabbed her multiple times using his preferred murder tool, the knife, and left the body somewhere along the road to Digby, Nova Scotia.

The body was found a month later.

His desire had been satiated, for now. More importantly, he had not been caught. Nobody could trace the girl's death back to him. He was a free man. This gave him hope and it meant he was ready to try his killing ways again. McGray didn't kill again until 1987, or so it is claimed. His next victim was Mark Gibbons, who had been reported as an alleged accomplice in a major robbery that had taken place in New Brunswick. His body was found mutilated and stabbed multiple times as well.

The exact details of the total murders committed by Michael McGray were not revealed until after he had been caught and confessed. He later stated that he could provide details of 16 different murders that he had committed, in places such as Toronto, Seattle, Vancouver, Calgary, Montreal, and Saint John. All of these murders had remained unsolved as yet.

A common theme existed between all the murders; he mainly targeted people who could not put up much of a fight. Michael also made sure that his victims were killed in places where the chances of capture were minimal. Most of the murders that he carried out were committed in secluded places, after he would lure people away. However, he didn't always stick to this theme. For instance, in 1991, he stabbed to death two gay men. He had also killed an alcoholic in High Park and buried the man there. Later on, in the mid 1990s, Michael also confessed to killing two prostitutes. He also revealed that he had also managed to cross the border into the U.S. and carry out a couple of killings there as well. His terrorizing reign came to an end however, when he killed Joan Hicks and her 11-year-old daughter, Nena.

He claims that he already knew he was going to get caught after the killings. Michael stated that most of the victims that he killed were those who held no connection to him whatsoever. However, after a night of heavy cocaine use, he and another man went out to search for a victim to kill. They couldn't find anybody, and eventually ended up at the doorsteps of the basement where Joan Hicks lived with her daughter. Before the night had ended, both the mother and daughter had been brutally killed. Nena was hung in the closet after being killed, while the mother's body lay bloodied on the floor. Michael knew Joan Hicks through his girlfriend, and the two had met at a local homeless shelter some time before. In an interview later conducted by police, Michael clearly stated that they just "couldn't find anybody on the street."

Soon after the murders of Joan Hicks and Nena, Michael McGray was caught. The accomplice who was with him, (he was not charged), had given up Michael's whereabouts as well as the role that he had played in the murders. It was not long before the Royal Canadian Mounted Police apprehended him on February 29, 1998.

Michael Wayne McGray had finally been apprehended, though his killings were yet to stop.

***

McGray was 34 years old when he was put on trial and charged with four counts of murder, as well as being a suspect in a fifth homicide. RCMP Constable Mark Gallagher also sent out a public request to all divisions to look for missing links in murder cases all across Canada.

A psychiatric report revealed that Michael McGray was suffering from an extreme nervous disorder very similar to Tourette's syndrome. Alan Schelew, the defense lawyer, gave an interview to the New Brunswick Telegraph Journal, stating that Dr. John Bradford, who was the psychiatrist in Ottawa at that time, had believed that Michael suffered from a very rare and a very dangerous disorder that could result in inciting violence. Alan Schelew also went on public record to state that he would not dispute the facts of the murders that his client had committed back in 1998, mainly because of the brutality in which they had been committed.

While in prison, Michael had carried out conversations with other prison inmates and ended up revealing a bit more than he should have. This led to him becoming a suspect in two murders in Montreal, as well as that of a resident of Saint John back in the 1980s. The RCMP spent a significant amount of time opening up case files to determine if Michael was responsible for any other unsolved murders.

However, the police were unable to find definitive evidence that would link the murders to Michael McGray. On Monday, March 20, 2000, McGray was sentenced to life in prison, without the possibility of parole for 25 years. As he pleaded guilty to the murder of Joan Hicks and several other murders, the judge was shocked to hear the grisly details of what had actually transpired. The police described that Michael had "no remorse" over his actions. However, in a later interview, Michael Wayne McGray stated that he would provide details to the police that would resolve all of the 16 murder cases that were opened against him, as well as some others.

Even though Michael Wayne McGray was mainly convicted for the murder of Joan Hicks and her daughter, Nena, he clearly stated in a public interview that he had never hurt a child ever, even though he had killed a lot of adults in his time. However, the charge was stayed until further investigations could be carried out. He also gave the police a number of different statements that led to the resolution of several cases, such as the one in Saint John in 1987, as well as two others in Montreal for which he was accused of. He later stated that he only given those statements as a form of incentive for the police, and that he would not speak further until his demands were met.

His demands included that all the accomplices who were involved with him would not be charged for the murders, he would also not be punished for those murders, and the third condition was that he wanted psychiatric treatment for the 'demons' that lived inside him. Disturbingly, he also stated that if he was given the chance, he would murder anybody he could. He said he could kill a prison guard, a fellow prisoner, or anybody else that came in his sights.

He later stated that he didn't remember the exact details, such as names and dates on when he committed the murders, though he did say that he remembered the details. "Half of the fun lies in the details for me," he said. He also stated that he "really liked" killing. He stated that he was never sexually motivated by the killings and he would often carefully stalk his victims before dealing out the death blow. He also confessed to killing several homeless people in Toronto. Strangely enough, Michael stated that he was actually relieved that he was now behind bars. Many believed that the capture of such a high profile criminal would finally mean that the loss of life would stop. Unfortunately, this was not the case.

After ten years in lock up, in November 2010, Michael McGray struck again. He said he would murder again, and he remained true to his word. On November 21, he killed his cellmate, Jeremy Phillips, who was nearing the end of his six year and nine month sentence for aggravated assault. Now, the question that belies this situation is; how does a man who clearly stated that he would kill again end up with a cellmate? Apparently, it was due to a lack of space. Phillips was 33 years old at the time of his death, and was found dead with wounds to his nose and cheeks, as well as being killed from a ligature made from a cut bed sheet. Almost immediately, McGray, who was 46 years old at the time, confessed to the murder and even refused legal representation. He was charged with another count of first-degree murder, and is serving the remainder of his sentence in a medium-security prison in Quebec. Even so, many believe that there was very little point to moving somebody with McGray's reputation to a medium-security prison. Michael McGray's horrific case was one of the most gruesome cases of serial homicide in the history of Canada and just goes to show the extent to which a person can stoop to fulfill his own desires, or in his case, succumb to his 'demons.'

Chapter 3: Dr. Michael Swango
"The Sweet Smell of Homicide"
by Michael Newton

What makes a serial killer? And why do 10 percent of all serial killers spanning the past century gravitate to medical professions? Is it easy access to weak, helpless victims? The cover provided by seeming efforts to heal? Simply a personal addiction to the sight of blood and suffering? Experts present no final answer, but the case of Dr. Michael Swango lets us track one such killer's evolution from childhood to prison as we search for understanding of the strange and terrible phenomenon.

Joseph Michael Swango was born in Tacoma, Washington, on October 21, 1954, the middle son of three raised by army officer John Virgil Swango and wife Muriel. John's frequent moves from one post to another made life restless, while his rigid code of discipline and heavy drinking guaranteed that Muriel and their three sons were happier during his times away from home.

For reasons never clear, Muriel viewed her son Joseph as the special one, the most gifted of her three offspring. It couldn't have been his early interest in violent death, revealed around age three and carried on as he grew older by his fixation on the Nazi Holocaust. In grade school, he began to fill a scrapbook with newspaper clippings and photos of war crimes, fatal auto wrecks, and other gruesome death scenes. Only in adulthood would he learn that father John kept a similar scrapbook, even larger and more hideous than Joe's.

In 1968 the Swango family settled, finally, in Quincy, Illinois. Young Joseph celebrated by discarding his first name, demanding that teachers and peers call him "Mike." Local public schools were good enough for his brothers, but Muriel feared they would not provide sufficient challenge for her "special" son. To help him, she defied her own Presbyterian upbringing and sent newly minted Michael Swango to Quincy Catholic Boys High School, an institution with a sterling academic reputation, run by the Christian Brothers.

He seemed to prosper there, excelling in his classes and at music, singing beautifully while mastering the clarinet and piano. As a high school underclassman, Swango was welcomed into the Quincy Notre Dame band and toured nationally with the Quincy College Wind Ensemble. In 1972 he graduated with honors as class valedictorian.

For college, Swango chose Millikin University, a private co-ed school in Decatur, Illinois, attending with a full music scholarship. During his first two years at Millikin, he scored high marks and found a girlfriend, but she dumped him in 1974 and Swango's life took a sudden, startling turn. Abandoning his semi-formal dress in class, he switched to military fatigues and slacked off on study, shunned former friends, and quit playing music. His grisly scrapbook collection expanded. That summer, he dropped out of school altogether and joined the Marine Corps.

For a time military life, like college, suited Swango well. He proved himself in boot camp, then trained as a sniper, but America was bailing out of Vietnam and had no other wars to fight, no opportunity for him to make his bones. In 1976, when it was time for would-be lifers like his father to commit themselves, Swango left the corps and went back to school.

His choice, this time, was Quincy University, a private liberal arts Catholic university in the Franciscan tradition, near Swango's home in Illinois. To win admission, Swango lied on his application, dramatizing his military service with false claims that he had earned a Bronze Star and Purple Heart in combat. Once admitted as a premed student, he immersed himself in chemistry and biology classes.

A warning bell sounded in Swango's senior year at Quincy, when he wrote his chemistry thesis on the recent case of Bulgarian dissident author Georgi Markov, assassinated by agents of his homeland's secret police in London, by a covert injection of deadly ricin in September 1978. The Markov murder fascinated Swango and led his dark imagination down new pathways, toward the use of poisons as tidy, silent instruments of death.

Swango graduated from Quincy *summa cum laude*— "with highest honor"—in 1979. Next came med school, where he faced stiff competition as an applicant, but with his documented grades and fudging on the details of his military service, Swango won admission to the Southern Illinois University (SIU) School of Medicine. As at Millikin and Quincy, he was a standout student in his first two years but kept aloof from classmates for the most part, prompting them to look at him askance.

Those classmates were surprised when Swango took a night job with the American Ambulance Service, sacrificing precious study time to rescue victims of car crashes, stabbings, and botched suicides. American Ambulance paid him to get his hands bloody. Swango's scrapbook collection expanded from one book to several, including his personal cases. Life was good.

Swango's third year at SIU required more personal contact with patients and more intensive case studies. Classmates marveled—and whispered—at Swango's ability to keep up with course work while spending most nights on the street. Some suspected him of cutting corners, ethically and academically, but none stepped forward to accuse him. They had fun at his expense, though, when five successive patients died at SIU after Swango's visits. One of his colleagues tagged him "Double-0 Swango," referring to fictional spy James Bond's license to kill, and the nickname stuck.

In fact, Mike Swango didn't seem to mind.

John Swango died in 1982, his "gifted" son's last year at SIU. Despite their distance and the fear John had engendered in his children, they united for his funeral. Afterward, Muriel surprised Michael with a gift: his father's own bulging scrapbook of articles about combat, murders, and natural disasters. Perusing its contents, Swango smiled and said, "I guess Dad wasn't such a bad guy after all." Redoubling his own efforts, Swango purchased Chicago newspapers and scoured them for tales of mayhem. When a classmate questioned his grim hobby, Swango explained, "If I'm ever accused of murder, "this will prove I'm mentally unstable."

As graduation neared, Swango kept the post office busy with applications for internships and residency programs in neurosurgery, his chosen specialty. His SIU mentor and model, Dr. Lyle Wacaser, helped with letters of recommendation, expressing his personal confidence in Swango. Both were delighted by Swango's acceptance to the University of Iowa Hospitals and Clinics in Iowa City.

But first, he had to graduate, and that was problematic.

While polishing résumés and making ambulance runs, Swango had slacked off on study for his final SIU rotation in obstetrics and gynecology, skipped mandatory hospital rounds and surgical demonstrations, and generally seemed to have lost interest. When he ducked meetings with Chief Resident Dr. Kathleen O'Connor, she called American Ambulance to schedule a meeting with Swango off-campus. Again, he turned up missing, but his boss informed O'Connor that the company had restricted Swango's personal contact with patients. Why? The nightshift manager declined to say.

46

Dr. O'Connor finally confronted Swango, handing him a do-or-die makeup assignment, preparing a complete "H&P"—history and physical examination—on an SIU patient scheduled for a Caesarean section. O'Connor watched Swango enter the patient's room and emerge barely 10 minutes later, subsequently turning in an impossibly thorough report. O'Connor shared her findings with administrators and the word came down that Swango would not graduate. His internship in Iowa was history.

Swango fought back, retaining an attorney, while a group of hostile classmates signed a letter to the university proclaiming his incompetence, requesting that he be expelled. Fear of a costly lawsuit led to compromise: Swango would not be graduating with his class in 1982, but if he pulled his act together in the coming year he had a last chance to redeem himself.

Intimidated by the writing on the wall, Swango buckled down and completed his Ob/Gyn rotation without further mishap, while filling the mail with fresh applications for internship and residency programs nationwide. Despite a critical assessment from SIU Dean Moy, highlighting Swango's academic problems and poor attitude, Swango won a yearlong residency in general surgery at Ohio State University Medical Center, followed by a four-year residency in OSU's neurosurgery department. Around the same time his diploma came by mail, in April 1983, American Ambulance fired Swango for telling a heart attack victim to find his own way to a hospital.

**

Life started over at OSU in Columbus, but Double-0 Swango still had the same old problems. On his rotation for transplant surgery, in October and November 1983, the chief surgeon noted Swango's "brusque and indifferent manner with patients," threatening to fail him if his attitude and overall performance did not radically improve. Other interns and residents remarked on Swango's morbid personality and evident distraction from his studies, peppering normal conversations with irrelevant references to Nazi genocide in World War II. If that was odd, though, Swango's record with actual patients proved downright alarming.

Assigned to OSU's Rhodes Hall, Swango suffered a new wave of deaths among relatively healthy patients. One survived a grand mal seizure after Swango's visit, telling staffers that the intern had injected her with "something" moments earlier. Others were less fortunate, and nurses on the wing took note, reporting Swango's appearance in patients' rooms at odd times, followed by "Code Blue" alarms requiring emergency resuscitation. Administrators staged an investigation, but they seemed more intent on silencing complaints than solving the problem.

Despite exoneration, Swango received formal notice of his marginal academic status in early January 1984. Days later, on January 14, he began his one-month rotation in neurosurgery, and five "very questionable" deaths quickly followed. On his first night of duty, 19-year-old Cynthia Ann McGee spiked a 104° fever, and Swango was summoned to draw a blood culture. Thirty minutes later, nurses found her dying with a "pale, dusty bluish look." Swango was on the floor during McGee's Code Blue but failed to answer.

One week later, on January 21, 21-year-old Richard DeLong and 47-year-old Rein Walker died inexplicably on Swango's watch. At 10 a.m. on January 31, long after normal interns' rounds, Swango visited patient Ruth Barrick to "check her IV [intravenous] line." Attending nurse Deborah Kennedy noted the aberrant time, but left Barrick's room on orders from Swango. Twenty minutes later, she found Barrick struggling to breathe, blue-faced, and summoned physicians who managed to save Barrick's life—for the moment.

Swango returned to Barrick's room on February 6. Soon after he left, Nurse Anne Ritchie found Barrick struggling to breathe and sounded a Code Blue. This time, Swango observed as Barrick received mouth-to-mouth resuscitation, muttering, "This is so disgusting." And too late to save her life, as it turned out.

One day later, on February 7, Swango called on 69-year-old former nurse Rena Cooper, recovering well from back surgery. Student nurse Karolyn Beery stepped in to visit Cooper on her rounds and saw Swango injecting something from a syringe into Cooper's IV line. She did not question him, assuming that doctor knew best. Moments later, Beery found Cooper in respiratory arrest and sounded the code in time to save the patient. Groping for a notebook and pencil, Cooper wrote: "Someone gave me some med in my IV and paralyzed all of me, lungs, heart, speech." Later, in a televised interview, Cooper recalled her "tall blonde" would-be killer saying, "When it reaches your other elbow, you'll die."

Male nurse Joe Risley weighed in against Swango, describing how he'd seen Swango emerge from an unoccupied room with the Code Blue on Rena Cooper in progress, furtively rushing to a nearby restroom. Risley watched Swango exit, then entered the lavatory to find a freshly washed syringe, still dripping wet, in the trash. Risley wrapped it in tissue and gave it to Nurse Lily Jordan, the ward's night manager, but it made no difference. Under questioning, Swango denied ever entering Cooper's room on the night of her near-death encounter. Administrators chose to take his word over those of mere nurses and that of the patient herself.

Nonetheless, Assistant Director of Nursing Jan Dickson was on full alert, presenting her suspicions and the written statements from her staff to neurosurgery professor Joseph Goodman. Goodman listened, promised to investigate, and then urged Dickson to keep her nurses focused on their proper duties in the future. As for Dr. Goodman's personal investigation, begun and completed on February 9, he perused the files of seven patients but declined to question any witnesses or examine the suspect syringe. Instead, he conferred with Medical Director Michael Whitcomb and Dr. Michael Tzagournis, Dean of the College of Medicine, before concluding that Swango was "a victim of bad press." At the same time, persons unknown amended Rena Cooper's statement without her knowledge, changing her "tall blonde" male attacker to a "short female."

With Swango back on full duty from two days' probation, the carnage continued. On February 19 internal blood clots killed 72-year-old Charlotte Warner, hours after her attendant physician found her recovering nicely from surgery. The same day, after an examination by Swango, patient Evelyn Pereney hemorrhaged from every bodily orifice, eyes included, baffling the resident physician on call. On February 20, while recuperating from routine intestinal surgery, 22-year-old Anna Mae Popko received an injection from Swango "to increase her blood pressure." Popko's mother objected, but Swango led her from the room, then re-emerged moments later to say, "She's dead now. You can go look at her."

Patients were not alone in suffering from contact with Swango. Once, he brought fried chicken to work for the staff, leaving several residents violently ill. Strangely, although he shared the meal, Swango displayed no symptoms.

Although "exonerated" by hasty investigations, Swango

was running out of time at OSU. In March 1984, a residency review committee notified him that he would not be welcome as a resident physician when his internship ended in June. Furious, he stayed on to complete his tenure, then returned to Quincy in July and applied long-distance for a license to practice medicine in Ohio. The state's medical board reviewed his background, logging serious reservations from OSU Surgery Director Dr. Larry Carey, then granted Swango's license in September 1984.

***

While awaiting that decision, Swango hid his latest troubles from his family in Quincy, claiming that he left OSU due to personality clashes with staffers. He found a summer job with the Adams County Ambulance Company, dodging another background check that missed his dismissal from the American Ambulance Service one year earlier.

Working 24-hour shifts, sharing a suite of rooms with coworkers at Quincy's Blessing Hospital, he soon appalled colleagues with his bizarre scrapbook collection and excitement over televised reports of bloody crimes. In one conversation Swango told another paramedic that he loved practicing medicine because "It gives me an opportunity to come out of the emergency room with a hard-on to tell some parents that their kid has just died."

On another occasion, Swango sketched his ideal ambulance run: "It's like this. Picture a school bus crammed with kids smashing head-on with a trailer truck loaded down with gasoline. We're summoned. We get there in a jiffy just as another gasoline truck rams the bus. Up in flames it goes! Kids are hurled through the air, everywhere, on telephone poles, on the street, especially along an old barbed wire fence along the road. All burning."

Later, while watching a TV program about a notorious serial killer, Swango remarked to coworkers, "Wouldn't that be great? To travel around the country killing people? Just moving on, killing some more—a great style of life."

Despite such episodes, other paramedics trusted Swango on the job and in their private quarters until September 14, 1984, when he showed up with a box of doughnuts to share. Soon after eating them, four coworkers became violently ill and went home. Swango, who abstained, experienced no symptoms. Suspicion festered after Swango described poison as "a good way to kill people," and co-worker Kent Unmisig balked when Swango brought him an open can of soda from the suite's refrigerator. Asked why he had opened it, Swango replied, "Why not?" Against his better judgment, Unmisig began to drink the soda, and was soon stricken with painful stomach cramps.

Frightened now, the other paramedics searched Swango's duffel bag and found a box of arsenic-based ant poison. Laying a trap, the crew prepared a pot of coffee, leaving it untended with Swango present, then returned later and bottled a sample, delivering it to the county coroner for testing. Discovery of toxins in the brew led police to search Swango's apartment, where they found various poisons, books on poisons, syringes, knives and firearms. Their report concludes: "An eerie mini-lab set-up was observed. Detectives found numerous chemicals, suspected poisons and poisonous compounds...Handwritten recipes for poisons...were [also] observed."

Detectives arrested Swango on October 26, 1984, charging him with aggravated battery for poisoning his teammates. Swango waived a jury trial, leaving Judge Dennis Cashman to decide his fate when trial convened on April 22,

1985. Convicted on six counts, he received the maximum sentence of five years' imprisonment on August 23, 1985. Judge Cashman told Swango, "It's clearly obvious to me that every man, woman and child in this community or anywhere else that you might go is in jeopardy as long as you are a free person...You deserve the maximum under the law because there is no excuse for what you have done." Years later, in a TV interview, Cashman opined, "I think he wanted to take them to the edge of death. If he had wanted to kill these people he had plenty enough arsenic to do so."

Always planning ahead, with an eye toward salvaging his sullied reputation, Swango granted a prison interview with reporter John Stossel, from ABC's *20/20* news program, in 1986. Professing innocence on every accusation, he insisted, "I did not do these things. It is simply beyond my—well, beyond the sort of person I am to even think about doing something like that." The public had no reason to fear him when he was released, Swango said, but further journalistic probing at SIU and OSU appeared to tell a different story.

***

With time off for good behavior, Swango won parole on August 21, 1987, still facing one year's probation. With girlfriend Rita Dumas, a believer in his innocence, he moved to Hampton, Virginia, applying for a medical license there. Denied on grounds of his felony record, he worked odd jobs until early 1989, when he secured employment as a job counselor at a state career development center. In May, the center fired Swango for fiddling with his scrapbooks on company time and converting a basement utility room into sleeping quarters without permission.

Swango surfaced next at Newport News, Virginia, in July

1989, concealing his prison record to find work as a lab technician for coal exporter Aticoal Services (now Vanguard Energy). While there, he poisoned at least one co-worker, Jim Sandahl, damaging Sandahl's kidneys and pancreas, inducing full-blown diabetes. Other employees reported symptoms consistent with poisoning, several of them requiring hospital treatment.

On the domestic front, Swango married Rita in July 1989, but soon lost interest in their relationship, moving into a separate bedroom, refusing to pay household bills, and pilfering cash from Rita's bank account. Suspecting adultery, Rita left Swango in January 1991, a year after he legally changed his name to David Jackson Adams. Around the same time Rita left, Swango resigned from Aticoal.

Rita's suspicions had been accurate. Swango had found another lover, nurse Kristin Kinney from Riverside Hospital, whom he met while taking medical refresher courses there. Kristin fell in love and Swango faked it, dismissing rumors that he had been barred from hospital employment by some ancient scandal.

As their affair blossomed, with talk of marriage, Swango applied for residency at Ohio Valley Medical Center in Wheeling, West Virginia. OVMC's Director of Medicine, Dr. Jeffrey Schultz, accepted Swango's claim that he'd been jailed unfairly after a restaurant brawl. Supporting that lie, Swango forged prison documents amending his charges and a letter from Virginia Governor Gerald Baliles, restoring Swango's civil rights. Thankfully, Dr. Schultz double-checked Swango's story with Quincy police and rejected him upon learning the truth.

Another residency application went to the University of South Dakota in Sioux Falls, where Dr. Anthony Salem took the bait. Again, Swango portrayed himself as a hapless "fall guy," this time in a barroom scuffle that left several patrons injured.

His right to practice medicine had been restored, Swango declared, and Dr. Salem scheduled his first staff interview for October 3. It went well, and on March 18, 1992, Swango received his invitation to USD's residency program at Sanford Medical Center, beginning in June.

Swango celebrated by proposing to Kristin. They did not set a date, but moved to Sioux Falls in May and Kristin stepped into a nursing job at Royal C. Johnson Veterans Memorial Hospital. Her parents were skeptical, in light of a prior divorce, but she clearly loved Swango and wanted to bear his children.

Life was good in Sioux Falls, until Swango got cocky in October 1992. He applied to join the American Medical Association, whose background search proved more thorough than Dr. Salem's. The AMA reported Swango's poisoning conviction to USD's Dean, Dr. Robert Talley, and Swango was fired, followed closely by a rerun of his *20/20* segment in November.

The TV story frightened Kristin, but she stayed with Swango until December, when supportive friends threw them a Christmas party. Even there, however, Kristin saw the party's host trailing her fiancé whenever he approached the food or punchbowl. Kristin's stress and grief brought on a round of vicious migraine headaches—which immediately ceased when she left Swango in April 1993, moving back to Virginia.

***

Never one to take defeat in stride, Swango pursued Kristin and won her back with lies, while he began another round of doctored residency applications. Incredibly, New York's State University at Stony Brook accepted him on June 1, 1993, for a residency in psychiatry at the Northport Veterans Administration Medical Center.

Leaving Kristin in Virginia, he reported for work on July 1—and again, his patients started dying. Dominic Buffalino, hospitalized with a mild case of pneumonia, was first, stricken with unexplained paralysis of his heart and other organs on July 2. Next came Aldo Serinei, Thomas Sammarco, George Siano, and Barron Harris, all tagged by Swango with DNR notices: "Do Not Resuscitate."

Kristen Kinney, left behind, began to fall apart, withdrawing from friends and family. Police found her nude on the street one night, nearly incoherent, and dispatched her to a mental ward. Finally, on July 15, she walked to a local park and killed herself with a gunshot to the chest.

The AMA lost track of Swango in New York, but Dean Talley from USD tracked him down in October 1993 and warned his counterpart at Stony Brook, Dr. Jordan Cohen, who promptly showed Swango the door. Taking no chances, Cohen broadcast warnings about Swango nationwide, to 125 medical schools and more than 1,000 teaching hospitals.

Meanwhile, the FBI began investigating Swango, for his crimes at the VA facility. He surfaced next as "Jack Kirk," in Atlanta, working as a chemist at a wastewater treatment plant called Photocircuits, with direct access to water consumed by 1.5 million people. A visit from federal agents cost him that job, and Swango vanished again—this time fleeing all the way to Africa.

Swango began by approaching a group called Options, created to help altruistic American doctors find work overseas. Options accepted his fraudulent credentials at face value— omitting his criminal record, shaving 15 years from Swango's age to make him 27 again—and put him in touch with the Lutheran Church, which operated mission hospitals in several African nations. Dr. Christopher Zshiri was pleased to receive Swango's application at Mnene Lutheran Hospital in

Mberengwa, in November 1994, accepting him on condition that he undergo five months of specialist training in common African diseases.

Swango readily agreed, and he impressed Dr. Zshiri with his performance at Mpilo Hospital in Bulawayo. Dr. Ian Lorimer, at Mpilo, praised Swango for his empathy toward patients and his cool-headed response to medical emergencies. Swango occasionally fumbled relatively simple tasks—removing cysts, attending childbirth—but his supervisors wrote that off to his previous specialization in neurosurgery. A fast learner, Swango returned to Mnene Hospital in May 1995, seeming confident and imminently qualified.

But once again, a change was in the wind. Mnene's nuns and nurses soon complained that he was rude, lazy and careless in his duties, sometimes disappearing for unscheduled holidays and leaving no replacement at the hospital. That news distressed Dr. Zshiri, but he had a larger problem on his hands. Again, as in the past, patients were dying at the hands of "Dr. Mike."

First to pass was Rhoda Mahlamvana, hospitalized for burns suffered in a fire at her home. She was recovering well, looking forward to discharge in a few days, when Swango took over her case and Rhoda's condition swiftly declined. At her death, Swango could offer no coherent explanation.

Others followed. Katazo Shava was chatting with visitors after a routine operation on his leg, when Swango intruded and asked the others to leave. They had barely cleared the room when Shava screamed. Upon returning to the room, they found him in a panic, shouting that Swango had injected him with "something bad" from a syringe. Swango denied it, but Shava died that afternoon, his passing blamed on paralysis due to heart failure. Other victims of "heart failure" at Mnene Lutheran include Phillimon Chipoko, lost in the midst of a foot amputation, and Margaret Zhou, a young woman awaiting routine surgery.

As at his other hospitals, Swango also left surviving victims. Patient Keneas Mzezewa woke one night to the prick of a needle in his arm and saw Dr. Mike retreating, inexplicably waving good-bye. Agonizing pain and nausea soon followed, with the onset of paralysis. Mzezewa had the strength for one scream, which brought nurses running, and they saved his life. When he regained the power of speech, he said of Swango, "That man, he's no good! He tried to kill me!" Swango claimed Mzezewa was hallucinating and denied injecting him with anything, not knowing that a nun had found a hypodermic needle's plastic cap beside the victim's cot.

Expectant mother Virginia Sibanda nearly died in labor at Mnene Lutheran, with Swango in attendance. Moments into the delivery, she cried for help and nurses once again stepped in to save the day, delivering a healthy child and rescuing Sibanda. Later that night, Sibanda told a nun that when the nurses' backs were turned, Swango had pulled a hypodermic from a pocket of his lab coat and injected her with something that induced excruciating pain.

Dr. Zshiri was alarmed and facing pressure from a group of nuns who threatened to alert police if he did not. Another part-time doctor at Mnene Lutheran, Jan Larsson, added his voice to the chorus of complaints against Swango, convinced that Dr. Mike was "playing foul." At last, reluctantly, Zshiri approached Superintendent P. C. Chakarisa of the Zimbabwe Republic Constabulary, detailing the strange events occurring at his hospital. As a result, police obtained a search warrant and raided Swango's cottage on hospital property, seizing a large stash of drugs, poisons, and medical equipment, including syringes filled with toxic liquids.

58

Dr. Zshiri fired Swango on October 13, 1995, giving him a generous week to vacate the hospital's grounds. Instead, Swango hired David Coltart, one of Mberengwa top attorneys, and fought for his job, amazingly securing a settlement of 10,000 rand (about $1,000) for wrongful termination, plus restoration of his suspended license to practice in Zimbabwe. Pending Dr. Zshiri's appeal of that judgment, Swango was permitted to attend patients in Mpilo, where his Zimbabwean odyssey began.

Swango's victory in civil court would not protect him, though, as Superintendent Chakarisa pursued his investigation of five suspicious deaths at Mnene Lutheran and 15 more at Mpilo. Communication with the FBI and other law enforcement agencies in the United States convinced Zimbabwe's Minister of Health and Child Welfare to ban Swango from practice while police filed charges and prepared their case for court. With a preliminary hearing set for late August, Swango wrote to lawyer Coltart, announcing plans to leave town "for a few days."

He never returned, escaping from Zimbabwe through Zambia, fleeing all the way to Europe, where his trail again went cold. At home, the FBI was busy building its own case against Swango, telling Judge Cashman in Illinois that the defendant he once sentenced for aggravated assault was a suspect in 60 murders worldwide.

Barred from America and Sub-Saharan Africa, Swango now set his sights on the Middle East. In March 1997 he applied for a position at the Royal Hospital in Dhahran, in Saudi Arabia's oil-rich Eastern Province, submitting the usual false résumé. Again, he was accepted by administrators blithely unaware of Swango's record, but for some reason, instead of traveling directly to Dhaharan from Europe, he decided on a side trip home to the United States.

It proved to be his last mistake.

**

Stateside, authorities were waiting to receive him. In addition to the FBI, Agent Richard Thomesen of the U.S. Drug Enforcement Administration wanted a word with Swango concerning misuse of controlled substances, and Criminal Investigator Tom Valery from Virginia's Office of the Inspector General was interested in filing murder charges. On June 27, 1997, when Swango landed at Chicago's O'Hare International Airport for a connecting flight to Saudi Arabia, U.S. Immigration officers detained him on a warrant from New York, where he faced trial initially for lying on his application to the Northport Veterans Administration Medical Center.

Swango pled guilty to that charge in March 1998, receiving a 42-month prison term on July 12. His judge ordered that while in custody, Swango should not participate in any activity "that directly or indirectly require the preparation or delivery of food."

On July 11, 2000, less than a week before Swango's scheduled release from a Colorado lockup, federal prosecutors on Long Island, New York, filed fresh charges including three counts of murder committed on government property, one count of assault, three counts of making false statements, one count of defrauding by use of wires, and one count of mail fraud. Should that case fall through, Zimbabwe's Ministry of Justice and Legal Affairs stood ready to extradite Swango on five counts of murder at Mnene Lutheran Hospital. If convicted there, the gallows waited for him.

Formally indicted in New York on July 17, 2000, Swango initially pled not guilty, then considered his prospects for survival in Zimbabwe and changed his mind, pleading guilty as charged before Judge Jacob Mishler on September 6, 2000. At his sentencing hearing, prosecutors read aloud from Swango's personal diary, including his reference to the "sweet, husky, close smell of indoor homicide" and an admission that murder was "the only way I have of reminding myself that I'm still alive."

On October 18, 2000, Swango received three consecutive life sentences from Judge Mishler. Back he went to Colorado, this time caged at Administrative Maximum Facility (ADX) Florence, a federal "supermax" prison in Fremont County. He remains there today, listed as "Michael J. Swango," Inmate No. 08352-424—still playing the system in a small way, with reversal of his first and middle names. Fellow inmates include the leaders of various drug cartels and organized crime families, members of Al-Qaeda, FBI traitor Robert Hanssen, CIA turncoat Harold Nicholson, neo-Nazi cult leader Matthew Hale, and killer escape artist Richard McNair.

Parole from federal prisons was abolished with passage of the 1984 Sentencing Reform Act, condemning Swango to end his days at ADX Florence. That statute renders moot his sentences imposed by other courts: life with parole after 20 years in Ohio, and life without parole in New York State.

In leaving Dr. Mike, we have no final answer as to why he killed. Some medical murderers portray themselves as "angels of mercy," relieving the misery of terminal patients, but few if any Swango victims fell into that category. Others harbor a "hero" complex, inflicting near-fatal trauma in hopes of "saving the day" with emergency treatment, but Swango plainly desired for his victims to die. Forensic psychologist Dr. Jeffrey Smalldon, whose list of serial-killing subjects includes John Wayne Gacy, diagnosed Swango as a narcissist, driven to murder by "a preoccupation with control and manipulation." By any definition, he appears to be a psychopath, devoid of conscience and remorse.

Since being jailed for life, Swango admits that he selected human prey without regard to age, gender, or race. Any patients in his path were fair game. Likewise, he chose his poisons for convenience and availability. In New York, he injected victims with epinephrine (used therapeutically to treat allergic reactions and cardiac arrest) and succinylcholine (used to induce muscle relaxation and short-term paralysis). In Ohio he killed at least one patient with potassium, a substance naturally released—and thus concealed from forensic pathologists—by the cells of a dying body. For coworkers and "loved ones," he was often satisfied with arsenic derived from common pesticides.

Whatever Swango's final psychiatric diagnosis, he was deadly and would certainly have gone on killing for as long as he remained at liberty. More terrifying than the random nature of his crimes is one more fact: within the field of modern medicine, Swango is not alone.

Chapter 4: David Russell Williams - Colonel (Revoked)

"Stripped of His Medals and Female Panties"
by Kelly Banaski

Some of the most notorious serial killers hide out in plain sight. These sadistic and perfidious animals, like Dennis Rader and Gary Ridgway are not social misfits, but can blend in and hold significant positions in the community.

When a news headline features an upstanding citizen who at night transforms into a deranged killer, the community is shocked. Perhaps even more importantly, how did his family and co-workers not suspect anything?

In the following case, not only was the community shocked, but the country of Canada, the military, government and even the royal family. Why? Because this man was one of the highest-ranking officers in the Canadian Air Force. How can a high-ranking trusted soldier and officer be a serial rapist and serial killer?

***

David Russell Williams had a largely unremarkable childhood. He was born in England in March of 1963 to Cedric David Williams and Christine Nonie Williams. The family moved to Chalk River, Ontario, Canada shortly after his birth. His parents divorced in his sixth year and his mother married a family friend, Dr. Jerry Sovka. Russell (or Russ as he was known at the time) soon took on Sovka's surname. Early photos show a smiling and happy Russ throughout childhood, despite his parent's divorce. No accounts exist of remarkable traumatic incidents, which would have possibly led to a scarred and disrupted psyche. By all accounts Williams was a pleasant child, if a bit peculiar.

In 1978, Russ Sovka began high school at Toronto's Birchmount Collegiate. His mother and stepfather traveled to South Korea to attend to his stepfather's work. Due to his parents' frequent travel, young Russ was required to finish high school as a boarding student at the prestigious Upper Canada College where he was elected prefect for his boarding house in 1982, his final year. His friends and instructors have regaled newspaper reporters with tales of his practical jokes and wily wit, including a retelling of an incident in which Russ filled his supervisor's office with reams upon reams of crumpled paper, reaching the ceiling and tumbling from the open door.

After finishing high school, Russ Sovka enrolled in the University of Toronto, where he ultimately graduated with degrees in economics and political science. He broke the mold of the typical college kid. He was both a nerd and a social butterfly. He made exemplary grades and excelled in everything he did, but that included his social life. He had many friends and was well liked. While in college, he began his career as a pilot after taking lessons at Toronto's Buttonville Airport. It was also during this time that, for reasons unknown, Russ Sovka resumed use of the surname Williams. Perhaps it signified his coming into his own as a man.

The female staffers at The University of Toronto took a shine to the strawberry blonde, part-time hire Russ Williams. He is described as having been pleasant, polite and easy to be around. In 1987, he joined the Canadian Forces and in 1990 he was awarded his flying wings. Soon after, he was dispatched to 3 Canadian Forces Flying Training School, based at Canadian Forces Base Portage La Prairie, Manitoba, where he spent the following two years serving as a flight instructor.

Williams excelled in the military just as he had in high school and only a year after receiving his wings he was promoted to Captain in 1991, the same year he married Mary Elizabeth Harriman. By all accounts, Russell and Mary had a happy marriage. They didn't fight in public (or private from their accounts). They were seen out together often, always smiling and happy. The two were avid outdoorsmen and particularly good at golf. Russell enjoyed running, photography and fishing as well. To the world, they were a happily married couple. To Mary Elizabeth, they were a happily married couple. Perhaps to Russell they were too.

Williams's admirable reputation grew with each successful mission as he flew the CC-144 Challenger in electronic warfare and coastal patrol. He mentored younger cadets and was known for treating everyone with respect. He became known as a model military official and the status followed him throughout his 23-year career in the military. He transferred to the 412 Transport Squadron in Ottawa in 1994 and was trusted to fly foreign dignitaries and government VIP's. By 1999, he was promoted to Major and was transferred to Director General Military Careers in Ottawa where he began a new position: multi-engine pilot career manager.

In 2004, Williams obtained a Master of Defense Studies from the Royal Military College of Canada. He exhibited leadership and drive in everything he pursued and his fifty-five page thesis supporting proactive, anticipatory war strikes in Iraq ensured his promotion to Lieutenant Colonel in July of the same year. He quickly became Commanding Officer of 437 Transport Squadron at Canadian Forces Base Trenton, Ontario and remained at that post for the next two years.

Williams was a rising military star who seemed only to continue in his successes. Not only was his opinion sought after and greatly respected, he was highly trusted by his superiors. In 2006, he became the Commanding Officer of Camp Mirage, which is believed to be a secretive logistics facility located at Al Minhad Air Base in Dubai, United Arab Emirates. Camp Mirage is said to provide support to Canadian Forces operations in Afghanistan. He was the man on the inside, a secret agent man. He had an ideal life.

Russell and Mary moved to a suburb of Ottawa, Orléans in 2006, shortly after Russell became the Directorate of Air Requirements at National Defence Headquarters. In 2009, he was made Wing Commander at the biggest and busiest air base. In all respects and by anyone's measurement, he was at the top of his game. Unbeknownst to those who revered him, however, a monster lurked beneath his trustworthy, respectful facade.

***

That's when the real evil began to emerge. Between 2007 and 2010, Russell Williams began a downward spiral into a depraved lifestyle. Beginning with voyeurism, stalking, fetish burglaries and vile pornographic pictures, Williams's crimes grew in barbarity to sexual assault, rape and finally murder, all to satisfy a growing disease of perversion inside him. He catalogued and documented his deeds and kept a collection of photos showing his bizarre actions in an amassment of journals, computer files and memorabilia.

Williams would watch neighborhood women undress through the windows at night, often nude himself. This voyeurism became criminal when he began breaking into these women's homes while they were away and stealing their panties, sex toys and personal items. Often, he would leave chilling messages for his victims. Williams had pedophilic tendencies and many of his early victims were little girls. He stole the panties of girls as young as nine years of age.

Williams photographed himself lying in a pink ruffled bed surrounded by stuffed animals, masturbating in a little girl's panties. A 2008 photo depicts him spraying semen across a 15-year-old girl's dressing table and touching her makeup brush to his penis, which he left at the scene. The word *"merci"* was found on the computer screen of a 12-year-old girl, whose panties he had ejaculated into. He enjoyed not only committing the acts themselves, but also reminiscing about them later. He took great pleasure in the fact that his victims knew he had been there, and that he had invaded their privacy and their sense of safety. He kept newspaper clippings, which headlined his acts and listened intently at neighborhood lunch counters to hear the exchanges of his frightened neighbors.

Perhaps Williams's military training also offered a framework for his systematic methods when committing and documenting his crimes. His good side and bad side mixing together in a sick abusive marriage. He photographed his crimes in the same manner every time, with the same precision and chronology. The first photos would be of the young woman's undisturbed bedroom, how she had left it. Next were photographs of the underwear in the drawer neatly folded and then spread skillfully upon the bed. Thirdly, Williams would photograph himself wearing the panties, bras and undergarments, each time with his back turned and gazing back at the camera, followed by a front facing photo. Finally, photos were taken of him masturbating with the undergarments. Williams amassed hundreds of these photographs, which he hid in hard drives in his ceiling and in deeply hidden folders on his computer. He kept thousands of pairs of underwear. So many that, periodically, he would take them into a field near his home and burn them. Hundreds were found in his home at the time of his arrest.

Williams broke into many of these neighbors' homes repeatedly, five to nine times. He was never caught in the act, and at times he left the home completely undetected, most commonly in the early years of his debauchery. He became very adept at erasing all evidence of his presence, only leaving what he wanted his victims to find. Anne Marson-Cook, a repeated victim of Williams, found the words, "Go ahead, call the police. I want to tell the judge about your really big dildos," displayed on her computer screen. Angela McCanny, whose Ottawa home was broken into several nights consecutively, reported every pair of women's panties in the house stolen. Nothing else was disturbed.

Williams would photograph his victims' belongings, such as pictures of family and friends, books and documents. He photographed dressing tables and objects such as hairbrushes and papers lying about. These pictures served as a link for Williams to connect the victims with his crimes. Ultimately, Williams was charged with 82 counts of breaking and entering into 47 homes in Tweed and Ottawa.

Eventually, the break-ins and masturbation weren't enough to satisfy Williams. His statements to police revealed his growing need to take more chances and bigger risks. The salaciousness which had overcome him was growing and he was powerless, or unwilling, to stop it.

In September of 2009, Williams did intensify the risk of his crime. He broke into the home of a young woman while she and her newborn baby slept. He beat and raped her for two hours, taking photos during the act. Williams committed a similar crime in the Ottawa area. He broke into a woman's home and beat her, raping her and taking photos throughout the several hour horrific ordeal, which resulted in two charges of sexual assault and forcible confinement.

He'd had a taste of the thrill that he experienced when

sexually abusing women, but now Williams wanted more. He was insatiable. The evil desire within him had grown more powerful than the respectable military man could control. He needed more thrill, and more risk.

***

The first murder with which Williams was charged was that of Corporal Marie France Comeau. Williams first met Comeau as a Commander on a military flight. Using his administrative access to her personal information, he obtained her address and broke into her home. Court transcripts state that he parked approximately 600 meters from her home and snuck around to a basement window to gain access.

Corporal Comeau was on a trip at the time of this first break-in, and Williams took his time in her home. He spent over an hour in the house, making sure she lived alone, modeling her underwear and playing with her sex toys, taking over eighteen photos in his meticulous pattern. Upon returning home, the Corporal noticed that her underwear had been disturbed but blamed her boyfriend, who denied the allegations according to later statements to police.

Corporal Comeau's death was like a true-life horror movie. Between 10:30 and 11:30 p.m. on November 25, 2009, Williams entered Comeau's house through the same basement window and tucked himself behind the furnace to wait for her to retire. He waited 30 to 40 minutes in silence with a mask covering his face. However, instead of going to bed, Comeau began to look for her cat, which sat at Williams's feet, staring up at him.

Comeau noticed Williams and ran for the stairs. Williams caught her and smashed a flashlight into her face and head several times, subduing her and securing her wrists to a post. Photo evidence of marks Comeau made when secured to the post was admitted in trial. He then went upstairs and prepared the house for the savage rape and assault, covering the windows and removing lights.

Williams recorded the assault and murder of Corporal Comeau on video. In the tape, she repeatedly begged for her life. At one point during the assault, Williams left Comeau for a moment to check a window. Comeau took the opportunity to attempt escape, but was caught and severely beaten. Throughout the many rapes and assaults, she repeatedly asked him to let her go and to please have a heart, promising not to tell anyone about the assault. Even in her final moments, duct taped and naked, Williams's hands pressing a pillow case against her face, Comeau broke free one final time, screaming that she didn't want to die, didn't deserve to die, refusing to give up.

After Williams had ensured that Comeau had taken her last breath, he spent the next hour taking photographs of her body, and of himself, as he cleaned up the crime scene and washed the sheets with bleach. He placed her lifeless body on the bed, covered it with a blanket and made his exit through the back door, leaving it unlocked. Comeau's body was later discovered by her boyfriend, who went searching for her when she did not show up for a dinner date.

Twenty-seven-year-old Jessica Lloyd vanished on January 28, 2010. An administrator of a school bus line at Tri-Board Student Transportation Services, co-workers became concerned when Lloyd did not report to work. Because this was uncharacteristic behavior, Lloyd's family was contacted. Upon arrival at Lloyd's empty house, family members found her car in the driveway; beside it was her purse containing her ID, glasses and wallet. There was no sign of Jessica Lloyd; she

70

would remain missing until February 8, 2010.

Williams had first spotted Lloyd as he jogged in his neighborhood. He watched her home until he ascertained that she lived alone, and then broke in while she slept. Binding her with duct tape at the wrists and ankles, he repeatedly raped and assaulted her in her home before driving her to his Cosy Cove Lane cottage. Williams continued to beat and assault Lloyd at the cottage, at times pausing to take photographs. The photos show her modeling lingerie and in stages of undress.

Williams recorded a video of Jessica Lloyd's murder as he had done with the murder of Comeau. One scene depicts Jessica, naked and shivering in the shower, begging for clothes and to be taken to the hospital. She warns Williams she might die because of her injuries, to which he responds, "Hang in there, baby. Hang in there."

The ordeal lasted hours. Williams fed Lloyd bits of fruit to sustain her through the abuse and taunted her when she asked that he tell her mother she loved her. Eventually, as with Corporal Comeau, Williams used a flashlight to hit Lloyd in the head from behind, before pouncing and strangling the life from her. He hid her corpse in his garage before disposing of it on a roadside not far from his cottage.

The police began to search for Jessica and an investigation was opened. Jessica's car and personal belongings had been in her driveway, intact if disheveled, which led investigators to believe she was taken against her will. Evidence was collected from various tire impressions in and near the driveway. One set in particular was unusual for the area. Canvassing every motorist who used the roads near her home in the days she was thought to disappear, police eventually encountered Russell Williams, whose tire treads matched the unusual pair from the crime scene.

***

Russell Williams epitomized the anomaly of duplicity. Serving as Commander of Canada's largest air force base, Canadian Forces Base Trenton, Williams concealed his identity as a serial murderer and rapist of particular sexual deviance. He regularly conferred with senior politicians and was quoted publicly and often about issues in Afghanistan. He piloted visiting dignitaries, such as Queen Elizabeth II and Prince Phillip, in his role as a decorated military pilot. His career as an esteemed pilot was abruptly halted, however, when in 2010 he was arrested for the murders of two women. Charges brought against Williams included forcible confinement, sexual assault and 82 counts of breaking and entering during which he stole women's undergarments and wore them himself.

On February 7, 2010, Russell Williams was asked to come in for questioning by the Ontario Provincial Police. Police confronted him with the tire track evidence and Williams eventually confessed. In a ten-hour videotaped confession, Williams explained his crimes and described how each had fueled his desire to commit more, sicker crimes. He detailed each break-in, assault, rape and murder. When pressed for a motive, he replied that he did not know the answers and was pretty sure they didn't matter. At the conclusion of his confession, he signed a written copy and then wrote a long apology letter to his wife, asking her to take care of their cat. He claimed to have confessed solely for her, to make things easier. In the early morning hours of February 8, Russell Williams directed police to the remains of Jessica Lloyd, on a rural road near his cottage home in Tweed.

A search of Williams's homes found profuse quantities of evidence to document his confession. Over 500 pieces of underwear were retrieved from his home, 87 of which belonged to one particular little girl. Thousands of photographs were retrieved as well as several video clips.

For each of the murdered women, Williams was charged with two counts of first-degree murder, two counts of forcible confinement, two counts of breaking and entering and sexual assault. Another 82 charges relating to breaking and entering were subsequently added. He was relieved of his military duties as base Commander at CFB Trenton. He pleaded guilty on October 18, 2010.

Horrific photos and videos were shown to members of the jury, many of whom cried. Several spectators left the courtroom. During most of the trial, Williams sat demurely, seeming to display shame and embarrassment; only looking up when photographs of him in his victim's underwear were shown. He made a tearful statement to the judge and to the victims' families expressing deep regret and shame. He acknowledged the pain he had caused his victims and their families, and concluded by also acknowledging his betrayal of his own family, the community and the military. Could it be he genuinely regrets his actions? How far could his good side stretch? Is it possible he has feelings, emotions? Ontario Justice Robert F. Scott expressed belief in Williams's regret and tearful statement to the court but also called him "sick and dangerous." He told the courtroom there has been no equal to the depths of William's depravity as he sentenced him. His normal façade could take him only so far.

For the first-degree murders of Cpl. Marie-France Comeau and Jessica Lloyd, Williams was sentenced to two life terms without possibility of parole until 25 years had been served. In addition, he received 10 years' prison time for each of the two charges of sexual assault and the charges of forcible confinement. He was sentenced to one year each for the 82 breaking and entering charges.

All of Williams's belongings associated with the crimes were burned, including the Toyota he had used to dispose of Jessica Lloyd's body. His military uniforms and belongings were burned as well. He was stripped of his commission and all military benefits.

Williams was remanded to Kingston Penitentiary in Ontario, and before long attempted suicide, as hundreds of inmates at Kingston have done. The attempt was unsuccessful, and he has since become more accustomed to prison life.

Though Williams is safely locked away from the public, his story still haunts public consciousness. The terrifying paradox of upstanding citizen beside deranged killer is made more horrifying when one realizes that this criminal could be anyone. The crimes of Russell Williams leave one with the nagging reminder that not everyone—whether neighbor, coworker or friend—may be who they seem.

David Russell Williams

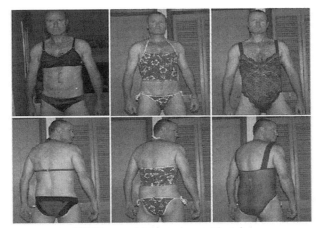

Williams (the perverted side)

Jessica Lloyd (L) and Corporal Marie-France Comeau (R)

Chapter 5: Joanne Dennehy

"The Mum Who Killed for Kicks"
by Sylvia Perrini

Joanne Dennehy was a sweet faced, angelic child who was born in August of 1982 in St Albans, Hertfordshire, U.K. to Kevin and Kathleen Dennehy. She had a secure middle class upbringing in Harpenden, Hertfordshire and was doted upon by her parents. When she was two years old, she was joined by a younger sister: Maria. As children, the two girls were very close.

At age eleven, Joanne became a pupil at Roundwood Park School in Harpenden. She was considered a bright academic pupil and was expected to go to university. As a child, she loved to read and held ambitions to become a lawyer. She played on the school's netball and hockey teams and was also a keen flute player.

Things began to go wrong in Joanne's early teens when, according to her parents, she got involved with older kids and began drinking and smoking cannabis, frequently turning up at school inebriated. She began to skip school and run away from home, only to be brought back by her parents. At the age of 14 or 15, she met John Treanor, who was five years older than she. Her parents strongly disapproved of the relationship and tried to put a stop to it. This resulted in Joanne running away with John. Her parents found her and again brought her home, forbidding her to have any further contact with John. However, in 1998, at the age of 16, she left home for good and set up house with John in the nearby town of Luton, Bedfordshire. Here, Joanne, aged just 17, gave birth to their first daughter. She informed her parents that if they wished to see their grandchild they would have to pay. It was then that she became permanently estranged from her parents.

John, who was a tee-totaller, was delighted with the birth of his daughter, but Joanne regarded her as an intrusion in their lives and left most of the day-to-day care of the baby to John. He was later to say that this was the start of her decline into heavy drinking, hard drugs, violence, and casual sex with both women and men.

In 2001, the couple moved to Milton Keynes. By this time, Joanne's drinking was beginning to escalate, and the couple would frequently fight. Joanne would often disappear from home for days on end and then return to John and, using all of her charm and feminine wiles, would beg for forgiveness. John always relented and let her back into the home, as he strongly believed that a child needed a mother.

John and Joanne stayed in Milton Keynes for nearly four years. In 2003, during one of Joanne's disappearances, John, in a fit of frustration, moved with his young daughter to the quiet market town of Wisbech, Cambridgeshire, where he rented a bungalow. Joanne tracked them down and once again persuaded John to take her back. For a while, she managed to cut down on her drinking and drug taking, and in 2006 Joanne gave birth to their second daughter.

This event caused her to again start drinking and taking drugs heavily. She also began to self-harm, cutting her body, arms, and neck with knives and razor blades. Under her right eye she etched, by herself, a green tattoo of a star. She became increasingly violent and would kick and punch John when she was drunk.

Joanna Dennehy (Cambridgeshire Police)

Neighbors, who were fond of John, finding him nice and polite, would frequently see Joanne drunk whilst with her daughters. She once shaved her eldest daughter's head completely telling neighbors that it was because her daughter had head lice, but the neighbors were skeptical.

Another neighbor later told of how she had seen Joanne arguing with John in their back garden and how Joanne had picked up a cricket bat and begun battering John with it as he desperately tried to shield himself. Neighbors said they frequently saw John with marks on his face and black eyes.

Joanne resorted to her former behavior of disappearing for days or weeks on end and never telling John where she was. When she returned home, she was inevitably in a drugged or alcoholic state.

Whilst Joanne's decline into drug and alcoholic abuse escalated, her younger sister, Maria, was in Afghanistan serving with British troops. When Maria returned from duty, she tracked Joanne down to her home in Cambridgeshire. Maria had not seen Joanne, her beloved elder sister, for seven years, and with all her fond memories of their childhood, wanted to make contact with her. Maria was appalled at the state of her sister, who made it clear to her that unless she had money to give her she wanted nothing to do with her.

Joanne's behaviour became more and more extreme,

and she would often arrive at her eldest daughter's school paralytically drunk.

The final straw for John happened in early 2009, when Joanne suddenly produced a six-inch dagger with a decorated handle from inside her knee-length black boot. Gripping it tightly, with cold and blank eyes, she thrust it into the carpet by his feet and said she felt like killing someone.

John felt terrified for himself and his daughters and realised he had to get himself and the children as far away from her as possible. At this point, Joanne was drinking up to two liters of vodka a day. Later that day, John left the house with the children and went to stay with his mother in Glossop, Derbyshire.

After John left, Joanne's behavior deteriorated further, and she would often find herself in trouble with the police. She remained in East Anglia and moved from place to place, frequently stealing and resorting on occasions to prostitution to fund her alcohol and drug habits. She eventually settled in the Cathedral City of Peterborough, the largest city in Cambridgeshire, 75 miles north of London.

In February of 2012, during one of her brushes with the law, she was admitted to a Peterborough psychiatric unit. Here, she was diagnosed as having an anti-social personality disorder that manifested itself in aggression, anger, irresponsibility, and impulsivity, as well as having a history of self-harm and drug and alcohol abuse. Despite this diagnosis, she was released after a few days.

Needing a new place to live, she visited the offices of the Quick Let property firm, which specialized in providing accommodation to people with "limited resources." The company was owned by Paul Creed and Kevin Lee. Joanne told the two men that she had just been released from prison for murdering her sexually abusive father. A lie. Paul was reluctant to rent to Joanne, as he took an instant dislike to her, but Kevin, a married man with two children, thought they should give her a chance and rented a room to her in a house in Rolleston Garth, Peterborough. Kevin took a liking to Joanne and offered her the job of running the house in return for rent-free accommodation. Her job was to keep the house and the other tenants in order. There was other work that she did for him on other properties he owned which he paid her for. Within a short amount of time, Kevin and Joanne began to have sex together.

The murders

Lukasz Slaboszewski, 31, an ex-heroin addict from Poland who had recently moved to Peterborough where he had a job in a warehouse, met Joanne in March of 2012. After meeting her, he proudly told his friends that he had an English girlfriend. The day after he met her, he received a series of sexually suggestive texts from her inviting him to her home. On March 19th, Lukasz, happily made his way to the address she had provided, expecting sex to be on the agenda. Upon entering the house, Joanne launched a vicious attack on Lukasz, stabbing him through the heart with a pocketknife. She then fetched a wheelie bin, somehow managed to put his dead body in it, and then placed it outside the house.

The following day, a 14-year-old girl, a friend of Joanne's, called at the house and Joanne lifted the lid on the wheelie bin and showed the shocked girl the dead body. Joanne also confessed to her friend and sometimes lover, Gary Stretch, what she had done and asked him if he would help her get rid of the body. Gary was a 7 foot 3 inches tall petty criminal who had served several prison terms for burglary. He agreed to help her.

A couple of days later, Gary arrived at the house in a green Vauxhall Astra which he nicknamed "the hearse" and he and Joanne drove Lukasz Slaboszewski´s body to the outskirts of Peterborough and dumped it into a ditch.

Just ten days later, in the early hours of the 29th of March, Good Friday, Joanne attacked John Chapman, aged 56. John was another tenant in the house. He was originally from Leeds and had been in the Royal Navy and fought in the Falkland's War. He was an alcoholic but had a reputation as a "friendly drunk." He did not like Joanne and was scared of her. He had described her to friends as the "man woman" due to her intimidating personality. Joanne stabbed him twice in the heart, once in the neck, and three times in the chest with her pocketknife.

Joanne then phoned Gary Stretch and said, "Oops, I've done it again."

Gary, along with a friend of his, Leslie Layton, arrived at the house shortly afterwards and helped her clean up the mess. They then drove the dead man's body to the same ditch on the outskirts of Peterborough in which they had tossed Lukasz Slaboszewski´s body and tossed John's in beside it.

Later on that day, Kevin Lee was shopping for CDs and cards as Easter presents for his wife, children, and for Joanne. He had met up with a friend a couple of days beforehand and had confided in him about his affair with Joanne. He had told him that Joanne had wanted to, "Dress me up and rape me." He told his friend that she reminded him of Uma Thurman from Kill Bill.

After completing his shopping, Kevin drove to his property in which Joanne lived. It was the last time he was seen alive. On entering the house, Joanne attacked him with her pocketknife and savagely stabbed him to death. After killing him, she dressed him in a black sequined dress.

She again called Gary for help in disposing of the body. Gary and Leslie arrived in "the hearse" and removed Kevin's body from the house. The three of them drove the body to a ditch near Newborough. Here, Joanne arranged Kevin's body so that the black sequined dress left his naked buttocks exposed.

The following day, Kevin's body was discovered by a farmer.

When Joanne and Gary heard the body had been found, they jumped in "the hearse" and drove to a friend of Joanne's, Gillian Page, in North Norfolk.

Gillian later said that when Joanne saw a police television appeal for information about her and Gary, she began "jumping around" with joy and excitement. She likened herself and Gary to the American outlaws Bonnie and Clyde and proclaimed she wanted to kill more. She said, "I want my fun."

After leaving Gillian's, they picked up a friend of Gary's, Mark Lloyd, and set off for Hereford via Worcester. Joanne said to Mark, as he sat on the back seat in the car, "I've killed three people; Gary's helped me dispose of them, and I want to do some more; it's fun."

Joanna Dennehy
(Cambridgeshire Police)

On Tuesday the 2nd of April, they arrived in the attractive Cathedral city of Hereford about 16 miles east of the border with Wales. Joanne posed provocatively for a photograph holding a jagged-edged knife.

In the afternoon, they drove slowly through the town as Joanne began searching for a victim. She spotted a 64-year-old man, Robin Bereza, walking his dog. She told Gary to stop the car. Joanne walked up to the man and with her pocketknife stabbed the man twice: once in the shoulder area and once in the chest.

Mark Lloyd, watching, had thought Joanne was going to mug the man before it dawned on him that she just wanted blood. He heard the man saying to Joanne, "What are you doing?"

She replied, "I'm hurting you. I'm going to fucking kill you."

A passerby, seeing the attack, approached to intervene. Joanne hopped back into the car smiling happily and gave Gary a kiss, as if to say thank you, and they drove off.

Ten minutes later, Joanne spotted another man, 56-year-old John Rogers, who was walking his lurcher dog. Once again, Joanne commanded Gary to stop the car. She clambered up and approached John Rogers from behind and stabbed him viciously in the back with her pocketknife. As he turned to face her, she began stabbing him in the chest. John asked, "What's this all about?"

Joanne replied, "You're bleeding. I better do some more."

Altogether, she stabbed him 40 times in his arm, back, chest, and stomach before leaving him for dead lying on a cycle path and taking the dog with her.

Luckily for both victims, they were taken to the hospital and miraculously their lives were saved.

Arrest

It was not long before the police found Gary and Joanne in their car and arrested them. The following day, on April 3rd, the bodies of Lukasz Slaboszewski and John Chapman were discovered.

When the police informed Joanne that she was being arrested for murder and attempted murder, she glibly replied, "It could be worse! I could be big, fat, black, and ugly."

While in prison awaiting her trial at London's Old Bailey, she was assessed by various psychiatrists. When asked by one psychiatrist why she killed, she said, "To see if I was as cold as I thought I was. Then it got more-ish, and I got a taste for it."

One psychiatrist assessed her as suffering from the condition "paraphilia sadomasochism," which is a preference for sexual activity involving the infliction of bondage, pain, or humiliation.

The police investigating the murders and attempted murders could find no coherent, lucid motive for her attacks. Gary Stetch, when asked by a previous girlfriend why Joanne had committed the crimes, answered: "Well, she's just that way. You know what I mean – she's just off her head."

Trial

At her trial in November of 2013, Joanne pled guilty to three counts of murder and two counts of attempted murder and of preventing the lawful and decent burial of her murder victims. During the court hearing, Joanne laughed and chatted with Gary Stretch, ignoring much of what was being said by the various lawyers and judge.

When the judge addressed her and said, "You are a cruel, calculating, selfish, and manipulative serial killer,"

Joanne laughed and smirked.

The judge sentenced her to life in prison, and she became the first woman ever in Britain to be ordered to die behind bars by a judge.

Gary Stretch was found guilty of the attempted murder of Robin Bereza and John Rogers after helping Joanne select her victims in Hereford. He was also found guilty of helping Joanne dump the bodies of her murder victims in Peterborough.

Gary yawned loudly when the judge told him to stand for sentencing.

The judge sentenced him to life in prison, with a minimum term of 19 years. Gary said to the judge, "Thank you very much."

Joanne's other accomplice in Peterborough, Leslie Layton, was sentenced to 14 years.

Engaged

Sometime during 2014, a builder from Worthing, West Sussex, James Budd, aged 48, began corresponding by letters with Joanne. According to the British tabloid newspaper The Sun, in his letters he wrote about Chunky, his Staffordshire bull terrier, and in her replies to him she wrote about Hitler, her German Shepherd she owned before being imprisoned.

Despite having never met or spoken, James proposed marriage to Joanne in a letter posted in July. Joanne accepted James's proposal but supposedly warned him: "You are declaring yourself to be the soul mate of a notorious serial killing psychopath. LOL." She then described herself as not being exactly the "girl next door."

James received a conviction for grievous bodily harm in 1990. The couple plans on requesting Her Majesty's Prison

Bronzefield in Ashford, Surrey for permission to marry at the prison in 2015.

Joanna, who tortured one of her victims as she listened to Elvis Presley, is planning on an Elvis-themed wedding. Her wish is to walk down the aisle to the sounds of "Jailhouse Rock."

Conclusion

In looking at Joanna Dennehy's case, it is virtually impossible to come up with an explanation for her actions. She grew up in a respectable, middle-class home. She had many advantages that other children lacked.

Yet, there was the history of self-harm; her victim's were not the only people whose bodies she cut, which indicates to me that she felt pain and rage about something. Was it that she felt replaced as a small child in her father's affections by the birth of her younger sister? Were her murders of men some kind of symbolic act of revenge on her father who she felt had betrayed her infant love?

Why had she told people that she had served time in prison for murdering her abusive father when she had never been to prison and nor was there any evidence that she was abused by her father or anyone else?

It is highly likely that we will never know the reasons behind Joanna's murderous rampage. People who kill are not characters in fiction or stereotypes, but multifaceted human beings with complex histories. To label her as mad or bad, or place her in some other neatly labeled box, does not really help us to comprehend her actions or motivations.

I believe, though I cannot know for sure, that her needs and motivations were most likely as confused as her life was chaotic.

Chapter 6: Donna Perry
"Really! The Other Guy Did It"
by Katherine Ramsland

Parallel Killers

At first, the police believed that Robert Lee Yates was the killer of the three "Spokane River" victims. This 48-year-old father of five, who had flown helicopters for the Army, was arrested in April 2000 for the 1997 death of 16-year-old Jennifer Joseph. Blood, along with a pearl button that matched other buttons on Jennifer's blouse, were found in his white Corvette. A witness also placed Jennifer in this model and color of car before she'd disappeared.

With this arrest, Yates became a suspect in more than a dozen other murders in the Spokane area. Over the years since the late 1980s, there had been thousands of tips and millions of dollars spent on the investigation. Most of the victims were prostitutes. Three, who also were drug abusers, had been dumped along the Spokane River during the first five months of 1990.

According to news reports, the nude body of Yolanda Sapp, 26, was found on February 22 in the 4100 block of East Upriver Drive. She'd been shot three times with a small caliber weapon. A green blanket was wrapped around her feet.

Just over a month later, the clothed body of Nickie Lowe, 34, turned up on March 25 in the 3200 block of South Riverton, under the Greene Street Bridge. Her billfold and tennis shoes were missing and she'd been shot once with a .22-caliber weapon. Someone soon found the missing items in a dumpster, with a tube of "sterile jelly." Detectives lifted several fingerprints from these items, but could not match them to a suspect.

Six weeks passed before someone came across another dead prostitute along the river's west side. On May 15, the body of Kathleen Brisbois, 38, was found near Trent Avenue and Pines Roads. Her clothes were scattered in the area, and ballistic tests showed that she'd been shot with the same gun used to kill Lowe.

These cases were investigated but soon went cold. Only when Robert Lee Yates was arrested a full decade later was there a glimmer of hope for local investigators that they could now resolve them.

The real killer must have laughed when Yates was named as the prime suspect in the riverside murders. He knew how cops sometimes closed cases with the logic, "Good for one, good for them all." But he was nervous. It was the age of DNA, after all. If three of those women were fully processed, Yates could be cleared. The killer looked for another way out.

DNA linked eight murdered women in Spokane to Yates, and other evidence nailed him to four more. In October 2000, this family man whom hookers called "Bob," confessed to thirteen murders, including a double homicide as early as 1975, and one attempted murder. He did not include Sapp, Lowe, or Brisbois on his list. Yet he remained a strong suspect in these as well as in other murders that occurred in areas where he'd lived. He was sentenced to over 400 years in prison.

In 2005, Mark Burbridge, a detective with the Spokane Police, and Jim Dresbeck, a detective with the Spokane County Sheriff's Office, became cold case investigators. The three riverside murders from 1990 had yet to be definitively solved. The officers submitted biological evidence found under Brisbois' fingernails to the Washington State Patrol Crime Lab. It went in line behind more pressing cases.

Four years later, the lab developed a male profile and submitted it to the national CODIS database. There was no match, but the results were now in the database. If the killer were arrested for something serious, his DNA would end up there, too. That's how some cases were solved.

In September 2012, the cold case team got the call: the DNA removed from Brisbois had gotten a hit. It was a match to a man with a considerable record of assaults and firearms violations. His name was Douglas Perry. He'd been arrested in March on yet another violation and was in federal custody in Texas.

But the chief suspect had changed considerably. As Washington State officials prepared to move Perry to a cell in Spokane, they opened an unexpected can of worms.

Conundrum

In his criminal record, Perry had charges dating back to 1974. He'd persistently violated his parole terms, especially with weapons violations, and had served several stints in jail. At the end of April in 1988, he'd been arrested for punching his mother. Police found five pipe bombs in his possession, along with machine gun parts.

In 1989, Perry had been arrested for soliciting a prostitute. In 1994, frightened mental health workers called the police to report their fear that Perry might commit a mass murder. He'd described himself as being like Dean Mellberg, a gunman who'd recently killed four people and wounded 22 others at a hospital outside Spokane's Fairchild Air Force Base. Among his victims were a psychiatrist and psychologist, whose reports about his emotional problems had helped to discharge him from military service. Perry had described his guns as being his "family" and his "purpose." He looked like a textbook case of a mass murderer.

When investigators searched his home, they found 49 firearms and 49,000 rounds of ammunition (one source says it was 20,000 rounds). Officers recovered several .22-caliber handguns, the same type used on the riverside victims. But no one made the connection.

Perry was back in prison in the late 1990s, this time in Oregon, for an 18-month sentence.
He'd been pulled over in a red-light district. Police found a knife and stun gun. His comment was that he was trying to help "get prostitutes off the streets."

He'd supposedly confided to a cellmate that he was a sociopath and had murdered nine prostitutes because he resented them for being women with reproductive capabilities. This "gift" was wasted on prostitutes, who were "pond scum."

One woman who reported Perry to the police recalled being in his home and seeing his vast collection of weapons. He'd assured her that he "liked" her and thus wouldn't hurt her. She told this to the police.

In March 2012, Perry was arrested for the unlawful possession of firearms. A retired detective had seen Perry buying ammo and a pistol magazine at the White Elephant Store. He'd taken a photo of Perry's car and called the ATF. They learned that Perry had gotten sex reassignment surgery in Thailand in 2000 and had changed his name from Douglas to Donna. The new driver's license photo matched the detective's photo. A search warrant was executed at Perry's home at 2006 East Empire, where 12 illegal firearms and over 12,000 rounds of ammunition turned up.

The searchers also found something else: a bedroom closet, painted shut. When this was pried open, ATF agents looking for guns found several boxes of women's panties. They were old, too small for Perry (even as a woman), and looked like a collection of serial killer trophies. But the agents were there for the guns, so they did nothing with these items.

Then Perry's DNA matched the tissue from under Brisbois' fingernails. That October, the fingerprints lifted from the items found in the dumpster on the day Nickie Lowe was killed were also matched to Perry, now 60. This evidence made a strong case.

Perry was charged with the murders and transferred to the Spokane County Jail. But she had prepared a unique defense.

It Wasn't Me, It Was Him

She did not kill anyone, Perry insisted, because at the time of the 1990 murders, "Donna" did not exist. Whatever evidence the police had was associated with *Douglas* Perry, her former male incarnation.

A detective who interviewed Donna asked why she thought the murders had stopped.

"Douglas didn't stop," she said. "Donna stopped it." She admitted to being "paranoid and emotional," but insisted she would not hurt anyone. "I'm not going to admit I killed anybody," she stated. "I didn't. Donna has killed nobody."

When pressed about whether Douglas had committed the crimes, Perry replied, "I don't know if Doug did or not. It was 20 years ago and I have no idea whether he did or did not."

She did say that her gender reassignment surgery was a permanent way to decrease and control her aggression. Thus, she hinted at the possibility that Douglas was a killer.

Perry's stance made headlines across the country, as criminologists grappled with the implications. Could Perry, as a female, actually escape a murder rap? Her statements posed an intriguing philosophical puzzle.

Officers continued to look for evidence. Perry had owned a 1969 International Scout for several decades, but had sold it in 2007. The fourth new owner, who'd had it a year, wanted it for parts. The police offered to purchase it, but he wouldn't give it up. They got a warrant, confiscated it, and towed it to the crime lab for processing. Inside, under a passenger-side floorboard, technicians found a .22-caliber cartridge.

The evidence from two of the three seemingly linked murders was taken before a grand jury. By March of 2014, Perry was ordered to court.

She refused to come. Her court-appointed attorney said he had been unable to meet with her because he'd been told that Perry was not at the jail. However, she'd been listed under her prior name, Douglas. The mix-up was corrected and a new court date assigned.

On March 19, 2014, Perry made a brief appearance, but kept her head down on the table. She did not enter a plea. Previously, her attorney had said that she wanted to plead not guilty by reason of insanity. The judge recommended that she undergo a psychiatric evaluation. He considered entering a "not guilty" plea on her behalf, but the prosecutor suggested that both sides should research the matter further. The judge agreed. He ordered that she be held on a $1 million bond in the Spokane County Jail.

There has been nothing of a formal nature regarding this case since March 2014. It's not yet clear when Perry will go to trial. However, she must undergo a full psychiatric evaluation, and the issues regarding her criminal responsibility must be sorted out ahead of time.

Is Guilt in the Body or the Soul?

There are three distinct problems with Perry's proposed defense. First, she seems to think that reducing her impulse toward violence should allow her to avoid responsibility for the murders. However, imprisonment is as much about punishment as a consequence of a criminal act as about community safety. So, she addresses only one component of our corrections philosophy.

Second, Perry believes that a shift in hormones reduces her violent tendencies. However, while seemingly logical, this idea has found little research support. Hormone therapy does not necessarily diminish aggressive tendencies. In other words, there are more factors in the decision to harm others than just biological make-up and some have a strong influence.

Third, Perry seems to believe that changing to a different gender somehow changes her into a different *person* and therefore releases her from the consequences of the former person's behavior. Thus, she takes it into the same territory as legal arguments about dissociative identity disorder.

In various news reports, some experts weighed in:

Dr. Jack Drescher, a New York-based psychiatrist, was asked to comment because he'd been part of the committee on sexual and gender identity disorders for the fifth edition of psychiatry's bible, *The Diagnostic and Statistical Manual of Mental Disorders* (*DSM-5*). Drescher stated that viewing oneself as a different person after gender reassignment surgery (or gender confirmation surgery, as it's also called) is more metaphorical than actual.

"It's a certain way that they use the metaphor when transitioning for those who were very unhappy before and now are happy," he said. "But it's different when a person makes a claim that somehow they have no linkage to the person they used to be. That would be more of a disturbed presentation."

Transgendered professor Jack Halberstam recognized the "multiple personality" line of argument. To clarify this connection, he described the concept of the physical body as a host that various personalities can take over. "It's an idea that we are simply competing personalities or selves," he said.

Perry's case might then be compared to that of Billy Milligan. He was accused of a series of robberies and rapes at Ohio State University in the late 1970s. By the time he faced a trial, ten of his twenty-three "alter" personalities had reportedly surfaced. One had a British accent and could write in fluent Arabic. One was a protector, another a lesbian. Male and female identities had emerged from the same host body.

A psychiatric report for Billy Milligan indicated that one offending alter was a 23-year-old Yugoslavian named Ragen. He had taken over Milligan's consciousness to rob some people. But before he could, a 19-year-old lesbian supposedly grabbed control and raped the women. The other personalities, including "Billy," had no memory of this incident.

Both sides agreed to acquit Milligan by reason of insanity.

So, with Donna Perry, the legal system must likewise grapple with the tricky notion of identity, because it's germane to responsibility. This case raises the classic question about Jekyll and Hyde: If Jekyll willingly drank a potion that he knew would give birth to Hyde and his atrocities, then Jekyll should be held accountable for Hyde's acts. However, if Hyde erupts in a way that Jekyll cannot predict, be aware of, or control, then Jekyll should not be held responsible.

With gender reassignment, the legal system must decide if the male personality (A) associated with physical body (B) is the same as female personality (C) associated with physical body (B). That is, does A have a distinct center of consciousness from that of C, or is there an embodied continuum in B that Perry cannot escape?

As with dissociative identity disorder, punishment for a guilty alter (or consciousness A) would involve imprisoning the "host" body (B), which would entail punishing an innocent person (consciousness C). According to some theories, the "core" or "primary" personalities generally experience periods of amnesia and might even find themselves in a foreign place with no idea how they arrived. This is called an amnesic barrier. One "person" might have full access to the memory bank, while others get only glimpses, and some might be entirely unaware of the others.

This situation does not appear to match Donna Perry's condition. She does remember her time as Douglas, although she is cagey about the details. She experiences no barrier or disturbance of integration.

In sum, resolving a gender disorder does not erase personal responsibility for earlier acts, because significant personal factors remain the same. Neither science nor the law supports Perry's argument, so it won't be difficult for prosecutors to find mental health experts who will dismiss her notions about becoming a "new" person. Her ideas are mired in outdated and debunked notions about both gender and aggression.

Still, this is a case to watch. It raises provocative questions for law, psychology and philosophy.

Chapter 7: Dr. Harold Shipman
"Bad Medicine"
by Michael Newton

Harold Shipman mugshot

Kathleen Grundy was well known in Hyde, Greater Manchester, England. A wealthy widow and former mayor, she still brimmed with energy at age eighty-one, described by a friend as "a twenty-five-year-old in an eighty-year-old body." Grundy devoted much of her time to local charities, including Hyde's Age Concern Club, where she helped serve meals to pensioners. When she missed the club's meeting on June 24, 1998, friends knew something was amiss. Rushing to her home, they found Grundy lying on a sofa, fully dressed—and dead.

The first call went to Dr. Harold Shipman, Grundy's physician, seen by neighbors leaving her home a few hours prior to discovery of her body. Shipman explained his house call as a mission to draw blood for a study on aging. Returning to the scene, he pronounced Grundy dead while a friend called her daughter, Angela Woodruff. She inquired about an autopsy, but Shipman said it was unnecessary, since he'd seen Grundy shortly before she died.

Soon after Grundy's funeral, Woodruff received a call from her attorney, claiming to have a copy of the late mayor's will. It left £386,000 (some $650,000) to Dr. Shipman. Woodruff—a lawyer herself, author of Grundy's original will in 1986—rushed over to see the new document. Poorly typed and ungrammatical, it bore an oversized, awkward signature barely resembling Grundy's.

Unwilling to doubt Dr. Shipman at first, Woodruff suspected some unknown third person was trying to frame him for fraud. However, after speaking to the fake will's witnesses, she grudgingly concluded that Shipman had murdered her mother for profit.

Woodruff's next stop was the Tameside Division of the Greater Manchester Police, where she showed the suspect's will to Detective Superintendent Bernard Postles. "You only have to look at it once," Postles said, "and you start thinking it's like something off a John Bull printing press. You don't have to have twenty years as a detective to know it's a fake. Maybe he thought he was being clever—an old lady, nobody around her. Look at it; it's a bit tacky. But everyone knew she was as sharp as a tack. Maybe it was his arrogance."

Proof of murder required an autopsy, which in turn required an exhumation order from the coroner, issued only if the coroner himself is probing a suspicious death, or if police present a prima facie case for murder—something never done before in Greater Manchester. On top of that, the exhumation and autopsy had to be conducted secretly, preventing Dr.

100

Shipman from destroying any evidence that might incriminate him.

In the dead of night on August 1, in pouring rain, gravediggers hoisted Grundy's coffin from its not-so-final resting place. Tissue and hair samples were sent to several forensic labs for testing, seeking cause of death. Meanwhile, detectives pored over the bogus Grundy will, and got an unexpected bit of help from Dr. Shipman. When they asked about the document, he handed them an old manual typewriter, claiming that his late wealthy patient had sometimes borrowed it to type correspondence. That story seemed ridiculous—all the more so when analysts proved that Grundy's will and other fraudulent documents were typed on Shipman's machine.

Next came the autopsy report: Grundy had died from an overdose of morphine, injected no more than three hours before she expired. "I was surprised," Det. Supt. Postles said. "I anticipated that I would have had difficulty if he gave them something in way of poison lost in background substance. It was an unexpected bonus once I had checked that Kathleen Grundy did not take it herself."

Police went back to Shipman's home, armed with a search warrant. They found the house in squalid disarray, littered with dirty clothes and old newspapers, but they also collected medical records and unexplained pieces of jewelry. Shipman, still aloof, claimed Grundy had been a closet morphine addict, injecting herself at home, though no drugs were found there.

Postles was convinced he had his man, but now he had a nagging sense that Grundy might not be the doctor's only victim.

***

101

Harold Frederick Shipman was born in Nottingham on January 14, 1946, the second of three children for trucker Harold Shipman and wife Vera. Vera favored Harold Jr. over his siblings and sought to make him stand out from his peers, insisting that he wear a tie when other boys dressed for school or play in casual garb. In Vera's eyes, Harold had a more promising future than sister Pauline or brother Clive. Outside the Shipman home, Vera chose Harold's friends and scheduled his play dates.

That changed in June 21, 1963, when Vera died from lung cancer. During the latter stages of her long illness, Harold had rushed home from school each day to sit at her bedside, holding her hand, watching as doctor's eased her terminal pain with morphine injections. On the night she died, relatives say, he ran for twenty miles in pouring rain. Shipman's father lived on, but there was no love lost between them. At his death, Harold Sr. split his meager estate between Pauline and Clive, leaving nothing to his namesake.

At school, Harold was a plodding, mediocre student, but he excelled at soccer and track. Aside from sports, he was a loner who looked down on his peers, despite his own modest circumstances. "It was as if he tolerated us," a former classmate later said. "If someone told a joke he would smile patiently, but Fred never wanted to join in. It seems funny, because I later heard he'd been a good athlete, so you'd have thought he'd be more of a team player." As for romance, an ex-teacher said, "I don't think he ever had a girlfriend. In fact, he took his older sister to school dances. They made a strange couple. But then, he was a bit strange—a pretentious lad."

In 1965, Shipman enrolled at Leeds University Medical School. He had failed his first entrance exam, then secured a passing grade on his second attempt. A year later, he gave up chastity after meeting Primrose May Oxtoby, three years his junior. She was five months pregnant when they married, in 1966. Their first child, daughter Sara, arrived in early 1967.

Shipman graduated from medical school in 1970, receiving provisional registration with the General Medical Council and becoming a pre-registration house officer—the equivalent of an intern—at Pontefract General Infirmary in Pontefract, West Riding of Yorkshire. Today, investigators believe he killed his first victim the following year.

Margaret Thompson, age sixty-seven, was recuperating from a stroke when she died under Shipman's care—and in his presence—on March 2, 1971. Other lost patients, now presumed victims, included fifty-four-year-old Thomas Cullumbine (April 12); eighty-four-year-old John Bewster (April 28); and seventy-one-year-old James Rhodes (May 22). Eighty-two-year-old Kate Sharpe entered Pontefract General in March 1972, complaining of chest pains; one week later, Shipman certified her cause of death as asthmatic bronchitis and coronary thrombosis.

Seven months later, on October 11, cerebral palsy patient Susan Garfitt checked into Pontefract General with pneumonia. Her mother recalls Dr. Shipman saying that Susan would die, and that further treatment would only extend her suffering. Ann Garfitt asked Shipman to "be kind," stepped out for tea, and returned to find her daughter dead. Today, she wonders if Shipman took her request as a plea for euthanasia.

A father of two by 1974, Shipman moved his growing family to Todmorden, on the Lancashire-West Yorkshire border, accepting a general practitioner's position at the Abraham Ormerod Medical Centre. The change of scene also appeared to change his personality—at least in public, where neighbors and fellow physicians saw him as outgoing, friendly, even charming. Shipman's office staffers told a different story, describing their boss as rude and belittling, prone to calling his employees "stupid" when they displeased him.

***

On March 17, 1975, seventy-year-old Eva Lyons died in Todmorden, under Dr. Shipman's care. Around the same time, Shipman began to experience blackouts. Confronted by his partners, he confessed to suffering from epilepsy, but the truth surfaced when receptionist Marjorie Walker noted anomalous entries in a pharmacist's log of controlled narcotics. Dr. Shipman was writing frequent, large prescriptions to his patients for pethidine, a synthetic opioid painkiller.

That, in itself, might not have been incriminating: 60 percent of all Western doctors prescribed pethidine for acute pain in 1975, while 22 percent prescribed it for chronic pain. However, Shipman was also writing prescriptions in the medical center's name, compiling an excessive stockpile of the drug. Dr. John Dacre led the investigation at Abraham Ormerod, discovering that many of Shipman's patients, listed as receiving pethidine, never required or got the painkiller.

Finally, Dacre and his colleagues confronted Shipman at a staff meeting, described by Dr. Michael Grieve. "We were sat around," Grieve said, "with Fred sitting on one side and up comes John on the opposite and says, 'Now young Fred, can you explain this?' And he puts before him evidence that he has been gleaning, showing that young Fred had been prescribing pethidine to patients and they'd never received the pethidine, and in fact the pethidine had found its way into Fred's very own veins."

Caught red-handed, Shipman first begged for a second chance, then, when that was refused, stormed out of the meeting, flinging his medical bag to the floor and threatening resignation. Stunned by his outburst, the partners were still discussing options a short time later, when Primrose Shipman barged into the staff room, declaring that her husband would never quit the practice. "You'll have to force him out!" she snapped, before leaving.

And so it was. Criminal charges followed, prompting Dr. Shipman to seek treatment at a counseling center in York, where he remained from early October until late December 1975. Prosecutors were waiting when he emerged, convicting Shipman in 1976 of dishonestly obtaining drugs, forgery of National Health Service prescriptions and unlawful possession of pethidine. Despite the serious charges, Shipman's medical license was neither revoked nor suspended. He paid £600— about $1,000 today—in fines and restitution to his former partners and went looking for another job.

Despite his new criminal record, Shipman soon found work as a clinical medical officer, the equivalent of a physician's assistant, in South West Durham. In 1977, he joined the Donneybrook House Group Practice, located on Clarendon Street in Hyde, Cheshire, as a general practitioner, resuming his life and career as if nothing had happened in Todmorden.

Acceptance of Shipman in Hyde was amazingly simple. Dr. Jeffery Moysey at Donneybrook House later said, "His approach was that I have had this problem, this conviction for abuse of pethidine. I have undergone treatment. I am now clean. All I can ask you to do is to trust me on that issue and to watch me." Once employed, Shipman donned the familiar solicitous mask, ingratiating himself with colleagues and patients, while subordinates soon felt the sting of his arrogant sarcasm. As for drug abuse, he showed no symptoms.

Over the next six years, authorities believe Shipman

killed at least ten patients in Hyde. Those publicly named as victims include Sarah Hannah Marsland, deceased on August 7, 1978; Mary Ellen Jordan, on August 30, 1978; Harold Bramwell, on December 7, 1978; Annie Campbell, on December 20, 1978; Alice Maude Gorton, on August 10, 1979; Jack Leslie Shelmerdine, on November 28, 1979; May Slater, on April 18, 1981; Elizabeth Ashworth, on August 26, 1981; Percy Ward, on January 4, 1983; and Moira Ashton Fox, on June 28, 1983.

In 1983, Shipman was interviewed for Granada television's *World in Action* documentary series. The episode, titled "A Serious Medical Emergency," aired on October 31, including Shipman's comments on how the mentally ill should be treated in their communities. Today, the irony is bitter.

Between January 1984 and December 1991, Shipman killed at least sixty-one patients from Hyde, Denton, and Dukinfield. Forty-four were women, ranging in age from fifty-one to ninety-three; the rest were men, aged forty-one to eighty-seven. They died by lethal injection, with Dr. Shipman listing various natural causes on their death certificates. In each case, advanced age or chronic illness made the official verdict seem plausible.

As with the early murders in Hyde, there are gaps for Shipman's later time at Donneybrook House. Despite thorough investigation, no victims have been named for the twenty-one months between January 1991 and September 1992, when Shipman left Donneybrook to establish his own solo practice in Hyde, at 21 Market Street. He called it The Surgery, but it might as well have been named The Slaughterhouse.

***

Dr. Shipman had barely moved into The Surgery when he

106

resumed killing patients. The first to die, on October 7, 1992, was Monica Rene Sparkes. Shipman's fifteen known victims for 1993 include Hilda Mary Couzens and Olive Heginbotham, both killed on February 24; Amy Whitehead, on March 22; Mary Emma Andrew, on April 8; Sarah Ashworth, on April 17; Marjorie Parker, on April 27; Nellie Mullen, on May 2; Edna May Llewellyn, two days later; Emily Morgan, on May 12; Violet May Bird, the following day; Jose Kathleen Diana Richards, on July 22; Edith Calverley, on August 16; Joseph Leigh, on December 16; Eileen Robinson, on December 22; and Charles Edward Brocklehurst, on New Year's Eve.

The killing pace slacked off a bit in 1994, with eleven known victims for an average of one murder every thirty-three days. January's victims were Joan Milray Harding and Christine Hancock. Elsie Platt died in February. May saw the loss of Mary Alice Smith and Ronnie Devenport. Cicely Sharples and Alice Christine Kitchen died under Shipman's loving care in June. Maria Thornton succumbed in July. November claimed Henrietta Walker and Elizabeth Ellen Mellor, five days apart. John Bennett Molesdale's murder capped the year, on December 29.

Dr. Shipman picked up the killing pace in 1995, more than doubling the previous year's tally with twenty-eight known victims. We cannot say with certainty if Shipman had begun to rob his patients, though some articles of jewelry recovered from his home suggest it. He claimed his first victim of 1995, Alice Kennedy, on January 9. March witnessed seven murders, including two victims—Netta Ashcroft and Lily Bardsley—slain on a single day. Four more patients died in April, one in May, four in June, one each in July and August, two in September, one in October, two in November, and two more on the same day in December.

The Surgery's high mortality rate might have been

alarming, but Shipman's victims were prime candidates for the cemetery, ranging in age from sixty-five to eighty-eight, many of them frail, some chronically ill. The year's tally included nineteen women and nine men, all mourned by families who trusted Dr. Shipman and saw no reason to challenge his diagnoses as to cause of death.

Nineteen ninety-six was another busy year for Dr. Death, with thirty known victims murdered. As usual, female victims predominated, with twenty-three dead versus seven men. Two died in January, two in February, one in March, two more in April, four in May (with two only one day apart), five in June (with Nellie Bennett and Margaret Mary Vickers both killed on June 25), six in July, one in August, two in September, one in October, two each in November and December.

Nineteen ninety-seven was the worst year yet for Dr. Shipman's trusting patients. At least thirty-seven died at his hands, thirty-three of them women ranging in age from fifty-eight to eighty-nine. The four male victims—David Alan Harrison, Charles Henry Killan, John Louden Livesey, and James Joseph King—offered a wider spread of ages, from forty-seven to ninety. Shipman averaged one killing every ten days that year, but even that was not enough to satisfy his compulsion. Three months—January, February and December—saw murders spaced only one day apart, and he claimed two female victims, Elsie Cheetham and Jean Lilley, on April 25 alone.

Nineteen ninety-eight was well on track to be another record year for Shipman, with sixteen patients slain in the first three months, but his high mortality rate was finally making waves in Hyde. Mabel Shawcross and Norah Nuttall died four days apart in January. In February, death knells sounded for Cissie Davies, Pamela Marguerite Hillier, Laura Frances Linn, Irene Berry, Maureen Alice Ward, and Joan Edwina Dean.

March brought funerals for Harold Eddleston, Margaret Anne Waldron, Irene Chapman, Dorothy Long, Lily Higgins, Ada Warburton, and Martha Marley.

The problem with a small town is its size. Hyde is not tiny, but it's small enough that most of Dr. Shipman's patients were referred to one mortician, Alan Massey, who began to note the death rate and a certain sameness to the dear departed. "Anybody can die in a chair," Massey later remarked. "But there's no set pattern, and Dr. Shipman's always seem to be the same, or very similar. Could be sat in a chair, could be laid on the settee, but I would say 90 percent was always fully clothed. There was never anything in the house that I saw that indicated the person had been ill. It just seems the person, where they were, had died. There was something that didn't quite fit."

Alarmed by that anomaly, Massey called on Shipman at The Surgery. As he described that meeting to reporters, "I asked him if there was any cause for concern and he just said, 'No there isn't.' He showed me his certificate book that he issues death certificates in, the cause of death in, and his remarks were 'nothing to worry about, you've nothing to worry about' and anybody who wants to inspect his book can do."

Massey took Shipman at his word, but Massey's daughter and partner, Debbie Brambroffe, remained unconvinced. She consulted Dr. Susan Booth, from Hyde's Brooke Surgery, who had examined one of Shipman's late patients under a statute requiring a physician from an unrelated practice to countersign cremation orders. Booth shared Brambroffe's concerns with Dr. Linda Reynolds, who in turn spoke to South Manchester District Coroner John Pollard. Pollard contacted police, who reviewed Shipman's records— unaware that he redacted patient files after each homicide—

and gave The Surgery a clean bill of health. Oddly, detectives failed to note his criminal record from Todmorden.

Authorities closed their investigation of Shipman on April 17, 1998. Over the next ten weeks, he claimed three more victims: Winifred Mellor on May 11, Joan May Melia on June 12, and Kathleen Grundy on June 24. The last case, bungled with a clumsy fling at forgery, would end the doctor's silent reign of terror.

***

Greater Manchester Police arrested Dr. Shipman on September 7, 1998. Dismissing for the moment victims who had been cremated, authorities focused on patients who had died soon after Shipman's house calls. At the same time, computer analysts scoured Shipman's hard drive, noting numerous discrepancies. We see the noose tighten in Shipman's interrogation regarding the death of Winifred Mellor.

> *Police Officer*: I'll just remind you of the date of this lady's death—11th May '98. After three o'clock that afternoon, you have endorsed the computer with the date of 1st October '97, which is ten months prior, "chest pains."
> *Dr. Shipman*: I have no recollection of me putting that on the machine.
> *Officer*: It's your passcode; it's your name.
> *Shipman*: It doesn't alter the fact I can't remember doing it.
> *Officer*: You attended the house at three o'clock. That's when you murdered this lady. You went back to the surgery and immediately started

110

altering this lady's medical records. You tell me why you needed to do that.

Shipman: There's no answer.

Shipman's trial convened in Preston, Lancashire, on October 5, 1999, before Justice Thaynes Forbes. Prosecutor Richard Henriques led the crown's case, while attorney Nicola Davies defended Shipman. The doctor was charged with fifteen counts of murder—for victims Marie West, Irene Turner, Lizzie Adams, Jean Lilley, Ivy Lomas, Muriel Grimshaw, Marie Quinn, Kathleen Wagstaff, Bianka Pomfret, Norah Nuttall, Pamela Hillier, Maureen Ward, Winifred Mellor, Joan Melia and Kathleen Grundy—plus one count of forging Grundy's will.

In preliminary motions, Davies led for the defense with three petitions. First, she asked that the trial be stopped entirely, on grounds that Shipman's case was irrevocably prejudiced by "inaccurate, misleading" media coverage. Second, if it must proceed, Davies requested that the case be broken into *three* trials: one for Grundy's case, with the lone allegation of murder for greed; another for patients whose remains were still available for scientific testing; and a third for cremated patients, where retroactive determination of what caused their deaths was impossible. Finally, she wanted evidence from Volume 8 of the police report on Shipman's case ruled inadmissible in its entirety.

Concerning pretrial publicity, Prosecutor Henriques objected on grounds that media reporting had been helpful, alerting survivors of Shipman's patients to possible irregularities. Regarding severance of cases, Henriques objected on grounds the murders were interrelated, displaying a longstanding pattern of criminal behavior. Finally, with respect to exclusion of evidence, Henriques reminded Justice

111

Forbes that Volume 8 contained extensive evidence of Shipman hoarding morphine from twenty-eight patients, prescribing drugs for patients who required no analgesics, and for others who had died.

Forbes denied all three defense motions. The trial would proceed, examining all sixteen charges against Shipman, and Volume 8's evidence would be admitted. Forbes then adjourned the court until October 11, when jury selection began.

Richard Henriques delivered his opening statement on October 11, telling jurors:

> The prosecution allege that he has murdered fifteen of his patients by administering to them substantial doses of morphine shortly before they died, thereby causing their deaths. None of those buried, nor indeed cremated, were prescribed morphine or diamorphine. All of them died most unexpectedly. All of them had seen Dr. Shipman on the day of their death. The defendant killed those fifteen patients because in the submission of the prosecution, he enjoyed doing so. He was exercising the ultimate power of controlling life and death and repeated the act so often he must have found the drama of taking life to his taste.

Over the next ten weeks, Henriques proved his case with a parade of witnesses including Angela Woodruff, whose investigation of her mother's death caused Shipman's downfall; Marian Hadfield, a neighbor of Marie West, who sat in an adjoining room when Shipman made his fatal house call; Elizabeth Hunter, who saw Shipman leaving Jean Lilley's flat after killing her; handwriting expert Michael Allen, identifying Shipman as the person who forged Kathleen Grundy's will; Det. Sgt. John Ashley, explaining postdated entries to Shipman's medical files on slain patients; pathologist John Rutherford, walking jurors through the details of multiple autopsies; Winifred Mellor's son, swearing that his mother had no critical health issues; Kathleen Wagstaff's daughter, who found her mother dead with her sleeve rolled up, her arm bruised; Det. Sgt. Philip Reade, who heard Shipman call victim Ivy Lomas "a nuisance"; Michael Woodruff, who deemed mother-in-law Irene Turner "fine" thirty minutes before Shipman's house call; Bill Catlow, long-time friend of Betty Adams, who felt her pulse still beating after Shipman told him, "She's gone"; Margaret Walker, a neighbor of Kathleen Wagstaff, who placed Shipman at Wagstaff's flat moments before she died; Jacqueline Gee, daughter of Pamela Hillier, whom Shipman blamed for negligence in watching over her mother's condition—the list went on and on.

In week seven, on November 25, Dr. Shipman took the witness stand in his own defense. Denying any criminal activity, he claimed to have noticed signs that Kathleen Grundy was a drug addict. A note penciled onto her medical chart read: "Query drug use. At her age?" Shipman explained, "I was just being suspicious that she was actually abusing a drug. It had to be something like an opiate—codeine, pethadone, perhaps morphine." His final visit to Grundy, he said, was to take a blood sample and screen it for drugs. Earlier that week, he testified, Grundy had visited his office and asked him to witness her signature on legal documents. "I jokingly said if it was her will and if she was going to leave me some money I couldn't do it," Shipman told jurors.

Nicola Davies asked her client, "Did you think there were any monies being left specifically to you?" Shaking his head, Shipman replied, "No. I thought the patient fund would benefit by one or two hundreds pounds."

Returning to the stand on November 26, Shipman testified that two of his late patients—Winifred Mellor and Bianka Pomfret—complained of chest pains shortly before they died. "I was upset by Bianka," he said, "because she hadn't trusted me enough to tell me about the pain." Pomfret also smoked two packs of cigarettes per day, prompting Shipman to say, "A patient who has heart disease and who smokes is silly and is looking to die."

As for Marie Quinn, Shipman testified that he had found her lying on her kitchen floor when he arrived for a house call, apparently suffering from a stroke. "I had to decide whether to attempt resuscitation or let nature take its course," he said, telling jurors he decided to wait briefly. "But two minutes later there was no sign of life and she had died." It was sad, of course, but "Patients who do survive often have a loss of personality, a loss of use of the body. Mrs. Quinn was an extremely independent likeable patient and for her to go from that to being dependent on people she didn't know was something I couldn't imagine."

Ivy Lomas, Shipman testified, was "gray and sweating and she looked unwell" during her final visit to The Surgery. He was about to give her an electrocardiograph test when she collapsed. "She was not conscious," Shipman testified. "I could not detect an artery on the neck. I thought the diagnosis was then confirmed that she had had a coronary thrombosis."

Were police correct in saying that Shipman considered Lomas "a nuisance"? "Far from it," he replied. "Like any GP I had a small number of extremely regular attenders who are not curable and you have to accept they are in the surgery on a regular basis. With some of them I joked that perhaps we should put a plaque above their seat and that was the case with Ivy Lomas. In no way was it said except in a friendly, jocular manner."

Jean Lilley's death had come as no surprise to Shipman, since she suffered from lung disease, high cholesterol, hypertension, and circulation problems linked to heart disease. "Any one of the illnesses she had could kill her," he testified. He had visited Lilley twice on the day she died. First, he found her in poor health, complaining that she "felt awful." Shipman told jurors, "I impressed upon her the seriousness of her chest condition." Twenty minutes later, he was called back to Lilley's home, where ambulance attendants had found her dead.

Muriel Grimshaw, Shipman said, was under treatment for hypertension when she died. His last house call, the day before her death, had involved a complaint of back pain. As for discrepancies on Laura Wagstaff's death certificate, Shipman testified, "I don't think I was quite clear in my own mind when I completed this document. This was one of the few times I was possibly more upset than the relatives." And with that, he burst into tears.

Shipman faced stiff questioning from Prosecutor Henriques over drugs found in his home. He had "no sensible answer" for why he destroyed six out of ten diamorphine ampoules, but kept four. And again, when asked why six time-release morphine tablets were missing from a box of fifty, he had "no idea." When he prescribed 1,000mg of diamorphine for a patient in 1994, why had she never received it? "I gave the lady the prescription," Shipman said. "What she did with it afterwards is up to her." Why had Shipman told nurse Marion Gilchrist that his only error in Kathleen Grundy's case was failing to recommend cremation? Shipman called it a "black joke," then hedged. "I am not being funny. You can't dig up ashes," he said. Of course, he did not fear Grundy's exhumation, "because I had done nothing wrong."

Jurors felt otherwise. On January 31, 2000, after six days of deliberation, they convicted Shipman on all counts. Nicola Davies requested immediate sentencing, and Justice Forbes obliged. Before imposing fifteen life sentences, plus four years for forgery, Forbes told Shipman, "Each of your victims was your patient. You murdered each and every one of your victims by a calculated and cold-blooded perversion of your medical skills, for your own evil and wicked purposes. You took advantage of, and grossly abused their trust. You were, after all, each victim's doctor. I have little doubt that each of your victims smiled and thanked you as she submitted to your deadly ministrations."

In parting, Forbes added, "In the ordinary way, I would not do this in open court, but in your case I am satisfied justice demands that I make my views known at the conclusion of this trial...My recommendation will be that you spend the remainder of your days in prison."

Ten days later, Britain's General Medical Council formally revoked Shipman's license to practice, striking him from its register. Despite prior sensational trials, Shipman remains the only British physician convicted of murdering patients.

***

The case was not closed with Shipman's conviction and sentence, however. On February 1, 2000, Britain's Secretary of State for Health announced an inquiry into further possible murders under Section 2 of the National Health Service Act of 1977. Dame Janet Smith, a High Court judge, chaired the inquiry, convening its first public hearing at Manchester Town Hall on June 20. Proceeding through four stages, the investigation continued until March 24, 2005, when it finally closed. By then, authorities had concluded that Shipman killed at least 215 of his patients between 1975 and 1998. Dame Janet acknowledged that there were "many more" suspicious deaths, including that of a four-year-old girl, during Shipman's early practice in Pontefract. At least 250 slayings were suspected, while a total of 459 patients died under Shipman's care. In roughly half those cases, there was no way to determine if he was the sole physician certifying death.

Dr. Shipman missed the latter part of the expanding scandal. At 6:20 a.m. on January 13, 2004, a guard found him hanged in his cell at Her Majesty's Prison Wakefield. Another inquiry followed, determining that Shipman "was showing no signs whatsoever of pre-suicidal behavior at all" prior to death. Guards reported that Shipman was "obnoxious and arrogant to the prison staff. Just before Christmas his enhanced status was reduced to basic. He was deprived of the television set in his cell and had to wear prison uniform rather than his own clothes." To this day, Shipman's widow and three sons insist that he was innocent of any wrongdoing.

After his suicide, *The Sun,* a London tabloid, ran a gloating headline. It read, "Ship Ship hooray!"

Chapter 8: Lonnie Franklin Jr.
"Grim Sleeper"
by RJ Parker

Lonnie Franklin, Jr. mughot

This might seem like a tale taken directly from old crime novels—a serial killer preying on young, beautiful women of the same ethnicity as his own, and eventually ending up murdering them. However, this is much more than just a mere series of killings. These are the heinous actions of a murderer who was at large for 23 years, and during this time, managed to take the lives of many women. More importantly, he carried out his actions in the heart of the City of Angels, Los Angeles, in California. However, unlike conventional serial killers, this one was different.

Even though his active years show up as starting in 1985 and ending at 2007, this murderer went on a hiatus for 14 years, from 1988 to 2002. As a result of this prolonged period of inactivity, he was given the nickname 'Grim Sleeper.' However, despite the name, he was an efficient killer. It took the police almost 25 years to finally apprehend the person behind the nickname, and he turned out to be Lonnie Franklin Jr., somebody who had once been a mechanic for the LAPD as well as a sanitation worker for the city of Los Angeles. Moreover, he was a happily married man, living with his wife of 32 years, as well as two children.

The Grim Sleeper had finally been caught, or so it seemed. The trial that followed the events after his capture has yet to get fully underway, and at the time of this writing, the families of his victims are still unable to rest peacefully because he goes unpunished as yet. This is perhaps one of the most gruesome tales of murder and evasion, one that has been recounted to many aspiring detectives that joined the Los Angeles Police Department.

For a very long time, nobody was able to put a face to the Grim Sleeper. There were many deaths, and according to the police, he is liable for ten counts of murder and will be convicted accordingly. Many thought that a firm judgment would be reached by now, but nothing has really transpired.

It is said that each of us carries a secret identity, one that only comes to light when we are alone. However, in the case of Lonnie Franklin Jr., the identity seems to be as far fetched as possible. Words fall short of the horrific nature of the crimes that he committed. The police have charged him with the murders of ten women, while another charge of attempted murder was also placed upon him. A media frenzy ensued upon his capture, and global media coverage was received by his case. Yet, few could have been able to accurately predict the extent to which this man could have gone in order to satisfy his killing desire. What follows is a recount of the murders that he committed, how he was captured, and finally, how he was put to trial.

The Murders

In the mid 1980s, there were a number of different active serial killers within California, most of them preying on women. A number of them even later stated that they found it "quite easy to take a stranger home." However, the case of the Grim Sleeper was slightly different. The women that were found murdered were usually found covered underneath dirty carpets or mattresses, well hidden from plain sight. Their bodies would be stashed deep inside dark alleys that were seldom visited, which made it quite difficult for the police to locate them. Often times, the only way that the bodies were found was when the smell of effluvium from the decomposing body became so strong that it alerted passerbys. Some were even stashed deep in trash bags and stowed in dumpsters.

There was a pattern, however, in all of the killings, which ultimately led the police to determine that this was the work of a new killer. First of all, apart from one man, they were all women. Most were young, while others were middle aged. Another clear indicator was the fact that all of these women were black. A significant percentage of the women had been shot primarily at close range with the use of a small caliber handgun, but there were also some that had actually been strangled to death. A large majority of these women suffered from drug problems, but most importantly, most of them had also been raped before they were killed.

In those times, the streets of Southern Los Angeles, also known as South Central, were primarily forgotten. The people had become tired of the police ignoring them. And worse of all, the crack epidemic was in full flow during those times. A majority of prostitutes were also killed during those times, mainly because they were the ones who had to make the most use of the streets. There were approximately 800 murders every year from 1985 to 1989, and these numbers mainly blended into the average counts. However, it took quite a while for the police to really figure out that they had a serial killer amongst all of this.

The first victim reported was Debra Jackson, who was 29 years old at the time. She worked as a cocktail waitress, and had only just left her friend's apartment and was walking to the bus stop when she was apprehended and killed. Three gun shot wounds were found in her chest. The body was found on August 10, 1985. Then, silence for a year.

Henrietta Wright was the next victim. Her body was found only a few miles away from where Jackson's body was discovered. This time, the body had been victim to sexual assault, and had then been shot in the chest as well. Her body was found on August 12 in 1986. No more than two days had passed when the LAPD uncovered another body, this time of a man. The pattern had been broken. Thomas Steele was 36 years old and was reportedly working as a pimp who was visiting from San Diego when he was shot and his body was left in the middle of an intersection.

A large number of the victims were simply out for a casual stroll, or were running an errand. After Steele, the next body that was discovered was that of a young 23-year-old by the name of Barbara Ware. Her body was found on January 10, 1987. Bernita Sparks was his next victim. She had only just gone out to grab some cigarettes, but unfortunately never returned home again. She was 26 years old. Her body was found on the same day, on April 15, 1987.

The Grim Sleeper was actively hunting young black women, and by this point in time, the police had put up flyers of all sorts in order to make sure that women were made aware of what was going on in the streets. Bernita's body was found stashed in a dumpster on Western Avenue. She had been beaten, strangled and finally shot in the head. It was a brutal attack. The next victim that the Grim Sleeper targeted was Mary Lowe, who was 26 years old at the time of her death. She had gone out to celebrate Halloween Night at the Love Trap Bar and was picked up by the killer at some point during her travel to or from the bar. Her body was found on November 1 in a dark alleyway, again on Western Avenue. Her death was significant however, because a neighbor had seen her getting into a red or orange Ford Pinto with a racing stripe on the hood. The neighbor was also able to identify a rough image of the driver, stating that he was male, young, and black.

Lachrica Jefferson was the next victim to fall on this gruesome list. Her death was also significant in the grand scheme of things. Her body was found on January 30, 1988. She was just 22 years old at the time. However, the way her body was displayed showed that the killer was trying to create a medium of communication via his victims; Jefferson's body was also found in an alley, with her face covered with a napkin. The napkin however, had writing on it, with the word 'AIDS.' The police were unable to find any sort of clues as to why or how this might have happened.

Investigations were underway at this point, and the community members had already set up the Black Coalition Fighting Back Serial Murders. The main purpose of this organization was to create stricter measures in order to ensure that serial killers were caught and apprehended as soon as possible. This organization began to apply pressure on the police to create a dedicated task force in order to locate the Grim Sleeper, and they also began handing out thousands of fliers on the streets in order to make people aware of the murderer. The flyers were distributed throughout South Central, and some even went as far as Beverly Hills, raising awareness of what was happening in those areas.

The city government also established a reward after the Coalition pressed them to take serious efforts into apprehending this serial killer. This resulted in the police disclosing that several serial killers were at large and killing women. An arrest was even made, as a Sheriff's detective by the name of Ricky Ross was captured. However, the police later released him, stating that a major error had been made in ballistics.

Continuing on, the next murder occurred on September 11, 1988. Eighteen-year-old Alice Monique Alexander lost her life to a brutal strangulation and gunshots to the chest. She had also been raped prior to her death.

A major break was made in the case on November 20, 1988, when the only survivor of the Grim Sleeper managed to live to tell her tale. Enietra Margette, a pseudonym that was given to avert attention from the media, managed to survive the horrific attack. She was on her way to the store, and was going to a party when a well-dressed man in an orange Pinto with white racing stripes on the hood crossed her path. He asked to give her a ride, though she politely refused. However, when he commented that "black women think of themselves very highly," she eventually relented.

As she sat in the car, she was very impressed. The interior of the car was as neat and clean as could be, and had been maintained to near perfection. She later said that the conversation was getting awkward, and she eventually invited him to the party. Along the way, the man made a stop for ten minutes to meet with someone, and then returned back to the car. An argument ensued, and soon after the man took a gun from a pocket located in the driver's side of the car, and shot her point blank in the chest. She also stated that he had chronicled his actions with a Polaroid camera. She'd blacked out at first, but the flash of the camera caused her to open her eyes.

She begged this handsome black man to let her go, to drop her off at the hospital, but instead, he threw her out of the car while it was still moving. Obviously, he thought that she would not live to see the light of day, but call it a miracle or an act of the divine, Margette managed to get to her friend's house. As her friends returned from the party, they immediately took her to the emergency room where she was able to survive.

Her testimony was very important. She told the police about the man, which led the police to believe that this man was targeting prostitutes. The ballistics from the bullet matched the prior killings. Perhaps this botched incident spooked the killer—because for the next 14 years, the Grim Sleeper slept.

Fast-forward to 2002, and all that changes again.

The next three killings occurred in 2002, 2003, and the last occurred in 2007. Young Princess Barthomieux lost her life at the age of 15, whereas Valeria McCorvey was killed at the age of 35. The last victim, Janecia Peters, died at the hands of the Grim Sleeper at the age of 25. However, it was the evidence uncovered by Barthomieux's murder that led to a break in the case. Yet, it wasn't until 2010 that an arrest was finally made. Janecia Peters was found in a dumpster, tied up in a garbage bag and her body was discovered on New Year's Day. With firm DNA matches made from the murders that had occurred 14 years ago, the police came to the conclusion that the old murderer had finally returned, and it was time to put a permanent stop to his activities.

The Aftermath and Trial

This was the time when the nickname 'Grim Sleeper' was also introduced. A series of new information was put out to the media, which included updated information regarding the murderer. Familial DNA analysis was carried out, which ultimately tied the murders to Lonnie Franklin Jr.'s son, as it was a partial match to the DNA found on the bodies. Franklin was trailed for quite a while in an attempt to get his DNA match. However, this was proving to be pretty difficult.

The Los Angeles District Attorney at the time, Steve Cooley, eventually made use of a piece of discarded pizza to find the missing link. Franklin's first mistake was that he went out to buy pizza without noticing that he had a tail. Then, he left the discarded pizza along with the utensils on the table only after eating, which was later used to trace his DNA. The waiter at the restaurant where Franklin ate was an undercover officer.

Three days later, Lonnie Franklin Jr. was caught in a major arrest that involved more than thirty cops on the scene and led to global media coverage. An original film was also created of the scene, entitled the 'Grim Sleeper.' However, the case was far from over.

In March of 2011, Lonnie Franklin Jr. was indicted and charged with the murder of Monique Alexander, along with that of nine other women that he had killed. This extended to a charge of 11 murders, along with one attempted murder. Later, a map was created of the crime scenes, and it showed that the house of Lonnie Franklin Jr. fell almost right in the middle of the field where the murders were committed. It was expected that the grand jury indictment was going to bring the trial to a speedy end. Unfortunately, that was not the case.

Franklin, having been placed in a solitary cell at the Men's Central Jail, has created a very robust defense so far. He has even managed to bring his loyal wife, Sylvia Franklin, who is a school employee at Inglewood, into the life he leads in prison. And, he has also attracted the visits of Victoria Redstall, a pretty blonde actress and author who often likes to befriend serial killers. Even today, Lonnie Franklin Jr. continues to draw from his pension of $1,700 each month, which was given to him courtesy of the L.A. medical pension program. He has even made disjointed remarks to the families of the deceased, subjecting them to further trauma.

The case has been delayed continuously. When you think about the fact that Lonnie Franklin Jr. was 61 years old when he was apprehended, it goes to show that he has lived virtually his whole life without any retribution. If this continues, it is likely that he will live the rest of it without any retribution either. Many of the victims' families thought that once Franklin had been captured, the worst was now over. There would be no more killing, and they would get deserved justice, as Franklin would be put on death row. Unfortunately, that has not happened.

Seymour Amster is the defense lead in the case for Lonnie Franklin, and he has created a number of procedural halts and delays in the case. Even though evidence has been available for months, it still remains unclear as to whether the defense team has finished up with their DNA testing. The police have also uncovered further information, and have now made Franklin the prime suspect in the killing of at least six more women, which would mean that the loss of life attributed directly to his actions would be around 18. This number is also expected to grow.

It was also discovered that the number of survivors who

have managed to live through the attacks by Lonnie Franklin Jr. have also grown. Even though the police are refusing to put a final death count on the number of cases linked directly to Franklin, it is expected that this number revolves around the 100 mark. His trial was expected to begin on July 14, 2014, though at the time of this writing, that date has come and gone and a new date has not been set.

Since his arrest, Franklin has lost more than 40 pounds. He is in a solitary cell, alongside another serial killer who has been charged with killing three prostitutes and a hitchhiker. He also awaits a new trial in which the police have accused him of murdering six more people. The case files are spread over a total of 20,000 pages, making it a massive investigation. It remains to be seen as to whether the courts and this famed system of law will actually bring justice in this case.

Chapter 9: Rosemary West
"The House of Horrors"
by Sylvia Perrini

Gloucester is an attractive English cathedral port city. It sits on the banks of the River Severn close to the Welsh border. It is overlooked by the Cotswolds Hills from the east, the Malvern Hills to the west and is a short distance from the Forest of Dean.

It was in this city that Beatrix Potter based her favorite character 'The Tailor of Gloucester.' The city also became well known from an old English nursery rhyme.

"Doctor Foster"
Doctor Foster went to Gloucester
In a shower of rain;
He stepped in a puddle,
Right up to his middle,
And never went there again.

Gloucester, however, was really put on the world map by events that began to unfold towards the end of February 1994. On the 25th February 1994, Gloucester police officers began to excavate the garden and ground floor of a house at 25, Cromwell Street, belonging to Fred and Rosemary West. The excavation of the house and garden lasted fifty-five days and a total of ten bodies were found buried, before the search widened to two more locations.

As news of the excavations spread, the world media descended upon the ancient city of Gloucester and headlines around the world detailed the unfolding gruesome discoveries.

129

ROSEMARY WEST

If someone were to just look at a picture of Rosemary West, they probably would assume she was just an ordinary, everyday housewife. She, by all appearances, just seemed to be a woman who was doing the best she could to take care of her husband and her many children. The house in which she and her family lived was just a regular town house at the end of a terrace; one that people walked their dogs past and thought nothing of. A narrow walk way separated the house from a Seventh Day Adventist Church. The couple was well regarded in the community in which they lived and, in fact, there may have been some people even jealous of the outward life Rosemary led.

Behind the plain exterior, however, the house held a dark, disturbing, and chilling secret for many years. It was the location for the torture and murder of at least ten girls, all at the hands of Rosemary and her husband Fred. It was a secret that would be kept for almost twenty years. These were scenes of some of the most depraved crimes in British history that shocked even the most hardened detectives. As time passed, the couple grew bolder and more confident in their killings, often taking their victims from a nearby bus stop. Despite the numerous opportunities the police and public had to stop the house of horrors, it seemed Rosemary and Fred couldn't be touched. And, for a while at least, they were absolutely right.

Rosemary had a rough childhood growing up. She was subject to many forms of abuse at the hands of her father. When she had the chance to leave her abusive household, she ran to a new man who was no prize, either. As a result, Rosemary would do what she could to take the pain away from herself, choosing instead to channel it into her stepdaughters, her own children, and random women who were lured in off the street. It was a cycle that would repeat itself over and over again, but would never be brought before the authorities in a meaningful way until twenty years had passed.

The fault of the murders, of course, lies on Rosemary's shoulders, but there were several opportunities the local law enforcement had to put a stop to things, but they never did. Several people reported the abuse and the torture, but the police neglected to act upon the information. In one instance, they actually believed Rosemary when she said that certain sexual acts were all consensual. In another instance, a couple of people had the chance to go to the authorities when one of Rosemary's daughters came to them for help; instead, they chose to tell the West's themselves what the child had told them, which ultimately resulted in the death of the young girl.

People have speculated for many years as to why Rosemary helped to torture and murder girls on numerous occasions. Some people think they were the result of a simple case of jealousy: she didn't want anything or anyone to come between her and her husband, Fred. Other people theorize it was because she simply didn't know any better, having grown up experiencing abuse nearly all her life. And still more people think she was just prone to fits of rage and depression, using those as excuses to hurt or harm those around her. Rosemary has stated that she didn't want to be responsible for so many children, especially ones that weren't biologically hers. Yet, do any of these theories or speculations really explain her atrocious behavior?

Once the cycle started, Rosemary seemed to be unable to stop herself. With each victim entering, and rarely leaving her home, Rosemary had to take more and more steps to protect her secret. Her fear caused her to harm or kill several more girls, because the last thing Rosemary wanted was to be caught and brought to justice.

Ultimately, however, these things have a way of working themselves out. And even though Rosemary may have gotten away with murder for the better part of twenty years, it turned out she couldn't outrun the police forever.

Childhood and early life

Rosemary West was born in November of 1953 to Bill and Daisy Letts. She was one of seven siblings. Bill Letts liked the idea of being the king of his castle and expected his wife and children to fall in line behind him. He was strict and rigid, often to the point of violence if he felt he was not being respected or obeyed. Likely, due to his upbringing, Bill felt it was his duty as the man of the house to provide for his family, but he had trouble holding onto steady work. As a result, the family was often financially broke, and Bill would take his frustration out on his wife.

Due to the constant verbal and emotional abuse, Daisy was severely depressed, which led to her hospitalization shortly before Rosemary was born. Part of the treatments Daisy received included electroshock therapy while she was pregnant. Even though it has never been definitively proven, Bill blamed a lot of Rosemary's problems on this treatment.

When Rosemary was born, the family noticed almost right away she was not like her older siblings. Whenever she was alone, such as in a stroller or chair, Rosemary developed the habit of rocking herself for comfort. As such, the family labeled her "slow" and treated her as less-than-intelligent.

Compounding Rosemary's problems was the fact that she was overweight and thus thought of herself as unattractive. As a result, as she grew older, it appeared she would do whatever she could to get a boy's attention. As soon as she hit puberty, she began dressing in provocative clothing. As she hit her early teens, her father forbade her to date boys her own age. Rosemary wasn't too bothered by this restriction, however, choosing to find a loophole in her father's rule and set her sights on older men. She later claimed that she was raped by two older men when she was just fifteen years old.

Despite her heaviness and lack of book smarts, Rosemary ended up being her father's favorite because she was quick to obey his every order and she rarely talked back. This allowed her to escape her childhood with relatively few physical beatings, unlike her siblings. Or perhaps it was because her father took an entirely different interest in her. As she entered puberty, he would come into her room and sexually assault and abuse her. In part due to this abuse, and in part due to her lack of interest in school, Rosemary became increasingly withdrawn and sullen. She didn't have many friends at school and stopped caring about academic work altogether.

When Rosemary was a young teenager, her mother left her father and took Rosemary with her, although it remains unclear if it was because she found out about Rosemary's abuse or if she was simply tired of being abused herself. During that time, Rosemary and Daisy lived with Daisy's oldest daughter, Glenys, and her husband in the nearby town of Cheltenham. Rosemary, at this point, was so used to her father's abuse and desperate for attention from older men that she tried to hit on her brother-in-law. When that didn't work, Rosemary would sneak out at night and seek solace with other men.

When Rosemary was fifteen, she moved back in with her father – without her mother. According to some sources, it has been thought Rosemary actually missed living with her dad and did not see what he did to her as abuse. It had gone on for so long that to Rosemary it was as if they were in some kind of romantic, if incestuous, relationship with one another.

As soon as Rosemary moved back into her father's house, the sexual abuse picked right back up. Her father would come into her room several times a week to have sex or sexually molest her. Actions that were, to Rosemary, part of everyday normal life.

FRED WEST

Just before she was sixteen, Rosemary met Fred West, a jack of all trades, and the two instantly connected. As it would turn out, Fred was almost exactly like Rosemary's father: abusive and insulting. Despite the stark similarities between Bill Letts and Fred West, Rosemary's father resented the younger man and felt he was not a good fit for his daughter. At the time, Fred was already using the revolving door at the local jail, usually doing time for things such as thefts, failure to appear in court, and refusal to pay fines. The tension between the two men, Fred and Bill, got so bad that at one point, Bill actually went to Fred's house to attack him. When that didn't work, he tried to report Fred and Rosemary's relationship to social services, another act that proved to be ultimately fruitless.

Fred was older, wiser, and more experienced, at least in Rosemary's eyes. He had already been in a serious relationship with another woman, Rena Costello, and had fathered two children with her. And while Rosemary recognized he wasn't the perfect man – in fact, he was far from it, she still felt this inexplicable desire to be with him and take care of him. Fred appeared to awaken some maternal instinct in her. She recognized that Fred needed her more than her father did and shortly after her sixteenth birthday, she agreed to leave Bill Letts' house and move in with Fred at 25 Midland Road. Once having moved in, she became a stay-at-home mother, in charge of Fred's daughters, Charmaine and Anna-Marie, whom he'd had with Rena Costello.

Rosemary would soon follow in Rena's footsteps, quickly becoming pregnant at the age of sixteen with Fred's child: a daughter named Heather. Shortly after Heather was born, Fred was sent to prison, convicted of petty theft and tax evasion. Rosemary became deeply stressed with her new life, left all alone to care for three children; something for which she was woefully unprepared.

While all of this was going on, as if that weren't enough, Rosemary's father would still visit and have sex with her on an almost weekly basis. Rosemary was so accustomed to this happening that she still failed to recognize it as abuse. Even worse, when Heather and some of Rosemary's other daughters grew up, both Fred and Bill would sexually abuse and assault them. Rosemary blinded by either her childhood upbringing, her love of Fred, or just fear, would often go along with these trysts. In many cases, she would either instigate or actively help Fred and Bill live out their sadistic fantasies with Rena's children, complete strangers, or even her own children. And when one of the children got on to her bad side, she had no qualms about killing them and hiding their bodies. It was a pattern that would repeat itself for many years to come.

The first murder

In 1971, when Fred was in jail, Rosemary grew increasingly depressed with her lot in life and felt alone in the world. She would frequently lash out at the children, especially the two born to Rena Costello. Rosemary had never intended to get stuck raising someone else's kids on her own, and she resented every moment of it. She would place the blame solely on the kids for what her life had become; none of the vitriol went towards Fred. Instead, Rosemary would yell at Charmaine and Anna-Marie, verbally berate them, and abuse them. The children, under constant threat, would say nothing of the happenings at the house to anyone. It has never been proven that even the girls' biological mother, Rena Costello, knew what was happening under Rosemary's rule.

One day in June of 1971, Charmaine went missing and the truth wouldn't come out about what had happened to her for many years. Rosemary simply told people that her mother had come and taken her away. It was a story Rosemary would tell for many years, and the police and other authorities believed what she said. As a result, no formal investigation was ever conducted concerning the missing young lady.

In more recent years, however, the real truth of Charmaine's disappearance has since been discovered.

During one of her fits of rage against the girls, Rosemary killed Charmaine. It remains unclear if it was pre-meditated, on purpose, or simply a horrible accident. Regardless, after the young girl was murdered, the way Rosemary acted afterwards hinted at panic – that is until Fred West came home a couple of weeks afterwards and helped her stay the course—a course that she would never leave again.

Once Charmaine was dead, Rosemary hid the body until Fred was released from jail. History is a little hazy on if she confessed or if he discovered the dead child on his own but, either way, he didn't seem all that heartbroken about the death of his eldest daughter. It is thought that maybe Charmaine was his stepdaughter rather than his biological daughter.

Once he learned of what she had done, he helped

Rosemary dismember Charmaine's fingers and toes before burying the rest of the body under the kitchen floor. Though there are many theories as to why he dismembered the extremities, the most popular ones are either he was trying to cover up the victim's identity, or he wanted a sick souvenir. However, throughout the years, missing fingers and toes would become a trademark of most of the murders connected with Fred and Rosemary West. So maybe they were, in fact, sick souvenirs of their conquests.

For the rest of their married life, Fred would hold this dark secret over Rosemary's head, threatening to turn her into the authorities every chance he got. At one point, Rosemary's father, Bill, showed up to try to get her out from under Fred's thumb, but all Fred had to do was remind her of their little secret and the now terrified Rosemary would remain by Fred's side.

A wedding and a new baby

On January 29th, 1972, when Anna-Marie was eight years old, Rosemary and Fred got married and soon after, they had another daughter: Mae.

Not long after the wedding, Fred bought the family a new large town house at 25 Cromwell Street, which was more suitable for their growing family, and they moved out of the house in Midland Road, leaving Charmaine's buried body behind. It has been speculated that at least ten murders took place in the new abode.

THE HOUSE OF HORRORS

For a while, things seemed to be getting better for the couple. Fred would work while Rosemary took care of her two daughters and the remaining daughter, Anna-Marie, from Rena Costello. After a few scant months, things began to once again unravel in the West household.

Rena Costello came looking for her eldest daughter. Fred and Rosemary must have panicked when they saw her on their doorstep, afraid she would go to the police. To prevent this, they murdered her and dismembered her fingers and toes in the same way they had done with Charmaine. Fred took her body and buried it in a field near the small village of Kempley in the Forest of Dean twelve miles northwest of Gloucester.

It remains unclear if Rosemary had anything to do with the murder of Rena Costello but she at least knew about it and hid the fact from the authorities. The odds are extremely high, however, that with Fred's knowledge of the murder of Charmaine, he used that as a form of blackmail to get Rosemary to cooperate with whatever he wanted to do.

After this episode, in order to bring in a bit of extra money, Rosemary would prostitute herself out, so there were many nights that the children were left alone with her husband. Fred, by all accounts, knew all about her business and actively encouraged it. In their new home, Fred even made space in the basement for Rosemary to entertain her clients so Fred could watch. These rooms he fitted with listening and recording devices. In a bizarre kind of way, he seemed almost proud of himself and his wife for choosing to partake in the oldest profession in the world.

Fred and Rosemary West

While all of this was going on, Fred had his own plans for the other parts of the family basement, which was windowless and had thick walls, thus making it virtually soundproof. This part became equipped with all sorts of bondage and sadistic equipment, which Fred West would use on his daughter, Anna-Marie. Several times a week, he would bring her down to the basement, rape and torture her, and then send her on her way. On more than a few occasions, while this was going on, Rosemary would help either hold or tie the girl down. At some points, the abuse and rapes were so severe the young girl couldn't even attend school for days on end. During these years Anna-Marie apart from being raped, tortured and abused, got pregnant and contracted syphilis. Anna-Marie was threatened with death and more beatings if she ever revealed her secrets and thus didn't tell a soul. Despite the difficulty in keeping the family's dark interior to herself, doing so may have just spared her life.

CAROLINE OWENS

Caroline Owens was only seventeen years old at the time she met Fred and Rosemary. She was lured in by the promise of a live-in nanny position. The West's even met Caroline's parents and promised them that she would be safe, cared for, and protected while under their roof. It seemed like a great deal all the way around and so young Caroline had no qualms in accepting their seemingly generous offer.

Caroline was an attractive young woman and quickly gained the attention of both Rosemary and Fred. In fact, at times, it seemed like they were almost in competition with each other to see who could win the young girl's heart. After a few short weeks of this, Caroline grew increasingly repulsed by their advances and announced to the Wests that she was planning to quit her job and leave.

Rosemary and Fred were having none of that. They quickly got Caroline down into the basement, tied her up, and raped her over the course of several hours. Before they let her go, however, she was threatened with death and a gang rape if she ever told a soul what had happened beneath the West house. Fred boasted to her that there were other young girls buried beneath the floor that the police hadn't found and if she talked, she would join them. Relieved to still be alive, Caroline quickly agreed and was set free.

Her silence didn't last. Caroline almost immediately went to the police and told them her whole ordeal. Rosemary and Fred were arrested and a trial was held in the beginning of 1973. For some baffling reason, the Wests were able to convince the judge that every act between them and Caroline was consensual and she knew what was going on and enjoyed herself the entire time. So instead of going to jail, Rosemary and Fred each received a small fine for their role in sexually abusing and raping young Caroline Owens.

Even though they received an alarmingly low punishment for their crime, Rosemary and Fred regretted the fact that they let Caroline go at all. It was a mistake that they would try to ensure they would never make again.

A string of murders

Over the next few years, several young women were lured into the house of Rosemary and Fred West on Cromwell Street. Many of them were taken in by either the promise to be a live-in nanny or to simply rent a room from the couple. Either way, each one had thought they had found the ideal situation for themselves, and each time they paid with their lives.

The first person to fall victim at the Cromwell Street house was a young lady named Lynda Gough. She had been a seamstress and had struck up a friendship with Rosemary and Fred, visiting their house and going to lunch (and all of the other things friends do in that type of relationship). When Rosemary and Fred presented her with the idea of being a live-in child minder, Lynda all but jumped at the chance. Though the details are unclear, at some point Lynda was lured down into the basement and raped. Learning from their experience with Caroline, Rosemary and Fred ultimately strangled Lynda. As with before, Fred removed Lynda's fingers and toes before burying the rest of her body underneath the garage.

It was a pattern that would repeat itself time and time again. Carol Ann Cooper, Lucy Partington, Therese Siegenthaler, Shirley Hubbard, and Juanita Mott all were lured into Rosemary's and Fred's house, tortured and raped for about a week, and then killed, dismembered, and buried somewhere within the property. With each victim, Rosemary's and Fred's sadistic urges grew more baroque. They weren't satisfied simply tying someone up and raping them—that was too mundane. Instead, they would think of new ways to torture the young women. In some cases, they would wrap plastic bags around their heads, with straws shoved up their noses as a source of air. In others, they would suspend their victims from the ceiling, torturing them that way until the final form of suspension: a noose.

All of these women were under the age of twenty-two, with the vast majority being teenagers. In each case, their families would either come looking for them or would report their daughters missing to the police, but the police just couldn't make the connection between the young women and Fred and Rosemary West. It turned into a source of frustration for the cops, but until some evidence presented itself, there was really nothing to be done about it.

One particular victim of Rosemary and Fred's ended up being a special case – Shirley Robinson. Shirley was eighteen years old, a prostitute, and bisexual. She was seemingly the perfect match for Rosemary and Fred, as they each engaged in a sexual relationship with her. After a short while, Shirley became pregnant with Fred's baby. Fred was thrilled. Rosemary, on the other hand, was not so excited. She felt threatened by this young, beautiful, pregnant woman. Rosemary was terrified she would be replaced and decided Shirley had to go. Fred, for some unknown reason, went along with this plan. As with the other young ladies, he killed Shirley and the unborn child. True to form, he dismembered her fingers and toes and then buried their corpses in the yard of their house.

While all of this was going on, Fred would constantly be making improvements to the house in which he and Rosemary lived. In order to pay for these home projects, Fred resorted to stealing. On more than one occasion, the police were called to the West household to investigate these minor crimes and, alarmingly, never suspected the horror they would have found if they had looked just a few feet beneath them.

Fred West enlarged both the basement and the garage,

supposedly making more room for his victims. With all of those bodies around, he must have been simply running out of room to house them all. Fred would, of course, work on the house at night or at other times when it wouldn't be noticed. If any of the neighbors thought something was amiss, they never said a word.

A growing family

During the years of the makeshift torture chamber, Rosemary gave birth to several more children. Most of them were Fred's babies, but at least two or three of them were with one or another of her prostitution clients. She gave birth to a daughter named Tara, a daughter named Rosemary Junior, and a daughter named Lucyanna. Rosemary got pregnant with Lucyanna around the same time Fred got Shirley Robinson pregnant. Instead of feeling jealous, however, Fred was excited that Rosemary was pregnant by another man – especially a black man. For some reason, Fred loved the idea of having a mixed-race baby in the house.

Over time, more children came into the picture, until the Wests had a total of nine. With so many kids to take care of, Rosemary became increasingly depressed and tired, and her temper would flare at the slightest provocation. She would severely beat the children on a regular basis. Rosemary grew irrational and paranoid, afraid she was going to lose Fred at any moment. Every time something happened to make her fear grow, she would take it out on the kids.

The children, unfortunately, knew practically everything that was going on in the house. They knew about the torture chamber, and they knew Anna-Marie was subjected to rape and torture at the hands of their father. The kids also knew their mother was a prostitute and became used to strange men wandering through the house at any given moment.

HEATHER

At some point, Anna-Marie aged to maturity and moved out of the West household to live with her boyfriend. Fred, having no regular victim to torture, set his sights on his and Rosemary's oldest daughter, Heather. He promptly had her take Anna-Marie's place down in the basement, torturing and raping her several times a week. Along with Heather, Fred would also bring down his second-eldest daughter, Mae, and perform the same unspeakable acts with her as well.

Heather, knowing something was amiss with this arrangement; ended up telling a friend of hers of the torture she was receiving, either to protect herself or her sister. This friend told her parents, who ended up telling Rosemary and Fred what they had heard. As a result, in June of 1987, Rosemary and Fred ended up killing sixteen-year-old Heather, dismembering her, and having their eldest son, Stephen, dig a hole in the backyard to bury her in. They were quickly running out of room at the Cromwell Street house to hold more victims and so Heather West became the last body buried at that house.

Police closing in

Even though Rosemary and Fred took measures to hide what they were doing, eventually, the situation came before the police through another abused daughter, who had told a friend at school and whose mother reported it to the police. This, coupled with a statement from another young woman Rosemary and Fred had tortured, who told the authorities about the house of horrors and what she had endured, led in

1992 to a search being made of the house on Cromwell Street.

This happened over twenty years after Rosemary's first murder—the one of Fred's stepdaughter, Charmaine. During the search of the house, detectives found evidence of child abuse and massive amounts of child pornography. Rosemary was arrested on the charge of assisting in the rape of a minor, and Fred was arrested for the rape and sodomy of a minor. Rosemary's and Fred's children were pulled from the West household and put into the care of the government. All of the children were questioned about the goings-on inside of the house, but Fred and Rosemary had told them they would end up like Heather if they breathed a word about what was happening and so they kept their silence.

The case against Fred and Rosemary collapsed when the two main witnesses changed their minds about testifying against them, and the Wests were both released.

One particular investigator on the case, Hazel Savage, had come across Fred before. She had known Rena Costello, and she had always wondered about her strange and sudden disappearance. Rena had also told Hazel about Fred's inclinations in the bedroom, causing Hazel to become even more concerned. DC Savage continued to be disturbed by what had been uncovered in the house and the fact that the Wests had been released without a trial.

She set her sights on investigating Fred and Rosemary more fully, but she needed more information.

Her first stop was to visit Anna-Marie, Fred's sole remaining daughter with Rena. Anna-Marie, probably due to her years of abuse and threats to what would happen to her if she ever spoke about her treatment, was reluctant to talk at first but eventually the truth came out. She highlighted everything that went on in the house, including her torture and rapes. Anna-Marie also expressed her suspicions about the disappearance of Charmaine, Rena, and Heather but didn't have any proof to offer up. Hazel believed Anna-Marie's story and questioned the other West children repeatedly, but they had been well trained by their abusive parents and failed to co-operate with the authorities.

When Fred and Rosemary were asked where Heather was, they claimed she had run away when she was sixteen. They described her as a difficult child with lesbian tendencies.

Finally, the police in their search for Heather obtained a warrant on February 23, 1994 to search the Cromwell house and excavate the garden. On the 24th of February, police officers visited Cromwell Street and informed Rosemary that her rear garden was going to be searched and dug up due to the disappearance of her daughter, Heather. On February 25th, Fred admitted to detectives he had murdered his daughter Heather and buried her in the back patio. He was remanded into custody.

Rosemary was then arrested on suspicion of the murder of her daughter Heather. She denied all knowledge of her daughter's disappearance or whereabouts. She claimed she was out of town the day Heather disappeared and had absolutely no idea what had happened to her.

Following Rosemary's arrest, Fred was taken back to his house on Cromwell Street and showed officers roughly where he had buried his daughter. The following day, he retracted his statement and denied murdering Heather. However, just three hours later, officers digging in his garden found Heather's remains plus the bones of another human corpse. This was the first time the investigators had any inkling there may be more to the story than just murdering those in the family.

Following this discovery, Fred admitted again to murdering Heather but claimed it was without Rosemary's knowledge.

146

Even though Rosemary had been arrested, she did not stay in prison for long. On the 27th of February in 1994 she was released on bail. As the search into the property on Cromwell Street was to be so intensive it was not a place she could stay, so she was provided with temporary accommodation and soon feared for her own safety.

The police had wanted to avoid media attention, but they had no choice but to start digging underneath the house. Fred had poured concrete slabs over the majority of the victims, so finding them became a task all on its own. The search and excavations at Cromwell Street lasted in total fifty-five days. As word spread throughout the media about the murder excavations in Cromwell Street, journalists and television crews from around the world descended upon the area. And the search for Rosemary, for journalists hoping to catch the hottest story or photograph, was on. Rosemary had to be moved to different properties on a couple of occasions to shield her from the media and hating public.

During this time, she made a couple of unsuccessful attempts at suicide. Instead, Rosemary turned to food as her sole source of comfort, gaining a significant amount of weight by the time she was put to trial for her crimes.

Fred knew it was only a matter of time before they found the rest of the victims; and find them, they did. Fred, during his time in custody, made a full confession to the murders at Cromwell Street and of his stepdaughter Charmaine in the Midland Road house. He also told police where he had buried the body of his first wife Rena and where the body of Anne McFall (his ex-wife's best friend and pregnant girlfriend of his) who was last seen in the summer of 1967, could be found in a field near Kempley. At this point, Fred claimed sole responsibility for all of the murders. He told the police Rosemary had no involvement whatsoever. Also, somewhat strangely, he never admitted to raping the young women; throughout the entire investigation and trial, he remained steadfast that the girls wanted to have sex with him and all of the acts between them were consensual. Maybe it was just complete insane fantasy in his mind but one that he genuinely believed!

Rosemary, in her mind, thought if she wasn't with Fred anymore, that she could distance herself from the investigation and could act like a horrified victim and get away with her crimes. The police didn't have enough evidence to prove she was in any way connected to the murders and especially not those of Rena and Anne. However, deep down, Hazel and the other detectives knew she was involved and it would only be a matter of time before they could prove it.

On Saturday, the 23rd of April in 1994, Rosemary was arrested for murder.

On Wednesday, the 27th of April in 1994, excavation work began on the house in Midland Road.

Rosemary maintained her helpless victim status throughout the rest of the investigation and even during the hearing. Even after the bodies of Charmaine and Rena were discovered, Rosemary maintained her innocence, stating she was under Fred's thumb and completely powerless to stop this monster from hurting her, the children, and the countless victims that ended up buried beneath their property.

Fred, however, was still enthralled with Rosemary and, despite everything going on around him, still wanted to be with her. At their court hearings, he attempted several times to make contact with her, trying to touch her, hug her, and console her throughout it all. Rosemary rebuffed each and every attempt, telling prosecutors she wanted nothing more to do with him and the mere sight of him made her feel sick. Fred was heartbroken at the way Rosemary treated him because he believed she still loved him. After numerous attempts to write her letters and win her back, and being shot down at every turn, Fred hanged himself in his jail cell on January 1, 1995. He would never have to face what he did in a courtroom; instead, he chose to take the easy way out.

Rosemary on trial

Rosemary was charged with ten counts of murder. The prosecution had no evidence to link her to the murder of Rena or Anne McFall. In fact, except for Charmaine who had been murdered while Fred was in prison, there was never any direct evidence to tie Rosemary West in with the rape, torture, or murders of any of the other victims. In fact, without a confession, the prosecutors didn't have a whole lot to go on, except for circumstantial evidence. Rosemary was convinced she would receive a lighter sentence and not be held accountable for any of the murders.

Rosemary West

That is, until several witnesses came forward to testify against Rosemary and all that she had done over the years. Anna-Marie, Caroline Owens, and a few other surviving victims all presented themselves to the court. As each one told their harrowing tale, the courtroom grew more and more convinced

149

of her involvement. The defense tried to argue that sexual assault and abuse was not the same as murder, and as such, the prosecution still had no direct evidence to link Rosemary to killing the young women.

Another woman, by the name of Janet, also came forward to testify. She had been involved in the investigation of Fred, serving as a witness to many of his interviews with the law enforcement officers. During these interviews, she said that Fred had privately confessed to her Rosemary's involvement in the murders, including the fact that she had killed Charmaine all on her own. He told Janet he had agreed to take the fall for the murders because he wanted to protect Rosemary at all costs. Janet, for her part, claimed Fred threatened her and terrified her to the point where she kept her silence for far too long. It was only after Fred's death that she felt confident enough to take the stand and repeat what he had said to her.

The testimonies of Janet and the young women almost completely torpedoed the defense's case. There was enough evidence to link Rosemary in with all of the crimes, but again, it was all hearsay and showed involvement with the torture and the rape of the victims, but not the murders themselves. The defense played a few tapes of Fred's interviews with the police, where he himself told them it was all his idea and Rosemary had nothing to do with any of it. Janet, however, had successfully shot down any credibility Fred may have had with those statements, and the jury knew to take Fred's confessions with a huge grain of salt.

The defense, in a bizarre final attempt to prove their case, decided to put Rosemary herself on the stand to try to clear her own name. It was a move that backfired in a spectacular fashion. Rosemary couldn't control her temper and quickly became belligerent every time evidence was

150

brought against her. All the prosecution had to do was make her angry, and she would self-incriminate. It was a pattern that happened within the courtroom over and over again. The jury quickly learned how bad Rosemary's temper could be and how dishonest she really was. As a result, she was deemed untrustworthy, which only served to damage her case beyond repair.

The verdict

After hearing all of the testimony and witnesses, the jury wasted no time at all finding Rosemary guilty of ten counts of murder. In fact, many members of the jury believed she was the mastermind behind everything. They thought she was dominant toward Fred and had orchestrated each and every murder, with Fred all too happy to go along with it. Rosemary appeared stunned at the verdict but had no choice but to comply.

Due to her involvement in the torture and murder of the victims, Rosemary was sentenced to life in prison with no chance of parole. She was immediately taken into custody and transferred to a penitentiary. It is there she still remains and will stay for the rest of her life.

Media

During the trial, Rosemary West got tons of media attention. It seemed the entire United Kingdom was hooked on this case and all of its bizarre twists and turns. Once the trial was over, however, a lot of the media attention died down; however, even to this day there is a fascination with this story that causes people to revisit it every now and again.

Over the years since the case, there have been many

talks of turning their story into a movie. Every time it has been brought up, the public outcry is large enough that it is shot down and nothing is ever made. It seems no one wants Fred and Rosemary West to get any more attention, fame, or money than they already have for their treatment of the young women.

However, a documentary was made about Rosemary and Fred, using photos from their house, including some crime scene photos and some pictures that once belonged to Fred. It was a controversial documentary because of the amount they showed and also because they gave Fred and Rosemary even more media attention that the public at large felt was not deserved.

Another reason this documentary was considered controversial was how the photos themselves got into the hands of the production company. After Fred's suicide, the estate was trying to raise some money to pay off some of the outstanding debts Fred owed and auctioned off a lot of his property. Among the items were many photos either Fred or Rosemary had taken throughout their stay at Cromwell Street.

The highest bidder for those pictures ended up being a production company, who then used them in the documentary. If Fred had not killed himself, those pictures would have remained in police custody. Once people realized how those chilling photos got into the hands of the production company, they tried to get a law passed to prevent things like that from happening in the future. They argued that, out of respect to the victims and their families, pictures like that should remain private and not available for public consumption. Ultimately, the bill didn't go anywhere and none of the laws were changed, but it at least brought this matter to the forefront of people's minds so they know to be aware of this practice of certain cut throat media companies. Quite a few books, however, have been written about the case.

One of the authors visited the Cromwell Street house and claimed some odd happenings going on during his time there. He became convinced that the property was haunted by some of the victims. When he brought up his concerns to the authorities, they agreed that there had been some strange sightings, but they couldn't find any logical explanation for it.

In the autumn of 1996, the Wests' house at 25 Cromwell Street was flattened and a public walkway was laid in its place. The decision to demolish the house was seen as one way of expunging the area of the sense of evil related to the house and its grim associations.

WITNESSES JANET AND ANNA-MARIE

Janet, the woman who sat in on the police interviews, ultimately ended up suing the police because of her involvement with this case. She said that hearing Fred confess to all of these murders, and the details of each, had caused her to suffer from post-traumatic stress disorder. She claimed that many of the law enforcement officers were able to receive psychiatric treatment but she, as a volunteer, was offered none of the same resources. She tried several times over the years to receive compensation for herself, but each time she was denied. The government claims she was strictly a volunteer and knew what she was getting herself into; they state there was nothing stopping her from seeking out the appropriate counseling on her own.

Anna-Marie, now married, perhaps had the hardest time adjusting to life outside of the West home, and with good reason. On multiple occasions, she tried to kill herself. At one point, she jumped from a bridge but was rescued by the police. Another time, she swallowed multiple sleeping pills.

She ended up being rushed to the hospital and having her stomach pumped.

In June 1996 she published a book Out of the Shadows: Fred West's Daughter Tells Her Harrowing Story of Survival.

After the trial, the five younger West children were sent to foster families and given new identities. All contact between them and their older siblings was stopped.

Stephen, an electrician, and Mae West, a mother, had a book published in December 1995 about their childhood entitled: Inside 25 Cromwell St. They both still live in Gloucester

Appeals

While Rosemary has been in prison, she has tried numerous times to file an appeal and overturn her conviction and life sentence. In March of 1996, Rosemary's lawyers submitted on her behalf an application for leave to appeal against her conviction. She and her lawyers promised there would be new evidence to support her claims that Fred West acted alone, without the consent or even knowledge of Rosemary. The appeal was denied.

In October of 2000, Rosemary's lawyers made an application to have her conviction reviewed by the CCRC (Criminal Cases Review Commission). Her lawyers were trying to prove that Rosemary had not received a fair trial.

In September of 2001, Rosemary decided she'd had enough of fighting with the courts and decided not to seek any more appeals. This means she has finally chosen to accept her fate and will remain in prison until she dies.

Life in prison

At one point, Rosemary and a thirty-something-year-old musician started writing back and forth. They became serious, so much so, that on January 19, 2003, it was announced that Rosemary West was to marry the bass player, Dave Glover, of the rock band Slade.

The press had a field day with this information, wondering why they would do such a thing and who in their right mind would marry a serial killer. Whether she was craving the attention, or it was an unwitting byproduct, she became the focus of many papers and news reports around the United Kingdom.

Less than a week later, the wedding was called off, and Dave Glover was dropped from the band.

When asked about the break-up, Rosemary stated that the young musician had been getting threatening letters and phone calls and, thus, she decided to end the relationship, stating that she didn't want to hold him back in his career.

Rosemary West is serving her sentence at a top security prison in Durham, North England at a cost to the taxpayer of $80,000 (£50,000). Her single cell is furnished with a TV, CD player, radio, and she has her own bathroom.

According to an article in the Daily Mail in 2014, Rosemary is very happy and content in prison, where she enjoys listening to the radio, playing Monopoly, cooking, embroidery, shopping from catalogues, and indulges in a host of lesbian affairs.

Conclusion

Rosemary West is an interesting character to say the least. Ever since she was born, she was fighting incredible odds to make something of herself. Having been abused and terrorized by her own father from such an early age, it's no surprise she ended up becoming a monster herself. As soon as she had the opportunity to get out from her father's watchful eye, she ran to someone who was just as bad or maybe even worse. Through these two men, Bill Letts and Fred West, it's no wonder Rosemary felt virtually untouchable. After all, nothing serious ever happened to her father or to her husband, despite all of the bad things they did over the course of their lives.

None of this excuses Rosemary's behavior, of course. It's crystal clear she knew right from wrong from the way she hid her dastardly deeds. Rosemary's first murder happened while Fred West was behind bars, serving time for theft. There is no way she was able to pin it on him and claim he made her take part in ending the life of a young girl, whose only crime was being born to the wrong parents.

Even when she was caught, and the evidence was stacked against her, Rosemary chose to lie to the police about her involvement, choosing instead to pin it on Fred. And Fred, in the name of love, either went along or helped instigate each and every instance of a girl being taken, tortured, and murdered. Despite all of this, the moment the cards were down, Rosemary turned her back on Fred.

Everything that went on in that house was villainous and simply pure evil. As a direct result of Rosemary and Fred's actions, nearly a dozen women and girls are dead, having no chance to live a life. Countless more lives were changed forever, either through the direct abuse or through the simple act of witnessing or hearing about what was done.

For many years, Rosemary evaded capture. Either the police didn't believe the victims or they just weren't aware of what was going on behind the walls of the house of Cromwell

Street. And with each victim Rosemary and Fred took, they grew more emboldened and surer they would get away with what they were doing forever. As with anything though, even these types of crimes had to come to an end eventually. As a result, Rosemary has ended up exactly where she should be: behind bars for the rest of her life.

Chapter 10: Felipe Espinoza
"Tale from the Old West"
by RJ Parker

The Mexican American War, also known as the Invasion of Mexico, was one of the defining moments of the 1800s. The war not only echoed throughout history, impacting the lives of many that were involved in it, but it also redefined the course of history, altering the United States of America as we see it. The war lasted one year and nine months, and was a pretty bloody affair. Most will give different reasons as to why the war started, but in truth, the main reason for the war was the annexation of Texas, which the Mexicans considered to be their own property.

Back in 1845, the United States annexed Texas and incorporated it as the 28th State. Texas had already declared independence from the Republic of Mexico back in 1836, and a lot of the people of Texas were actually in favor of annexation. However, the leaders of both the biggest political parties of America, the Whigs and the Democrats, were pretty much against the introduction of Texas as a state, mainly because the residents of Texas were known for owning a vast number of slaves. The introduction of a vast region of slave-owning people into a pretty volatile political atmosphere that was precariously balanced between pro-slavery and anti-slavery view points in the Congress was unlikely to have a positive effect.

Another reason why the leaders opposed the annexation of Texas was because it was almost a certainty that this would lead to war with Mexico, something the country wanted to avoid at all costs. The government of Mexico at that time had refused to acknowledge the sovereignty of the

159

province. However, by the 1840s, the economic conditions of Texas were deteriorating rapidly, and it was evident that a change had to be introduced. A number of talks were held with the government of Mexico, but all of this resulted in President Tyler offering immediate annexation to Texas by the year 1845. In December, Texas was annexed and incorporated as the 28th State of America.

Come April 1846, the Mexican American war began. The war was a bloody one, there's no doubt about that. The American forces were able to quickly capture the state of California as well as New Mexico, and were also able to invade parts of Northwest Mexico and Northeast Mexico. A blockade was also set up by the Pacific Squadron, which was stationed in the Pacific Ocean, and this led to the Pacific Squadron gaining control of a number of major garrisons set along side the Pacific Coast towards the southern side of Baja California. Situations became very dire for the Mexicans, and ultimately, another American army was able to capture Mexico City, which effectively resulted in the end of the war. After one year, nine months, one week, and one day, the Mexican American War had finally come to an end.

The Treaty of Guadalupe Hidalgo effectively spelled out the damage that had been caused to the Mexicans as a result of the war; New Mexico and Alta California were ceded to the United States for a price of $15 million. The Mexican border was moved to Rio Grande, as the country accepted that Texas was no more to be considered their own land. For the politicians, this was a major win. President James K. Polk's main purpose of invading Mexico all the way to the Pacific Coast was to expand American territory. The war also invoked controversy within the United States, as the leaders of the Whig Party and the anti-imperialists were all pretty opposed. There were heavy casualties on both sides and a significant amount of monetary damage was also incurred.

However, despite the significant political damage that was caused to both the countries as a result of the war, the damage caused to individual families was much worse. Since the Centralist Republic of Mexico was forced to concede New Mexico, the people who lived there found it quite difficult to adapt to the ways of the Americans. There was wide spread dissent amongst the people, mainly because the Anglo Americans were grabbing up land as much as they could, and had also begun to politically exploit the people. For the people who had their roots deep in Mexican culture, the change was proving to be an extremely challenging affair. Of the many families that had to suffer from moving away from their own homes and settle into poorer places because of the Americans, the descendants of Nicolas de Espinosa took it quite hard. This was a Nuevomexicano family hailing from the mestizo and coyote lineage that had first settled in New Mexico back in 1695.

So, you can well imagine the impact left on the family from the war. This was a family that considered the town, and its people, their own. For five generations, the Espinosas had lived peacefully in New Mexico until the war broke away everything. On top of the indignation that the family suffered, the Americans had begun taking away their lands and subjecting the family to their own terms. However, the story that you are about to read is one of the most remarkable tales in the history of the west. Few know the details of what truly happened, mainly because at that time, record keeping was not at a very advanced stage. The typewriter had not come in to use as yet, and in those days record keeping was primarily completed by those who had actually been affected by what transpired. The story that follows is of a man named Felipe Nerio Espinosa, and what he did. It also involves another key person, Tom Tobin, one of the most legendary trackers that lived in those times. The events that have been written in the following paragraphs have been compiled from the diaries kept by Espinosa and Tobin, as well as newspaper articles and retellings of the story. The events have been put together to provide an accurate picture of what actually transpired in those days.

***

Felipe Nerio Espinosa was born in 1832 to Pedro Ygnacio Espinosa and Maria Gertrudis Chavez. He was born at the San Juan Nepomuceno de El Rito in New Mexico, and was the eldest amongst five siblings. The names of his younger siblings were Maria Tomasa, Jose Vivian, Juan Antonio, and Maria Juana, who was the youngest of the lot. Even before the Mexican American War had started, the communities based in Northern New Mexico had expressed their dissatisfaction at having been largely ignored by the government of Mexico. This was mainly because of their remote geographical location as well as the internal political turmoil that existed within the southern parts of the country. By that time, the people of New Mexico felt themselves to be independent and strong willed, and felt that they were not governed by anybody.

When the Treaty of Guadalupe Hidalgo was signed, it stated that all the rights to property of the people of New Mexico would remain with the original owners. However, this was not the case. Numerous entrepreneurial Americans ventured into the land, manipulating and bribing their way across and using deviousness and chicanery, which ultimately caused the native people of New Mexico to lose approximately two-thirds of their land to the new Americans. One of the families that lost land to the invading Americans was that of

Felipe Espinoza.

Ultimately, by 1858, there wasn't enough land for Felipe Espinoza and his family to be able to provide for themselves. As a result, he was forced to move out, and ended up settling in Conejos County, Colorado. He settled in the town of San Rafael. Little is known of Felipe's physical appearance. The newspapers of those times claimed that he had a "jack o-lantern grin," comprised of misshapen teeth, with gaps among them. He would often claim that he was proud of his Castilian blood, and considered his heritage to be one of God's given privileges. Very little doubt remains over Felipe's education; he was certainly a learned man. However, little is known as to where he received his education, because those areas were pretty much devoid of schools. It is very likely that he was taught by his mother or someone from his family.

He was a religious man, and also considered himself to be highly patriotic. This was one of the main reasons why he considered being driven out of the land of his forefathers such a big form of injustice. He had often vowed amongst his friends that he would one day take his revenge. The influx of Presbyterians and the Baptists that moved into Nuevo Mexico left a lot of New Mexicans, along with Felipe, quite angry. This was the land of his family and it was their property that was being occupied. He was unable to do anything about it. And so, as mentioned, he did the only thing that was in his power, albeit with a lot of reluctance. He, along with his wife, Secundina Hurtado, and other members of his extended family finally settled in Conejos County, but that was not exactly what Felipe wanted.

The circumstances in Conejos County were not very good either. His brother, Jose Vivian, had also moved out with them, and it was sometime during this period that the Espinosa family met with such hardships and desperation that

Felipe Espinosa and Jose Vivian finally began to consider a career in banditry. Felipe, along with his brother Jose Vivian, started small at first. They began robbing freight wagons and stealing horses that passed along routes. For the next few years that followed, these acts began to define the Espinosa brothers. Once, there came a wagon along an empty route with just one driver. It was coming from Santa Fe and moving towards Galisteo, and was likely carrying freight goods. The two brothers at first thought they'd only just loot the wagon, but then decided to have a little fun. Tying the driver upside down with his head barely moving above the rocky surface of the earth, the two brothers pulled the wagon ahead. By the end of the journey, the driver was barely alive, though he managed to live, and ultimately described his assailants to the police. This was the first bounty that was put on the heads of the Espinosa brothers. And so began a period of time that resulted in murder, violence and hatred of a very high order. This was also the first time that they had been recognized and described to the police, as the wagon driver had once been a neighbor in Conejos with them.

The American officials situated at Fort Garland in California sent out a small group of men in order to arrest the Espinosa brothers at their home in San Rafael. Upon arrival however, the military men found that the Espinosa brothers were armed. A shootout then ensued, which ultimately resulted in the death of an Army Corporal. From robbery, the initial charge had now been increased to include murder too. The Espinosas were able to escape however, and moved into the safety of the Sangre de Cristo Mountains. In English, Sangre de Cristo means the 'Blood of the Christ,' a fitting name.

Meanwhile, the American military had decided to search the home of the two brothers and found the money from the previous robbery, as well as stolen goods from other robberies. All was taken back. When the two brothers returned from the mountains days later to ensure their house was all right, they found that the house had been stripped of the most basic possessions, and that the family was in dire straits. This led to the brothers becoming highly infuriated with the Americans, declaring a war against them. A pact was signed by the two to kill as many Americans as they possibly could.

According to history records as well as newspaper clippings from that era, the first kill made out of vengeance by the Espinosas was in March of 1863. At first, the Espinosas were quite successful. It wasn't long before they had been able to kill a number of Anglo Americans, starting from the area that is currently known as Fremont County in Colorado. The corpse of their first kill had been badly mutilated—the heart had been hacked out of his chest.

During the same summer, they had managed to kill around twenty-five more people, all in the same horrific manner. However, on May 9, 1863, the two brothers were followed back to their camp, where a shootout ensued and Jose Vivian received a fatal wound, dying soon after. Felipe, however, managed to escape.

He enlisted the help of his cousin as well as his nephew in order to fulfill his quest to murder as many Americans as he could. In this time period, he also wrote a letter to the Territorial Governor, John Evans, mentioning that he wanted to kill 600 "Gringos." He later demanded full pardons for himself and his family, as well as 5,000 acres of land in Conejos County along with appointments in the Colorado Volunteers. The letter also mentioned that in case his wishes were not fulfilled, the Governor himself was likely to die, along with 574 more "Anglos."

The military and police were soon up in action. Conejos County Sheriff Emmett Harding, along with Colorado Volunteer Commander S. B. Tappan, had been assigned to find Felipe Espinosa, though they were virtually unable to track down the men. A search party of sixteen men was formed to capture Felipe along with his compatriots, without success. Often times, they would travel for days and nights in search for Felipe, and once they were even able to find the campsite of the Espinosas, though Felipe was always able to escape from them. By September 5, 1863, more and more corpses had been found badly mutilated. A woman by the name of Dolores had barely survived the Espinosas, but Felipe and Julian had raped her. Her role here is crucial, she was able to provide the best possible description of the Espinosa family. The time had come for Commander Tappan and his men to put an end to the Espinosas.

Thomas Tobin, a famous adventurer, tracker, mountain guide, as well as a U.S. Army Scout, was called up by Colonel Tappan to Fort Garland, and asked to take up the hunt for the Espinosas. His first action upon entering the Fort was to carefully interview both Dolores, along with a member who was traveling with her, Philbrook. At first, Tobin insisted that he travel alone to find the company of Espinosas on his own. The request was obviously denied. Espinosa was no ordinary criminal.

He was offered a company of full militiamen at his disposal, though he politely refused, ultimately settling upon three party soldiers to help him. Tobin was an articulate, meticulous person. When he was able to find the first campsite used by the Espinosas, the experienced tracker would carefully consider each and every object and scent in the area before finding a path that followed. Soon, a chain emerged. They would reach campsite after campsite, with fresh ash smoldering in the fire pits. The party soon realized that it wouldn't be long before they would finally catch up to Espinosas.

Tobin refused to allow his company to light fires. He would also give them very little time to sleep. On the fourth day of their hunt, Tobin saw some birds flying about nearby. A kill had been made. Soon, Tobin and his men were able to see a ring of smoke in the distance. Instructing his men to lay low, he got down to the ground, and began to crawl on all fours like an army man towards the scene. For most of the day, Tobin crawled like this.

However, his slow approach came to an end when he saw Julian and Felipe sitting off in the distance, their faces illuminated by the dim light of the fire. A dead ox that had been murdered only a few hours before lay beside the two, about to be put on the skewer as dinner for the two men.

It was obvious that getting the proper shot was not exactly easy. The Espinosas had a powerful reputation, which meant that a missed bullet would definitely get Tobin killed. Fortunately, the bigger of the Espinosas stood up and began to stretch. Tobin took the chance. The bullet hit Felipe Espinosa directly in his sides, catching the man off guard and knocking the wind out of him. As Tobin reloaded, Julian began running for the woods. Tobin sent off a second shot, which caught Julian directly in his spine, killing the young Espinosa on the spot.

All this time, Felipe had managed to move himself away from the fire, and was resting against a log when Tobin approached the dying man. Felipe hurled curses at Tobin. However, Tobin severed his head and then the head of the younger Espinosa, and made his way back to Tappan. To this day, the assassination of the Espinosas makes Tom Tobin a famous man around Colorado. There was controversy afterwards, as the bounty placed on Espinosa's head was $5500, of which Tobin received not a cent, not from the government anyway. People believed that Tobin wanted the money, though he maintained that he did not know of any bounty until after he brought the men's heads back to town. He did receive a number of gifts however, along with money that was raised by the public. The reign of terror of Felipe Espinosa had come to an end, in what was probably one of the greatest untold stories of the west.

Chapter 11: Donald Harvey
"Angel of Death"
by Michael Newton

Each year, some 1.4 million patients die in American hospitals, an average of 3,835 deaths per day. In 1999, a report from the Institute of Medicine estimated that 98,000 of those annual deaths were preventable, caused by medical mistakes or negligence. More recently, in September 2013, an updated report raised that number to 440,000 preventable deaths per year, listing hospital medical errors as the third leading cause of death in the United States. Other studies place the annual toll of deaths from medical errors above 780,000.

Those numbers are enough to shake our faith in "healers," but they do not count another threat: the menace of deliberate murders committed by serial killers on hospital staffs. No trustworthy statistics exist for that plague, but headline-grabbing cases make the killer medics' names familiar: Orville Majors, Charles Cullen, Genene Jones, Efren Saldivar, Kristen Gilbert, Richard Angelo, Gwendolyn Graham and Catherine Wood, among others. Most prolific of them all, according to his guilty pleas and the supporting evidence, is Donald Harvey, convicted slayer of 36 victims, strongly suspected in 20 more murders spanning two states.

Harvey was born in Hamilton, Ohio, on April 15, 1952. Soon afterward, his parents moved to Booneville, Kentucky, a tiny town on the eastern slope of the Appalachian Mountains whose population was 81 souls in 2010. Mother Goldie Harvey described her only child as "a good boy," raised in a loving environment, but Donald would not escape his parents' home unscathed.

In October 1952, while holding Donald in his arms,

Goldie's husband dozed off and dropped the infant on his head. Donald's parents claimed no lasting injury, although his fontanel had not yet closed, but they may have missed it as their small-town life dissolved into rounds of furious bickering. In 1957, Donald suffered a second head injury, tumbling from a truck's running board and receiving a four-inch gash on the back of his skull.

A more significant long-running trauma began in 1956, when Goldie's half-brother Wayne began molesting Donald during visits to his grandmother's home. A year later, older neighbor Dan Thomas joined in the sexual abuse, both men taking turns with Donald over the next 15 years. Thomas purchased Donald's silence with cash, while Uncle Wayne relied on threats and shame. Debate continues as to whether Harvey, gay in adult life, was "turned" by those encounters starting at the age of four. In any case, there is no doubt that molestation fueled his bleak depression from an early age, producing frequent thoughts of suicide.

Despite all that, when Harvey entered Booneville's Sturgeon Elementary School in 1958, he seemed to be a normal, well-adjusted child. Principal Martha Turner later told the *Cincinnati Post,* "Donnie was a very special child to me. He was always clean and well dressed with his hair trimmed. He was a happy child, very sociable and well liked by the other children. He was a handsome boy with big brown eyes and dark curly hair. He always had a smile for me. There was never any indication of any abnormality."

Classmates took a different view, recalling Harvey as a loner and "teacher's pet" who shunned sports and other extracurricular activities in favor of reading and daydreaming. Perhaps books and fantasy offered escape from his grim life at home. Without a doubt, school honed his skill at keeping up a bright, non-threatening façade.

170

Harvey graduated from Sturgeon Elementary in 1967 and entered Booneville High School that autumn. He earned high marks in most classes without much effort, but was quickly bored and dropped out as soon as state law allowed. Instead of giving up on education, though, he enrolled with Chicago's long-distance American School and received his diploma in April 1968, subsequently passing the state's five-part test for his GED.

Nineteen sixty-eight was a tumultuous year in America, and it also marked Harvey's first fully consensual gay love affair. That occurred in Cincinnati, Ohio, where Harvey had landed a factory job, and while his first true romance was short lived, in 1969 it led to a relationship with Cincinnati resident James Peluso, continuing erratically for the next 15 years.

***

Downsizing cost Harvey his factory job in 1970, leaving him at loose ends. Coincidentally, his mother phoned days later, asking Harvey to visit his ailing grandmother, recently admitted to Marymount Hospital (now Marymount Medical Center), operated by the Sisters of St. Joseph of the Third Order of St. Francis in London, Kentucky. With nothing better to do, Harvey made the 138-mile journey and became a fixture at his grandmother's bedside, charming the nuns who ran Marymount. In May 1970, one of the sisters invited him to work as an orderly and Harvey jumped at the chance, starting work the next day, May 11.

Devoid of medical training, Harvey started out mopping floors, making beds, and emptying bedpans, then progressed to passing out medications, inserting catheters, and handling other chores to help the nursing staff. His first days were uneventful on the job, but Harvey later told police that roommate Randy White raped him during that period. Soon afterward, on May 30, he killed for the first time.

Marymount patient Logan Evans was 88 years old, senile, and sometimes combative. That Memorial Day evening, when Harvey entered Logan's room, the old man grappled with him, smearing Harvey's face with a handful of feces. "The next thing I knew, I'd smothered him," Harvey later confessed. "It was like it was the last straw. I just lost it. I went in to help the man and he wants to rub that in my face." While covering Evans's nose and mouth with a pillow and sheet of blue plastic, Harvey listened to the patient's failing heartbeat through a stethoscope. When it was still, he discarded the plastic, cleaned Evans up, and dressed him in a fresh hospital gown. "No one ever questioned it," Harvey recalled.

Despite Harvey's claim that he killed in a fit of anger, he had clearly rehearsed the procedure beforehand. Placing a plastic barrier between the pillow and his victim's face not only hastened suffocation, but also prevented Evans from inhaling fibers from the pillowcase that might have shown up during an investigation, had there been one.

A sense of power over helpless lives energized Harvey, compelling him to kill again. The very next night, May 31, he "accidentally" killed 69-year-old James Tyree, first inserting the wrong size catheter into Tyree's penis, then physically subduing him when Tyree cried out and struggled in protest. During that contest, Harvey compressed Tyree's abdomen with the heel of one hand to control him, claiming surprise when Tyree vomited blood and expired.

Again, there were no questions asked.

Harvey committed his first self-styled "mercy kill" at Marymount on June 22, 1970, targeting 42-year-old Elizabeth Wyatt. Years later, Harvey claimed that Wyatt "prayed to die" and he obliged her, switching off her bedside oxygen tank. Four hours later, a nurse found Wyatt dead. As before, no foul play was suspected.

On July 10, 1970, Harvey killed 43-year-old Eugene McQueen, turning the patient on his stomach for a sponge bath despite posted orders that McQueen should remain on his back. Observed by a nurse, Harvey remarked that McQueen "looked bad," but the nurse allegedly instructed Harvey to continue. So he did, watching McQueen suffocate on his own bodily fluids, continuing the bath as if nothing was wrong. Investigators later blamed Marymount for whitewashing McQueen's death, while ward nurses teased Harvey for bathing a corpse.

Two days later Harvey claimed another "accidental" victim, 82-year-old Harvey Williams. This time, a defective oxygen tank was the weapon, inducing cardiac arrest and death.

Another scuffle on the ward prompted Harvey's next murder. Ben Gilbert, 81 years old and senile, mistook Harvey for a burglar in his room, clubbing Harvey unconscious with a bedpan, then dumping its contents over Harvey as he lay on the floor. Roused by nurses, Harvey swallowed his rage and pretended to shrug off the incident, but he came back for revenge that evening, first inserting a No. 20 female catheter rather than the smaller No. 18 male model, then ramming a straightened wire coat hanger through the tube, puncturing Gilbert's bladder and bowel. Pain and shock plunged Gilbert into a coma, with infection claiming his life on July 28.

Soon after landing the job at Marymount, Harvey began a covert seven-month affair with Vernon Midden, a married mortician with children who kept his gay life "in the closet." In addition to their sexual liaisons, Midden reportedly taught Harvey details of how human bodies react to different forms

173

of death, an education that helped Harvey conceal evidence of his ongoing murders. Midden also introduced Harvey to Satanism, which increasingly began to prey on Harvey's mind.

A new romance, however, failed to stop his killings at Marymount. On August 15, 1970, he killed patient Maude Nichols by connecting an empty oxygen tank to her respirator. Harvey's stated motive: Nichols had severe bedsores infested with maggots which made bathing her repugnant.

Next came 58-year-old William Bowling on August 30. Hospitalized with breathing difficulties, Bowling died from a heart attack after Harvey, on a whim, replaced his old oxygen tank with a full one, but neglected to turn it on.

Death took a holiday at Marymount until November 4, when Harvey killed 63-year-old Viola Reed Wyan for "smelling bad." The patient suffered from leukemia and an electrolyte imbalance, but survived Harvey's initial bid to suffocate her with a pillow and a sheet of plastic when a nurse entered the room. Returning later to finish the job, he used his trusty defective oxygen tank.

Harvey graduated to poisoning on December 7, 1970, injecting 91-year-old Margaret Harrison with a cocktail of narcotic pain relievers—codeine, meperedine and morphine—prescribed for a different patient. Harvey stood listening through his stethoscope until Harrison's heart stopped beating, another elderly victim's death logged without investigation by the hospital's staff.

Harvey's secret relationship with Vernon Midden dissolved in January 1971, leaving Harvey depressed and angry, spinning visions of Midden strapped to his own mortician's table, screaming while Harvey pumped his veins full of embalming fluid. Lacking courage to fulfill that fantasy, Harvey resorted to the next best thing.

Sam Carroll entered Marymount Hospital at age 80,

with an intestinal blockage and pneumonia. Harvey showed him "mercy" on January 9, 1971, connecting Carroll's respirator to an empty oxygen tank. Six days later, he called on Maggie Rawlins, in for treatment of a third-degree burn on one arm. Harvey suffocated Rawlins with a pillow and a plastic bag. On January 23, after multiple failed attempts to smother 62-year-old kidney patient Silas Butner, Harvey succeeded at murder with an empty oxygen tank. The resultant autopsy failed to detect Butner's cause of death. The same method worked with 68-year-old cardiac patient John Combs on January 26.

Another moratorium ensued with Butner's murder, this one lasting six weeks and four days. Harvey emerged from hibernation on March 14, 1971, killing 90-year-old cardiac patient Milton Bryant Sasser with an overdose of morphine pilfered from the nurse's station on his ward. Uncomfortable with the new technique, Harvey tried to flush the murder syringe down a hospital toilet, but only succeeded in clogging the pipe. A maintenance man retrieved it, and while it raised questions, no one connected the stray hypodermic to Sasser's demise.

***

Whatever Donald Harvey hoped to gain from killing helpless patients—sexual release, some inner calm, even a sense of having "served" mankind—it did not fill the void inside him. His depression deepened, with recurring thoughts of suicide. His sex life was chaotic—breaking up with Midden, off and on with James Peluso, and a brief affair with new acquaintance "Jim," including fantasies of killing him, though Harvey balked, for now, at murdering outside the hospital's familiar halls.

At one point in this period, Harvey even attempted to

"go straight," giving sex a try with willing neighbor Ruth Anne Hodges. Harvey later blamed their one fumbling experiment on blackout drinking, saying he remembered nothing more than waking nude with Hodges in his bed. Harvey says that Hodges bore a son nine months later, naming him Donald, but his accounts of fatherhood are confused and contradictory. On one occasion Harvey claimed two living children, then backpedaled, denying any.

Drunk and raving, Harvey snapped on March 31, 1971. Arrested for an awkward burglary attempt in at his own apartment building, he babbled to police about his lethal crimes at Marymount, but the detectives laughed it off. In June, even more depressed than usual, Harvey set fire to a vacant apartment's bathroom, but neighbors quickly extinguished the blaze. Soon afterward, he pled guilty to a reduced charge of petty theft in the burglary case and walked out of court a free man after paying a $50 fine.

Harvey's judge had recommended psychiatric counseling for the defendant's "troubled condition," but he did not make it mandatory. Harvey ignored that suggestion and joined the U.S. Air Force instead, on June 16, 1971.

Many a wayward youth had trod that path before him, fleeing drab hometowns, legal entanglements and family strife to build new lives under the military's strict routine of regimented discipline. It has worked for thousands, who began careers as "lifers" or returned in time to civilian life with their unsettled past a fading memory, but such was not the case with Donald Harvey. He could not escape himself by stepping into uniform or spending eight weeks in boot camp. Depression and the memories of murder dogged his every step.

New recruits initially enlist in the Air Force for terms of four or six years. Harvey lasted 267 days before he was released from service with a general discharge, officially reserved for "members whose performance is satisfactory but is marked by a considerable departure in duty performance and conduct expected of military members." On separation from the service, recipients of a general discharge are required to sign a form acknowledging the possibility that they may face "substantial prejudice in civilian life" without a more respected honorable discharge. Harvey signed and went home to Kentucky.

The precise reasons for Harvey's exit from the Air Force remain classified. No grounds are stated on a general discharge, and published guesses as to why he left the service contradict each other. One account claims Harvey was discharged after trying to kill himself with Vicks NyQuil cold medicine, an effort that produced only a good night's sleep with some residual nausea. Another version claims that Harvey's superiors learned of his 1971 murder confession and chose to unload a ticking time bomb. In either case, he got no treatment for what ailed him and returned to the environment that had produced his mental problems in the first place.

As bleak depression had followed Harvey into uniform, so it trailed him back home. After a quarrel with his disappointed parents, Harvey tried to kill himself again, this time with a mixture of the sedative Placydil and Equanil, an anti-anxiety medication. Once again, he failed. This time a hospital stomach pump saved Harvey's life, after which he was transferred to a local Veterans Administration (VA) Medical Center in Lexington when his parents declared him *persona non grata* at home.

A general discharge bars military veterans from some post-service benefits, including higher education under the GI Bill, but recipients are still entitled to treatment at veterans' hospitals nationwide. Harvey was twice committed to the

Lexington VA facility, initially confined from July 16 to August 25, 1972, returning for a second stint from September 17 to October 17. While access to records of a living patient is restricted with good reason, Goldie Harvey says her son spent most of his VA time in restraints while receiving a total of 21 electroshock therapy treatments.

Electroconvulsive therapy (ECT) is prescribed as a last-resort treatment of various psychiatric ailments including major depressive disorder, schizophrenia, mania and catatonia. A normal course involves multiple applications of electricity to the brain, typically given two or three times per week until a patient is relieved of the worst outward symptoms. Although depicted as something akin to torture in novels and films such as *One Flew Over the Cuckoo's Nest,* modern ECT is conducted after patients receive anesthetic and muscle relaxants.

Whatever the value of ECT treatments to most mental patients, they had no apparent effect on Harvey. He left the VA hospital on October 17 as depressed as he was on arrival, and perhaps more so. Goldie Harvey claims that Donald tried to kill himself inside the hospital itself, and she condemns VA officials for releasing him uncured. Whoever was to blame for Harvey's condition—his family, childhood molesters, or Mother Nature itself—he hit the street with no intention of reforming.

***

After sanitizing his record, Harvey found work as a nurse's aide at Cardinal Hill Convalescent Hospital in Lexington, starting in February 1973. There, Harvey worked full-time until June, then cut back to part-time hours while taking a second job in the same capacity, at Lexington's Good Samaritan Hospital.

Somehow, he restrained himself from killing any further victims at either hospital during the remainder of his tenure, lasting until August 1974.

Some observers credit Harvey's 19-month abstention from murder to changes in his personal life. Soon after his second departure from the local VA hospital, Harvey met new lover Russell Addison and lived with him for 10 months. After their breakup in 1973 Harvey paired with Ken Estes for a sporadic five-year relationship, spending his free time on the study of satanic rituals. Despite his growing fascination with the dark arts, Harvey held himself aloof from joining an established coven in those months.

In August 1974, Harvey took a new job as a telephone operator in Lexington, then moved on to a clerical post at St. Luke's Hospital in Fort Thomas, Kentucky. That job denied him contact with the institution's patients, who were safe with Harvey in his sector of the premises until he quit and traveled back to Cincinnati in September of 1975.

His next stop was the Cincinnati VA Medical Center, hired as a nightshift employee with varying duties as a nursing assistant, autopsy assistant, cardiac-catheterization technician, and a housekeeping aide. Working with corpses proved particularly fascinating, prompting Harvey to steal various tissue samples "for study" at home. Some were incorporated into his satanic ceremonies, including rituals used to select his next victim.

Long out of practice but still with an urge to murder, Harvey soon picked up where he'd left off at Marymount in Lexington, claiming at least 15 veterans' lives over the next decade. With minimal supervision on the nightshift, he favored cyanide injections and spiking his victims' meals with arsenic or rat poison. He still utilized suffocation, as well, employing wet towels or plastic bags as the spirit moved him.

Through it all, Harvey kept a diary of his crimes, with detailed notes on each victim, and sometimes joked with nurses on the morning after murder, saying, "I got rid of that one for you." Their laughter seemed uneasy, still it prompted no complaints to management.

Despite its high toxicity, cyanide is found in many hospitals and pharmacies, stored up for a variety of uses. At the Cincinnati VA, Harvey tapped that supply to create his own arsenal, eventually storing 30 pounds of poison at his home. Prior to work, he would commonly mix a solution of arsenic or cyanide at his apartment, perform a black magic ritual to help him select his next victim, then carry the poison to work in his gym bag with other tools of the trade.

Authorities blame Harvey for five deaths on his ward during 1975, though details remain vague. He admitted reducing patient Joseph Harris's oxygen flow, resulting in death, but was never charged with that crime. In five other cases—those of victims James Twitty, James Ritter, Harry Rhodes, and Sterling Moore—Harvey would tell police that he "may have been involved" in their deaths, but denied any specific memories of the crimes.

In June 1977, Harvey finally joined a satanic coven, which, unlike some black magic cults, restricted membership to heterosexual couples, trading partners during ceremonies that involved release of sexual energy as a form of "sacrifice" to Lucifer. Harvey's cover was a female companion identified only as "Jan," who joined him for an initiation that included pairing off with strangers. Once, Harvey claimed cult couplings resulted in the birth of his second child, never identified.

In coven "workings," Harvey allegedly met his satanic spirit guide—an entity he called "Duncan," supposedly a doctor in his earthly life—who assisted in Harvey's selection of future victims. Sitting down with Duncan and a skull purloined from the VA's morgue, Harvey would chant and ultimately come up with the next name on his list of patients slated for a lethal dispensation of "mercy."

And on the side, he started hunting away from hospital grounds.

***

Early in 1980, Harvey began dating new lover Doug Hill. It was another in his long string of tempestuous relationships, but Harvey was no longer prepared to suffer in private without striking back. After one heated quarrel, he spiked Hill's ice cream with arsenic. The dose was not lethal, but it finished their affair.

Next, in August 1980, Harvey paired with Carl Hoeweler. They moved in together, but Hoeweler had a roving eye. Upon discovering that Carl's Monday nights out consisted of cruising local parks for other men, Harvey began to feed him small doses of arsenic on Sunday nights, to keep him sick at home the next day. A female friend of Carl's, known today only as "Diane," meddled in their relationship, inevitably siding with Hoeweler when he and Harvey quarreled. Harvey first tried to dissuade her by feeding her acrylic acid, a colorless organic liquid used in the manufacture of various plastics, coatings, adhesives, elastomers, as well as floor polishes, and paints. When that failed to kill Diane, Harvey stole samples of hepatitis B and the HIV virus from work, but neither infection took hold.

Increasingly restless and angry at home, Harvey next turned on 63-year-old Helen Metzger, another neighbor he regarded as a meddler in his life with Carl Hoeweler. First, Harvey gave Metzger a plate of leftovers dosed with arsenic, then followed up with poisoned mayonnaise and an arsenic-contaminated pie. Later, he denied any intent to kill Metzger, but the net result was paralysis requiring an emergency tracheotomy, after which Metzger suffered fatal hemorrhaging and died on April 10, 1983, without regaining consciousness. Physicians blamed her death on Guillain-Barré Syndrome, a disease of the peripheral nervous system, and ignored the "coincidence" of her relatives falling ill at a wake held in Metzger's apartment, after they ate Harvey's spiked mayonnaise.

Soon after Metzger died, Harvey quarreled with Carl Hoeweler's parents and began to dose their food with arsenic as well, beginning on April 25. Henry Hoeweler, age 82, suffered a stroke four days later and was admitted to Cincinnati's Providence Hospital. Harvey visited him there and added more arsenic to Henry's pudding, inducing lethal kidney failure on May 1. Harvey also made repeated efforts to murder Carl's mother, Margaret Hoeweler, over the next 12 months, but she proved more resistant to his potions and survived.

Carl's brother-in-law, Howard Vetter, was less fortunate. Harvey later claimed that he was using highly toxic methanol, also known as wood alcohol, to remove adhesive labels at home, keeping the colorless solvent in an old vodka bottle. One day in his absence, Harvey said, Vetter came calling on Carl, who mixed him drinks from the wrong bottle, somehow shelved with the normal liquor in their home. After imbibing several drinks, Vetter suffered a week of illness, then was stricken with a fatal heart attack, his death blamed on cardiac failure.

Enough was enough for Carl Hoeweler. In January 1984 he sent Harvey packing, although their on-again, off-again relationship would continue until May of 1986. During those months, grieving and furious, Harvey would try to poison Hoeweler several times, and while one attempt landed Carl in the hospital, none proved fatal.

Meanwhile, there were always other victims waiting for a visit from the bedside executioner.

***

On September 19, 1984, Harvey "accidentally" killed VA patient Hiram Proffit by giving him the wrong dosage of heparin, a highly sulfated glycosaminoglycan used in medicine principally as an injectable anticoagulant. After Proffit died, Harvey kept mum about his "error," and postmortem tests failed to expose him.

Seven weeks later, according to Harvey, 65-year-old ex-lover James Peluso was hospitalized for cardiac problems, and on release asked Harvey to "help him out" if he ever proved unable to care for himself at home. Harvey heard that plea as a request for immediate euthanasia, giving Peluso arsenic in a daiquiri and in pudding on November 9, 1984. Rushed back to the VA hospital, Peluso died that night with no investigation, in light of his poor condition.

With help from "Duncan" and his trusty skull, Harvey next set his sights on former landlord Edward Wilson, who had accused Carl Hoeweler of cheating on his utility bills. To spare Carl from embarrassment and possible eviction, Harvey visited Wilson on March 18, 1985, using the supposed social call to place arsenic in Wilson's Pepto-Bismol. Five days later, Wilson died and Hoeweler was "saved," while Harvey celebrated his own promotion to supervisor of the VA hospital's morgue.

Around that same time, Harvey joined the Chicago-based National Socialist Party of America (NSPA), a spin-off from the National Socialist White People's Party, which in turn was the direct descendant of assassinated fascist George Lincoln Rockwell's American Nazi Party. Founded in 1970 by

183

Frank Collin, the NSPA had been led since 1980 by Harold Covington, after media reports and criminal investigators exposed Collin as a closet Jew and predatory pedophile.

None of that dissuaded Harvey from joining the "Aryan" boy's club, although he later claimed he only joined the party to destroy it from within. If so, it seems he took no steps in that direction prior to his arrest, and in fact, flirtation between Satanists and Nazis had historic roots, dating from Germany's Thule Society and Heinrich Himmler's occult obsessions during World War II, to New Yorker James Madole's National Renaissance Party in the 1960s and on to the present day among neo-Nazi fringe dwellers.

Whatever Harvey's motive for becoming a dues-paying Nazi, he had little time remaining to preach the racist gospel to VA coworkers. On July 18, 1985, hospital security guards caught Harvey leaving work with a satchel containing a .38-caliber pistol, hypodermic syringes, surgical gloves and scissors, a cocaine spoon, two books on Satanism, and a paperback biography of globe-hopping serial killer Charles Sobhraj. A peek inside his locker revealed a slice of liver from the morgue, mounted in paraffin as if for microscopic study.

While most of those items raised eyebrows, packing a firearm to work on federal property was strictly forbidden. Harvey lost his job and paid a $50 fine, protesting to this day that the gun surprised him, suggesting it was planted by Carl Hoeweler to "frame" him. Wherever the weapon came from, no record of it or the other confiscated items appeared in Harvey's employment file as he moved on in search of a new job.

***

With no official blot on his record, and no ongoing

investigation to discover whether he'd committed any other crimes at the VA facility, Harvey stepped into a part-time nurse's aide position at Cincinnati's Daniel Drake Memorial Hospital on February 24, 1986. He did not start to kill again immediately, but when he did resume, after a calm six weeks of biding his time, he went at it with a vengeance.

In early April, steered by "Duncan" and his trusty VA morgue skull, Harvey targeted 65-year-old Nathani J. Watson, a semi-comatose patient surviving on nutrients injected through a gastric tube. Harvey later claimed that Watson was a once-convicted rapist, though research does not substantiate that charge. Harvey's first few attempts to smother Watson failed, but he finally succeeded on April 8, 1986, suffocating Watson with a pillow and a wet plastic garbage can liner. Afterward, he trashed the liner, dried off Watson's face, and went about his other business on the ward, leaving a nurse to find the corpse 45 minutes later.

On April 12, Harvey used the same technique to smother 64-year-old Leon Nelson. Seven days later, 81-year-old cardiac patient Virgil Weddle suffered a fatal heart attack after Harvey spiked his evening pudding with rat poison. Harvey also stole some cookies left by Weddle's family, consuming them during his next satanic prayer session with spirit guide "Duncan." On April 20, Harvey seasoned patient Lawrence Berndsen's dinner with rat poison, and while Berndsen grew ill, he did not die until April 23, after his transfer to another Cincinnati hospital.

May began with stress for Harvey, starting with Carl Hoeweler's May 2 accusation that Donald was "out to get him." Harvey dismissed it as paranoia, but Hoeweler terminated their relationship regardless. That same night, at Drake Memorial, Harvey killed 65-year-old Doris Nally by slipping cyanide into her apple juice. Meanwhile, Harvey faced his first job performance evaluation, but he need not have worried. When supervisor Daisy Key filed the report on May 5 she rated Harvey "good" in six out of ten categories, and "acceptable" in the other four.

Secure in his job for the moment, Harvey soon began poisoning patient Willie Johnson with arsenic, but four attempts in May and June failed to bless Johnson with Harvey's "mercy." While Johnson lived on to be discharged, Harvey was more successful with 63-year-old Edward Schreibeis, dispatching him with arsenic in his soup on June 20, 1986. Nine days later Harvey killed again, injecting a cyanide solution into 80-year-old Robert Crockett's intravenous line. Physicians sought no autopsy in either case.

On July 7, 1986, Harvey killed 61-year-old Donald Barney with a double dose of cyanide, the first fed through Barney's gastric feeding tube, the second lanced into his buttocks with a hypodermic needle. Next to die, on July 25, was 65-year-old James T. Woods, also poisoned with cyanide through his gastric tube. The same method worked with 85-year-old Ernst C. Frey, on August 16. After murdering Frey, Harvey stole an old pair of knitted booties from his victim as a souvenir.

Personal adjustments briefly stalled the killing spree at Drake Memorial, as Harvey moved from Cincinnati to Middletown, 28 miles farther north, on August 17, 1986. It took some time to settle in, but he was ready for action again by August 29, when he killed 85-year-old Milton Canter, injecting cyanide through Canter's nasal tube and afterward stealing his lap blanket. This time, Drake administrators requested an autopsy, but Canter's family refused in accordance with Jewish tradition.

On September 17, Harvey came for 74-year-old Roger Evans, again slipping cyanide into his victim's nasal tube. An autopsy *was* performed on Evans, but it failed to diagnose his cause of death. Three days later, Harvey fed 69-year-old Clayborn Kendrick cyanide through his gastric tube, then hedged his bets with a lethal injection into Kendrick's scrotum.

Another killing hiatus ensued, lasting until October 29, 1986, when Harvey murdered 86-year-old Albert Buehlmann with cyanide dissolved in a glass of water. It was poisoned orange juice on October 30, when 85-year-old William Collins followed Buehlmann to the grave. On November 4, Harvey dissolved cyanide in water and poured it through Henry Cody's gastric tube, killing Cody at age 78. Surviving members of the latest victim's family refused to grant permission for an autopsy.

November 1986 was a bleak month for Cincinnati's self-styled mercy killer. Harvey entered treatment with a psychologist, Dr. Mark Barbara, for depression over his breakup with Carl Hoeweler, but the sessions didn't help. Neither did more frequent séances with "Duncan" from the "Other Side." Around mid-month Harvey attempted suicide once more, veering his car off the brink of a mountain road, but he achieved only a new head injury and an expensive towing fee.

Only killing brought some measure of release from personal anxiety. On November 22, Harvey murdered 65-year-old Mose Thompson at Drake Memorial, feeding a cyanide solution through his gastric tube. The same technique killed 72-year-old Odas Day on December 9, while cranberry juice spiked with cyanide did the job with 67-year-old Cleo Fish. In that case, Harvey clipped a lock of the dead woman's hair for use in his next ritual with "Duncan."

Before year's end, Harvey poisoned two more patients, Harold White and John Oldendick, with arsenic on the hospital ward. Neither died, and Harvey came away from those failures convinced that his poison had actually "cured" Oldendick of whatever ailed him.

Although Harvey didn't know it yet, his time was running out. As if forewarned subconsciously, his pace of killing escalated in the final weeks remaining to him. The last spree began on January 10, 1987, when Harvey dosed 47-year-old Leo Parker's intravenous parenteral nutrition bag with cyanide. (An autopsy failed to reveal it.) On February 5, he killed 80-year-old Margaret Kuckro, using cyanide dissolved in orange juice. The same technique took longer with 76-year-old Stella Lemon: although poisoned in late February, she survived until March 16.

Meanwhile, on March 6, Harvey murdered 68-year-old Joseph M. Pike by feeding him Detachol, a liquid adhesive solvent recommended for use in removal of dressings, wound closure strips, tapes, tubes, and colostomy bags. One day later, pleased with that result, Harvey killed 82-year-old Hilda Leitz by feeding Detachol through her gastric tube and mixing it in her orange juice. Also on March 7, Harvey poisoned 44-year-old John Powell with cyanide, injected through his gastric tube.

It was the end of Harvey's run at Drake Memorial.

***

Because John Powell had been a relatively young man, expected to fully recover, Drake administrators requested permission for an autopsy and Powell's family agreed. Forensic pathologist Dr. Lee Lehman performed the postmortem and immediately recognized the bitter-almond scent of cyanide after he opened Powell's abdomen. Toxicology tests confirmed the poison's presence, and Dr. Lehman listed Powell's death as a homicide, promptly informing the

Cincinnati Police Department.

So began a painstaking investigation, including chemical analysis of John Powell's last hospital meal, plus interviews with his widow, friends, and hospital staff. During one interview at Drake Memorial, a nurse mentioned rumors that Donald Harvey had left his last hospital job in a hurry and under an ill-defined cloud of suspicion. Another staff member noted that coworkers sometimes called Harvey the "Angel of Death," for his frequent presence when patients expired.

Next up, police asked staff members to sit for polygraph examinations. All agreed, but on the day his test was scheduled Harvey called in sick. Detectives Ron Camden and Jim Lawson brought him to headquarters for further questioning, and after several hours obtained Harvey's confession to poisoning John Powell out of pity for Powell and his loved ones. Even then, he denied killing anyone else.

With Harvey's confession in hand, Camden and Lawson obtained a search warrant for his apartment in Middletown. There, they found copious evidence including jars of arsenic and cyanide, books on poisoning and Satanism, Harvey's personal grimoire filled with occult incantations, and his diary detailing multiple murders. On April 6, 1987, prosecutors charged Harvey with one count of aggravated first-degree murder, for killing John Powell. A judge appointed lawyer William Whalen as Harvey's public defender, recorded Harvey's plea of not guilty by reason of insanity, and ordered the defendant jailed in lieu of $200,000 bond.

The media in Cincinnati buzzed with news of Harvey's arrest, quickly spreading the ripples statewide and beyond Ohio. While William Whalen initially thought he was only defending his client on one murder count, Pat Minarcin, anchor for WCPO-TV evening news, thought the story might be larger. He questioned whether Harvey was suspected in any other deaths at Drake Memorial, but authorities denied it, saying cyanide could not be found in corpses once they were embalmed.

Minarcin dug deeper, wondering if "mercy killer" Harvey might have used varied methods during his 17 years of employment at different hospitals. On April 10, Minarcin received an anonymous call from a purported nurse at Drake Memorial, saying, "There's something going on here, and our supervisors won't do anything about it." The caller listed 13 other patients she suspected Donald Harvey might have slain, then hung up after promising to call back with more information the next day.

On April 11, the informant rang back, this time with a second Drake nurse on the line, adding three more names to the prospective victims' list. Both nurses said they had approached their supervisor with suspicions about Harvey, but were ordered to keep quiet. A third call, on April 13, put five Drake staffers on the phone, echoing accusations that Harvey was a serial killer. Reluctantly, the five agreed to meet Minarcin privately that night, prompting the veteran newsman to leave WCPO's studio 20 minutes before airtime, with the reluctant blessing of news director Jack Cahalan.

The covert meeting confirmed Minarcin's suspicion. His informants told him that Jan Taylor, Drake Memorial's chief administrator, had convened a meeting of Ward C staff members on April 7, one day after Harvey's arrest. There, Taylor informed all hands that Drake had conducted its own one-day internal probe of Harvey's case and "found no evidence" of any other homicides. In parting, he warned them all to shun reporters and avoid discussing the matter among themselves. Before he left the April 13 huddle, Minarcin's list of potential murder victims had grown from 16 to 33.

As Minarcin forged ahead with his one-man

investigation, Drake Memorial administrators learned of his interest and mounted a campaign to discredit Minarcin, branding him a "sensationalist" at staff assemblies and claiming Minarcin planned to sacrifice Drake Memorial's good name in pursuit of TV ratings. The whispering campaign only strengthened Minarcin's resolve, prompting him to track Don Harvey's movements from one ward to another, charting the rise and fall of patient death rates at each duty posting. Still, he didn't have enough hard evidence to air an exposé without risking a lawsuit from the hospital.

Late in May 1986, Minarcin phoned William Whalen, laying out his circumstantial evidence of multiple murders. Whalen replied with a cautious "No comment," then met with his client at the Hamilton County Justice Center, warning Harvey of a major TV story in the offing. Reluctantly, Whalen asked Harvey if he had killed patients other than Powell.

Harvey replied in the affirmative, but balked at giving a final number. Challenged by Whalen, Harvey explained, "It's not that I don't want to tell you, but I can only estimate." Sickened by the implications, Whalen asked Harvey to "pick a number in your mind that you know the number of deaths could not go beyond." After an hour's consideration, Harvey finally replied, "Seventy."

The answer stunned Whalen. Later, he wrote, "In the state of Ohio, two or more deaths qualify a person for the death penalty. If authorities could prove it, the actual number would be of little consequence. And if the number really was 70, how would one deal with that? The simple answer was to keep my mouth shut and hope it would go away." Pat Minarcin, of course, had other ideas.

The day after Harvey's jailhouse confession to 70 murders, Whalen obtained a copy of celebrity attorney F. Lee Bailey's 1971 book *The Defense Never Rests,* including a section on Bailey's defense of alleged "Boston Strangler" Albert DeSalvo. In that case, Bailey had informed police of DeSalvo's apparent "guilty knowledge" in 13 deaths, trading confessions for waiver of trial for murder and a life sentence imposed on lesser charges. Whalen regarded Bailey's action as unethical and as he later wrote, "I decided that I was not going to sacrifice Harvey."

Another conference persuaded Harvey to plead guilty on multiple charges, if Whalen could negotiate a prison term to keep him out of Ohio's electric chair. By 1987, no state inmate had been executed for a quarter of a century, but Harvey seemed to be the poster child for capital punishment, unless Whale could work out a deal.

On May 26, 1987, clinical psychologists Roger Fisher and Nancy Schmidtgoessling testified at Harvey's competency hearing, both agreeing that he was legally sane—i.e., that he knew the difference between right and wrong and was physically able to conform his conduct to the law's demands. Dr. Schmidtgoessling acknowledged Harvey's history of childhood molestation and depression, but found that he had never been psychotic. With that finding, Whalen was denied access to an insanity defense.

WCPO-TV aired its exposé of Harvey's case on June 23, 1987, including a tabulation of deaths at Drake Memorial during the 12 months from April 1986 to April 1987. While Harvey worked on Ward C-300, 34 patients had died on his watch. Four other wards, all filled with patients, lost a total of 43 altogether during the same period. The apparent clincher: in the 12 months prior to Harvey's assignment on Ward C-300, that ward's death toll totaled 13, on par with the other wards where Harvey never served. His arrival on the scene had increased sudden deaths by 62 percent with no other obvious variables.

Before the end of June, while Hamilton County Prosecutor Arthur Ney Jr. threatened to subpoena Pat Minarcin, Whalen approached Ney's office to negotiate a plea bargain. After brief hesitation, Ney agreed to waive execution in exchange for a full and honest confession. If Harvey omitted any crimes or tried to back out of the deal, he faced trial with his life on the line.

***

Harvey began confessing to police on July 9, 1987, describing 33 murders before he ran out of steam on August 11. While Harvey stood by his story of "mercy" killing, ducking any reference to his satanic rituals, a spokesman for the DA's office said, "This man is sane, competent, but is a compulsive killer. He builds up tension in his body, so he kills people." On August 18 a grand jury charged Harvey with 25 counts of aggravated murder, four counts of attempted murder, and one count of felonious assault. Harvey pled guilty on August 21, receiving four consecutive life prison terms plus $270,000 in fines, levied without hope of ever collecting a cent.

Next came Kentucky, with victims of its own and another electric chair waiting for Harvey unless he played ball with the state. On September 6, 1987, Harvey agreed to confess his crimes at Marymount Hospital, with taping of his recitation beginning three days later. He admitted 13 slayings, but police only corroborated nine with independent evidence, prompting Harvey's November 2 indictment on eight counts of murder and one count of voluntary manslaughter. Harvey pled guilty once again, receiving eight life sentences plus 20 years on the manslaughter charge, to be served in Ohio concurrently with his sentence for murders at Drake Memorial.

Nor was he finished yet. On January 21, 1988, Harvey

193

confessed three more murders and three failed attempts at Drake Memorial, drawing a six-count indictment on February 19. His guilty plea on those counts landed Harvey three more life sentences, plus terms of seven to 25 years for each of the attempted murders. With 36 murder convictions on record, and unverified confessions nearly doubling that tally, he surpassed current U.S. record-holder John Wayne Gacy's body count, but voiced disappointment when he failed to rate mention in Guinness World Records.

In the wake of Harvey's guilty pleas, residents of Hamilton County filed civil lawsuits totaling $235,000,000 against Daniel Drake Memorial Hospital, Jan Taylor, and the county's board of commissioners. The cases dragged on for years, with few published results, although widower Shelton Gillispie reportedly settled a $75 million lawsuit for $45,000 in 1991. Drake director Jan Drake faced four charges of tampering with evidence, pleading guilty on a solitary count of falsifying public documents on April 13, 1988, with no jail time imposed.

Interviewed by the *Columbus Dispatch* in 1991, Don Harvey gave some insight into his thought process during his long murder spree. "Well, people controlled me for 18 years," he said, "and then I controlled my own destiny. I controlled other people's lives, whether they lived or died. I had that power to control. After I didn't get caught for the first 15, I thought it was my right. I appointed myself judge, prosecutor and jury. So I played God."

Interviewed again by *60 Minutes II* in February 2005, Harvey explained his long run by blaming the doctors around him at various hospitals. All were overworked, he said, and some never bothered to visit lost patients after they died, in a search for answers.

Harvey resides today as inmate No. A-199449, at

194

Southern Ohio Correctional Facility, outside Lucasville. He is technically eligible for parole in 2048, at age 96.

Chapter 12: Brian Dugan
"Multiple Jeopardy"
by Katherine Ramsland

Patricia Nicarico was worried about her ten-year-old daughter. Jeanine had a tummy ache, possibly the flu. The other girls got ready for school as Patricia pondered what to do. Her husband, Tom, had already left for his job as an engineer in Chicago, so she couldn't ask him to stay home. Patricia considered calling a substitute to take her place as a secretary at a local elementary school.

"I'll be fine, Mom," Jeanine assured her. "I'll just stay in bed."

Feeling pulled in two directions, Patricia finally agreed. After this day, she would have cause to doubt herself for the rest of her life.

She would check in often, Patricia said. She made sure that Jeanine had everything she needed before she got into the car and drove to the school. She called during the morning to check, and Jeanine was still feeling sick but wasn't any worse. On her way home for lunch, Patricia stopped to buy Jeanine's favorite ice cream, chocolate chip with chocolate mint sauce. *This* would cheer her up.

At home, Patricia felt Jeanine's forehead. There was still a fever, but she seemed better. Patricia fixed her a sandwich and gave her a large bowl of ice cream.

"Someone from the gas company came," Jeanine reported. "I let him in."

Patricia was startled. "Jeanine," she said, trying not to sound too stern, "I don't want you to open the door to *anyone*. No matter what they say. Your father or I should

197

always be present before you let someone in. Promise me that you won't do that again. If someone comes, just call me at work."

"Don't worry, Mom." Jeanine gave her a hug.

It was Feb. 25, 1983, in Naperville, Illinois. Patricia went out in the cold and drove back to work. Jeanine called her as she arrived. The girl was bubbly. Tomorrow, Patricia realized with relief, Jeanine would be well enough to go back to school. It was just a temporary bug.

Patricia had no way of knowing that at this very moment her house was being targeted for robbery.

Forced Entry

Jeanine's thirteen-year-old sister, Kathy, arrived home from school around 3:00 PM. As she neared the house, she slowed down. Something was wrong. The front door stood open. Even in the summer, this would be disturbing, but it was cold out.

She went to the threshold and stood for a moment before entering. The door looked broken. Something was wrong with the frame. It was cracked.

"Hello?"

No one answered. Even the dog didn't greet her and it was quite cold inside, as if the door had been open for a while. Had the dog run away? She wasn't sure she should enter, but she went in and closed the door as best she could. Definitely, something was wrong. She saw some odd marks on the wall near the door that she'd never noticed before.

"Jeanine?" Kathy called out. She checked her sister's bedroom. It was empty, although clearly from the rumpled sheets and blankets, she'd been in it. Kathy checked her own bedroom. Things were disturbed in here as well. What had Jeanine been doing?

Kathy went through the house, growing alarmed. The television was on, but no one was watching it. She called for the dog. No response. The house felt empty. Kathy pulled her coat closer. Where was her sister?

Finally, she went into the lower level. The family dog came up to her, cowering and whimpering. Kathy had a definite sense that something was dreadfully wrong here. She was about to call her mother when she heard the car.

Patricia came in the back, ready to hug her sick little girl. In the kitchen, she saw an empty bowl. Good. Jeanine had eaten the ice cream. Then Kathy came in.

"The front door was open when I came home," she said. "I can't find Jeanine."

Panic rose in Patricia's throat. She remembered the gas meter reader. Had he noticed a girl alone and come back?

"Let's search," she said.

They went systematically through every room. Kathy said that someone had been in hers. She hadn't made her bed, but it was more rumpled than when she'd left that morning.

"Jeanine!" they called out. But the girl was not there. Patricia looked at the broken frame of the front door and noticed a boot print square in the middle of the door. Someone had kicked it in. She saw the marks on the wall — gouges. She peered at them. *From fingernails*. She rushed to the phone and called the police. Then she called Tom to urge him to come home as soon as he could. By now, she knew, she sounded hysterical.

That man, she thought. *That gas man. He must have done something to Jeanine!*

***

Officers arrived and organized a search. Patricia told them everything she knew and awaited word that her daughter had been found and was safe. As unlikely as it seemed, she thought that perhaps Jeanine had gone to one of her friend's houses. Patricia made some calls. No one had seen her.

By evening, the police informed the Nicaricos that their daughter had been kidnapped. A crime scene unit sealed off the house to process it. They found evidence of an intruder, forced entry, and a struggle. Jeanine's fingernails had made the scratches on the wall. They would do their best, they promised, to find her.

But as detectives left the Nicarico home, they knew that the odds of finding the child alive diminished with each passing minute. Someone had forcibly taken her, most likely a child molester. The meter reader was quickly ruled out through an alibi, which made things more difficult. Child abductions by strangers were difficult, sometimes impossible, to solve. They sent out alerts to other patrol officers, although they had no information about the kind of car they were looking for. Questions to neighbors turned up nothing useful.

Child Killer

Two days later, Jeanine's body was found six miles from home. She'd been dumped near the Illinois Prairie Path bike trail, by the East-West Tollway between Naperville and Aurora. Her head was wrapped in a towel and bound with jagged-edged tape. The autopsy found that she'd been sodomized and severely beaten to death. Her head had been split open with something blunt but forceful, like a bat.

The Nicaricos were horrified at the thought that Jeanine

had suffered the terror of being alone when an intruder broke in, not to mention his kidnap and treatment of her. They knew she must have been screaming for them, hoping for rescue. They couldn't believe how he'd treated her. And now they'd lost her.

Patricia blamed herself. She deeply regretted not calling in to work that day to stay home with her sick daughter. But who would have thought that someone would break into her home in a peaceful neighborhood in the middle of the day? Such a thing was unheard of.

The police were determined to find the intruder. A $10,000 reward was offered for information. Leading the investigation was John Sam, an experienced detective from the DuPage County Sheriff's Department.

A tip from street thug Rolando Cruz, eager to claim the reward, sent police looking for Alejandro Hernandez, who supposedly had information about the murder. (Another version indicates that he came forward on his own.) On March 14, Detective Sam questioned him.

Hernandez said that he was drinking with a friend named Ricky, who'd admitted to killing the Nicarico girl. He didn't know Ricky's last name, supposedly, and Sam was unable to find any person like he'd described. Sam wondered if Hernandez had meant Stephen Buckley, who'd also been present during this dark conversation. Sam showed Buckley a photo of the shoeprint left on the Nicarico's door and he said he had boots like that. He gave them up for analysis.

John Gorajczyk, a shoe print examiner in the police crime lab, concluded they didn't match. Tom Knight, chief of the criminal division of the DuPage County State's Attorney's Office, sent the print and boots to the Illinois State Police crime lab. They concluded the same thing, as did a print expert in Kansas, although this analysis was more tentative. Finally, the print and boots were sent to "shoe expert" Louise Robbins, who said it was a match. This was good enough for the investigative team.

Wrong Turn

Humans are wired to make order out of chaos. Add to this the public pressure of solving a child murder in a county with few such crimes and the stage is set for potential error. Although three experienced analysts could not find a match, the prosecutor ignored this and accepted the lone opinion of a supposed expert because it helped the case.

Detective work has long been done by hunches, anecdotes, gumshoe work, and brainstorming. Sometimes science is involved, but often it's done by instinct and "tradecraft." Problem solving consists of trial-and-error, sudden insight, and rule of thumb strategies.

Criminologist Kim Rossmo has made a study of how cognitive errors specifically affect investigations. He discusses how investigators arrive at scenes with a perceptual set, which helps them decide what to do next. However, if their decisions are premature or entrenched in a specific idea, they will see what they expect to see. "Tunnel vision results when there is a narrow focus on a limited range of alternatives," Rossmo states.

Tom Knight had his sights on Buckley.

Detective Sam now suspected Cruz as well. He stayed on the suspects, questioning them repeatedly. He let them know he believed they were the girl's killers. When he unsuccessfully tried to trick Hernandez into a confession, Sam began to doubt that Hernandez was involved. He concentrated on Buckley and

Cruz. No one caved.

Sam told what he'd learned to Knight and his team. Knight decided that all three men were implicated. Their original intent had been burglary, but once they broke in and saw Jeanine, they grabbed her for their own kicks. Sam wasn't so sure. He didn't think that three burglars would collectively want to rape, brutalize, and murder a child.

Knight ignored Sam's doubts and took his case to a grand jury. On March 8, 1984, over a year after Jeanine's murder, all three men were indicted.

Knight prepared for trial. Just before the trial started, he received a statement from a detective and a prison guard that Cruz had described a "vision" that proved he knew things about the treatment of Jeanine that only a participant would know. Five informants were prepared to testify that both Cruz and Hernandez had confessed to inmates, and two eyewitnesses would identify Buckley as the driver of a car that might have been used in the crime. Finally, the shoe expert would link Buckley to the intruder's boot print. Knight thought he had a strong case.

Yet Detective Sam was mystified about why none of the defendants cut a deal with the state. He thought that the pressure of possible execution would move *one* of them toward a confession. He watched and waited.

The trial began in January 1985. As it moved along without any deals, Sam finally acted. He resigned from the sheriff's department and offered himself as a witness for the defense. (He was not used.) He believed that these men were innocent.

On February 22, the jury found Cruz and Hernandez guilty, but was unable to reach a verdict on Buckley. Cruz and Hernandez were sentenced to death. Buckley was held for a new trial. Hernandez and Cruz went to death row at Menard

203

Correctional Center, to await the results of their appeals. Their assigned defenders were puzzled over the lack of actual evidence.

Then came a surprise. Later that year, an inmate serving a sentence for two other murders claimed that *he* was the one who'd raped and killed Jeanine Nicarico. He stated that he'd been alone and that the men who'd just been sentenced to death were innocent. His name was Brian Dugan.

But a confession was not enough. Nor was Dugan's criminal background and similar *modus operandi*. The DuPage prosecutor had a lot riding on the convictions he'd just won. He resisted any interference.

However, those who'd arrested Dugan thought he might be telling the truth.

Melissa

Dugan was aimlessly driving his blue Gremlin on a country road outside Somonauk, a village on the boundary of DeKalb and LaSalle Counties. It was a pleasant enough afternoon on June 2, 1985, and he spotted two young girls riding their bikes. He steered toward them.

No one was around. He believed he could get them both if he was lucky. Before they knew what he intended, he'd snatched one of the girls, Opal, and threw her into his car. As he ran down the other, Melissa Ackerman, Opal managed to get out and take off on her bike to get help.

But Dugan had Melissa in the truck and was driving too fast for anyone to catch him. He took the terrified seven-year-old to an isolated spot about 17 miles away. Near a creek, he raped her and, as she struggled to get away, he drowned her. He drove away, believing he'd get away with this one like he had with the other two.

204

However, Dugan's luck had run out. He'd forgotten to renew his vehicle sticker, which caught the attention of a patrol officer, who stopped him and told him to take care of it. When Melissa's friend later reported the abduction, the officer remembered the Gremlin he'd seen. The driver, in his late 20s, matched the girl's description.

The next day, at 6:45 AM, a SWAT team surrounded Dugan as he drove into the parking lot of Midwest Hydraulics, where he operated machines. They brought him in for questioning. In fact, they were interested not just in the missing girl but also in several recent rapes.

A month earlier, on May 6, a 21-year-old North Aurora woman said that a seemingly friendly man in his 20s had helped her to start her car. But then he'd pushed his way inside and flashed a hunting knife. He'd threatened her into being quiet before he gagged and blindfolded her. She'd sat still, terrified. He'd driven her to an isolated spot near Batavia and stopped the car. She'd waited, unsure what he'd do. He'd forced her into the back seat and raped her.

Three weeks later, on May 28, a 19-year-old woman was walking on Route 31 when a man had slowed his car next to her. She'd tried to ignore him, but he stopped, got out and tried to force her into his car. She'd struggled and managed to flee.

The day after, a 16-year-old girl had reported that a man driving around in Aurora had threatened her with a tire iron, insisting that she get into his car. She'd obeyed. He'd taken her to the next county, where he'd wrapped a belt around her neck and raped her. To her relief, he'd taken her back to Aurora.

They'd all described a similar man and a similar blue car.

Under questioning, Dugan admitted to the rapes.

However, he remained mute about Melissa Ackerman. The officers realized this could be bad news. They were certain from Opal's description that he'd kidnapped the girl. They now believed she might be dead. Dugan was charged with various counts of abduction and sexual assault.

A strand of hair was lifted from a sleeping bag in Dugan's car. They sent it to a lab, along with hair from Melissa. Two weeks later, Melissa's body was found. There was little doubt from the hair analysis that Dugan had raped and killed her. Melissa's friend had also identified him.

On June 25, they questioned Dugan again. The FBI, now involved, placed the crime scene photos in front of Dugan. He averted his eyes.

"I don't want to look at those photos," he said. "I don't want to think about that."

"She's an only child," he was told. "Whoever killed her has caused her parents overwhelming anguish."

Dugan squirmed, but he wouldn't budge. He was charged with Melissa's murder. He faced a possible death sentence.

Dugan's assaults had been impulsive and opportunistic, so he hadn't given much thought to being caught and punished. He was scared. He wanted to make deals. His public defender, George Mueller, told prosecutors that Dugan would confess to killing Melissa in exchange for taking the death penalty off the table. He'd also tell them about others that hadn't been linked to him.

A Serial Killer Identified

Early on July 15, 1984, a twenty-seven-year-old nurse, Donna Schnorr, had stopped at a traffic light on Randall Road near Aurora. A truck had come up behind her. She'd revved her engine and started to drive, and the truck had stayed close. Frightened, she'd tried to maneuver but was forced off the road near a Kane County quarry. She hadn't been able to protect herself against the man who'd come after her and beat her into submission before raping her. Finally, he'd drowned her in the quarry.

Dugan knew this story, because he was the man in the truck.

He received two life sentences in the Pontiac Correctional Center, but he'd told Mueller about yet a third murder. Dugan knew that two men had been wrongly convicted for it. Mueller contacted Knight to tell him that Dugan might have a connection to Jeanine Nicarico's abduction. He would confess to it in exchange for another life sentence.

Knight wasn't sure. He had a lot riding on the convictions he'd already won. Mueller said there had been no reason for Dugan to tell them anything, but he'd volunteered the information.

Knight's team developed questions based on items they believed that only Jeanine's killer would know. Mueller took them to Dugan and returned an hour later with his answers.

Knight looked them over. He was quiet, noncommittal. Finally, he said, "I'll get back to you."

Mueller knew there was a lot at stake, politically, for the DuPage prosecution team. If they accepted Dugan's confession, it meant that their approach had been seriously flawed. They'd spent a lot of taxpayer money and had put two men on death row. Dugan's confession put them in a bind. They would need a way to save face.

Before Knight would deal, he sent a team to question him.

In a cold manner, Dugan provided details:

He had burglary in mind when he approached the Nicarico house around 2:00 PM and knocked. Jeanine shouted that she was not going to open the door. He said his car was having trouble and he just wanted to borrow a screwdriver. She would not relent.

Dugan looked through the window at the frail young girl in a pink nightshirt walking away from the door. He saw words on the nightshirt, "I'm sleepy" and a Disney image of Sleepy the Dwarf. His lust kicked in. "I had to have her," he would tell detectives. He kicked in the door.

Jeanine was on the stairs going down. She turned in terror at the noise of the door breaking inward and froze. He grabbed her and carried her upstairs, where he saw an unmade bed in her sister's room. Jeanine kicked and tried to scream, but Dugan overpowered her. He tied her hands and used a sheet to wrap her up. She was secured enough for him to go to his car and get tape that he carried for burglaries. He moved his car into the driveway, so he could carry her out more easily.

Back with the weeping girl, Dugan placed a towel over her face and taped it in place. Then he carried her to his car, placing her in the back seat. He drove to an isolated spot near the Prairie Path, got into the back seat and anally raped the girl. He assured her that he would take her home.

When he was done, he moved her out of the car. He told her to walk ahead of him and as they went behind the car, he lifted his tire iron and hit Jeanine twice in the back of the head. As she fell, she hit her head against the car's bumper.

Dugan then smashed her in the forehead. He dragged the body into some bushes about twenty feet off the path.

Driving away, he took a wrong turn and got stuck in mud. It aggravated him that some toll workers noticed him as he worked his way out. There was nothing he could do about it. But to his surprise, no one ever came to arrest him.

During the interview, Dugan accurately described the jagged-edged tape he'd used to bind Jeanine's head. He knew she had short hair, recently cut. He told detectives where he'd purchased the tape (which they confirmed). He said he'd raped Jeanine anally because he'd been unsuccessful with vaginal penetration, and this was consistent with the autopsy findings. The type of tire iron he'd used to bludgeon her, which fit her wounds, came with the type of car that Dugan drove at the time, a 1980 Volares. Toll workers *had* seen his car near the Prairie Path, including the missing hubcap, and he fit their description of the driver. In addition, Dugan knew the locations of the Nicarico home and the body dumpsite, and he knew the house interior layout. Even under hypnosis and with a polygraph attached, Dugan's story remained consistent.

However, he'd made some factual errors. He hadn't recalled a sailboat parked in the Nicarico driveway, where he'd parked his car. He was also wrong about some of the interior details of the house. Jeanine's body had been found facedown, but Dugan recalled that it had been face up. He thought she'd had toenail polish on, but she hadn't. He said he'd entered the home around 11 AM, but this was off by three hours.

Not much was known in 1985 about psychopaths. Dugan showed no remorse for having done the terrible things he'd done, which made his confession seem less credible to his interrogators. They believed he could have learned about the details while behind bars or from reading the newspapers.

When the Nicaricos heard about the confession, they were torn. They believed in the prosecution team and thought that Dugan was lying. They counted 25 separate errors, which suggested to them that he'd heard or read about the crime and wanted to take credit for it. They called a press conference to affirm that they stood by Knight. They believed that Hernandez and Cruz had killed their daughter.

Jeanine's body was exhumed in March 1986 to corroborate what Dugan had said. Had there been any significant differences, the deal was off the table. But even if there were none, this did not confirm Dugan as the killer. The officials decided to use Dugan's factual errors as proof that he was lying. They thought he was not Jeanine's killer. Later, they decided that he'd been an accomplice to Cruz and Hernandez.

Back to Court

The decision was made not to retry Buckley, especially when FBI analysts found no match between his boots and the boot print from the Nicaricos' door. The shoe expert had been discredited, so the charges were dismissed. However, Cruz and Hernandez remained on death row.

Then part of the case crashed. In December 1987, Hernandez's cousin recanted his testimony. He said he'd been pressured to say what he'd said and none of it was true. In January 1988, the Illinois Supreme Court overturned the Cruz and Hernandez convictions, deciding that they should have had separate trials.

Within a few months, an analysis of several hair strands found on Jeanine showed Dugan's rare genetic abnormality. By May, blood tests from each of the suspects, including Dugan, implicated Dugan, exonerated Hernandez and Buckley, but were inconclusive about Cruz. Their attorneys publicly called the state's team dishonest. All the evidence pointed to Dugan. None pointed to their clients.

Still, in 1990, the county moved forward with new trials. Robert Kilander and Richard Stock replaced Knight and his team. Dugan wasn't charged but he was implicated as an accomplice. His confession was not used. Cruz was convicted again and sentenced to death. Hernandez had a mistrial.

In 1991, Hernandez went to trial for a third time. He was convicted and received 80 years.

Assistant Attorney General Mary Brigid Kenney, who was assigned to oppose Cruz's second appeal, found significant errors in the process, including perjured testimony. She sent a memo to Illinois Attorney General Roland Burris. He ignored her concerns, so she resigned in protest.

The Illinois Supreme Court affirmed Cruz's conviction in 1992, but reversed itself six months later and granted Cruz a rehearing. In 1994, the Court overturned Cruz's second conviction, stating that certain evidence about Dugan's MO should have been admitted. In 1995, an appellate court also overturned the conviction and ordered a new trial.

However, things went downhill. A police lieutenant now realized that he'd been on vacation at the time that he'd supposedly received a call from detectives who'd heard about Cruz's "vision." The conversation he'd recalled in previous trials had never happened. The judge acquitted Cruz and ordered that he be released. He was eventually issued a full pardon. A month later, the charges against Hernandez were dismissed. A special prosecutor was appointed to look into how the case had been mishandled. This was a momentous move.

Dugan was bemused. This would have been cheaper and easier if they'd just accepted his confession in 1985.

In 1996, a grand jury began to hear the results of the lengthy investigation against three DuPage prosecutors (Patrick King, Robert Kilander, and Tom Knight) and four investigators. All were indicted on 47 counts of misconduct, perjury, falsifying evidence and trying to frame Cruz. They became known as the DuPage 7. Central to the testimony was Cruz denying that he'd ever told a cop and a prison guard about a "vision" he'd had that implicated the others in the murder. Although the vision had played a strong role in the first trial, it had never been recorded or mentioned in any police report. In addition, it could not have happened on the date that officers claimed. Clearly, there was misconduct.

Still, all of the defendants were freed or acquitted in 1999, on grounds of insufficient evidence. All three defendants sued the county in civil court, settling for $3.5 million.

Cruz was pardoned just a few weeks before Governor George Ryan granted clemency to all of the 167 death row inmates in Illinois in 2003. He'd been shaken by the possibility that innocent men might have been executed. The Nicarico case demonstrated real problems in the legal system. Cruz and Hernandez had wrongly spent ten years in prison, and there had been a dozen more such cases.

The spotlight was back on Dugan. New DNA results showed that he was Jeanine's rapist, just as he'd stated. A grand jury indicted him in 2005, two decades after he'd confessed. At first, he pleaded innocent. In 2009, he changed his plea to guilty. Since he'd already confessed, the last stage was his sentencing. Would he get life...or death?

A Psychopath's Brain

The defense team's forensic psychiatrist, Jim Cavanaugh, from the Isaac Ray Center in Chicago, invited Dr. Kent Kiehl into the proceedings. Kiehl recorded their initial meeting in his book, *The Psychopath Whisperer*.

Cavanaugh explained the case complications in DuPage County, ending with the latest DNA analysis. The prosecutor, he said, would claim that Dugan posed a future danger to society. The defense was searching for mitigating factors. Cavanaugh thought they had it in getting Dugan a diagnosis of psychopathy. This was where Kiehl came in. He could explain to a jury the flaws in Dugan's brain.

Kiehl is at the forefront of neuroscience research on psychopathy. Mentored by Robert Hare, the creator of the Psychopathy Checklist-Revised (PCL-R), he directs the Mobile Imaging Core and Clinical Cognitive Neuroscience at the Mind Research Network. His primary focus is on groundbreaking research on the brains of incarcerated psychopaths.

Kiehl believes that psychopathy arises from a brain deficit and qualifies as a severe mental illness with serious emotional deficits. To his mind, expecting psychopaths to understand and control their actions is like expecting someone with dyslexia to read Faulkner. If psychopaths think differently, Kiehl believes, then they must have different brain structures. The research supports this idea.

Psychopathic brains show differences from normal brains in the prefrontal and paralimbic systems. The amygdala, linked through a complex network to brain regions that monitor all five senses, shares a communication channel with the prefrontal cortex.

If the amygdala is not functioning properly, the person can have a disturbed sense of emotional values. That is, if this brain region in psychopaths is sending the wrong signals to the prefrontal cortex, they would experience an impaired ability to respond to the threat of punishment, make clear moral judgments, and grasp the emotional implications of their behavior.

Cavanaugh hoped that a functional magnetic resonance imagining (fMRI) scan of Dugan's brain would show his diminished ability to control his aggressive compulsion.

Kiehl agreed to get involved. He looked into Dugan's history to learn more about him. Hundreds of pages were available from FBI files, detailing interviews with Dugan's relatives, coworkers, and former girlfriends.

Born in New Hampshire on September 23, 1956, Brian Dugan was the second of five children. There was reason to believe that he'd suffered brain damage during birth, because nurses had ignorantly tried to keep him from being born until the doctor could get there. As a child, he suffered further head trauma and constant headaches. His parents were both alcoholics, who often dealt severely with their children's misbehavior. As he grew up, Dugan began to torment his siblings and family pets. He became sexually promiscuous at 13. There was suspicion that he'd been sexually assaulted several times. Although his IQ was in the superior range, Dugan dropped out of high school at age 16 and became a habitual drug user, burglar, arsonist, and rapist.

Steve Greenberg was Dugan's defense attorney. He set up an interview for Kiehl, which ran four hours. Dugan was friendly and talkative. He described a time when he'd been abducted – he was 15 – and said that his abductor was Chicago-area serial killer John Wayne Gacy. [This has been contested.] He claimed that the incident didn't bother him. "His lack of emotion," Kiehl later wrote, "was as profound as I'd seen in any inmate I have ever interviewed."

Dugan denied having planned any of his rapes or murders. He'd acted on impulse. The items he'd carried, such as a knife and duct tape, he'd used for burglaries and car repairs. He offered no reason for why he'd killed his victims.

He just didn't know.

Kiehl was eager to do a brain scan. The medical campus of Northwestern University had the sophisticated type of MRI machine needed. The results showed an abnormally low density of grey matter in areas that monitor emotion, which suggested that Dugan might not have chosen as freely as many believed. "Brian's paralimbic gray matter values were even more atrophied than most psychopaths," Kiehl wrote.

At the hearing, Kiehl's testimony was restricted to generic diagrams rather than Dugan's actual brain scan, but he was allowed to describe the meaning of Dugan's high PCL-R score (37 out of 40). He believed the jury took this seriously.

A forensic psychiatrist familiar with neurological scans testified for the prosecution, saying that the analysis for psychopathy was oversimplified.

The jury returned a life sentence, but the judge sent them for more deliberation. They came back with a death sentence. Dugan's execution date was set for February 25, 2010. Greenberg filed an appeal.

In March 2011, Dugan's sentence was commuted when Governor Patrick Quinn abolished the death penalty.

Although Kiehl's testimony had made little impact on the Dugan case, it made waves in the legal system. Other defense attorneys were now aware of his work and have asked for his assistance. It's possible that future juries will accept psychopathy as a mental illness with emotional deficits. How this will impact the legal and correctional system remains unknown.

Chapter 13: Enriqueta Martí

"The Vampire of Barcelona"
By Sylvia Perrini

THE GROWTH OF BARCELONA

Barcelona, Spain in the autonomous community of Catalonia is a city with a rich history. The city was originally founded by the Carthaginians and Phoenicians in about 230 B.C.

Catalonia was an independent region of the Iberian Peninsula– with its own language, laws, and customs until the 15th century when it became part of Spain as we know it today. Various Spanish Kings attempted to impose the Spanish language and laws on the region. As a result, Barcelona began to lose the importance and power it once had, and there were many conflicts between Barcelona and the Spanish capital and seat of power, Madrid. The government in Madrid even went so far as to ban Barcelona from trading with its newly acquired American colonies.

In 1778, Madrid finally permitted Catalonia to trade with America, which boosted the city's shipping industry and led to the start of Barcelona's industrial revolution. Textiles, with the raw materials shipped from the Spanish New World territories, grew into a big business, along with the cork, iron, and wine industries. Barcelona, by the 1830s, was riding on a feel-good factor that lasted for most of the 19th century.

The population of Barcelona in 1800 was 115,000, but the city soon attracted poor immigrants from rural Catalonia and, later, from other regions of Spain, and by 1900, the population had grown to nearly 600,000.

Barcelona's commercial success and growing wealth

helped revive interest in all things Catalan, and Catalonia began demanding more political freedom from Madrid. Between 1822 and 1888, Barcelona held 14 exhibitions to promote Catalan industrial products and, hence, boosted its cultural identity.

However, the growing industrialization and wealth for the business classes did not filter down into the working class. By the mid-1800s, overcrowding in the city had become a major problem, along with poverty, disease, and unrest.

Working-class families lived in progressively putrid and overcrowded conditions. Poor diet, poor sanitation, and disease were standard in workers' districts, and riots unsurprisingly resulted. In 1842, one such riot was brutally quelled by government troops stationed in the 17th century Montjuïc castle on the steep Montjuïc hills, west of the city. The castle had been built to repress the citizens of the city.

Meanwhile, the Spanish empire, from 1840 until 1850, had their cities of Ceuta and Melilla in the North African country of Morocco under continuous and untiring attacks from Moroccan troops and tribes. From Catalonia, thousands of young men were recruited into the army to fight the Moroccans.

In 1854, Barcelona's old medieval city's walls were knocked down, which offered some relief to the city's overcrowding but the problems remained acute.

In 1869, a plan formulated to expand the city had begun. A civil engineer, Ildefons Cerda, created the plan for the new area known as l'Eixample. It was carefully incorporated with the old Barcelona city in a very contemporary way, with wide avenues built in a grid pattern, offering ventilation, natural lighting, an effective sewage system, green spaces, and the ease of movement between goods, people, and services. In this new area of the city, the flourishing bourgeoisie paid for lavish, ostentatious houses and buildings, many of them in the unique, Art Nouveau-influenced modernista style, whose leading exponent was Antoni Gaudi.

In 1888, Spain held its first International World Fair in the city of Barcelona. The fair was held on a 115-acre reconstructed site of the city's main public park: the Parc de la Ciutadella. The fair was opened on the 20th of May in 1888 by the Queen Regent Maria Cristina and Alfonse XIII of Spain. In all, twenty-seven countries participated including China, Japan, Russia, and the United States. More than 2 million people from Spain, the rest of Europe, and other international points of embarkation visited the exhibition before it closed on the 9th of December.

Barcelona was portrayed to the world as an international bourgeoisie and industrial city. There were many who objected to the International Exhibition. The journalist and writer Josep Yxart objected to the exhibition because of the local and national economic crisis that the city was undergoing at the time and the lack of a reliable urban transport and communication network, along with the decadence and decay of the old town. Antonino Suárez Saavedra, an electrical engineer, criticized loudly the colossal public investment of money instead of putting it to more "useful" schemes, such as urban sewage, street pavements, and water pipes. A local socialist newspaper, El Productor, declared the exhibition was a "bourgeois" display of luxury goods and waste, of no interest to the workers of Barcelona.

As the merchants and bourgeoisie grew wealthier, the gap between the rich and poor was growing progressively more obvious and a subculture emerged, creating in the city a twirling vortex of anarchists, bourgeois regionalists, republicans, gangsters, police terrorists, and hired pistoleros (gunmen). And so grew the city's reputation for excess and seediness. In 1893, a revolutionary extremist created widespread panic and disarray at the Gran Teatre del Liceu when he hurled bombs into the audience killing twenty people.

ENRIQUETA ARRIVES IN THE CITY

Near the beginning of 1888, an attractive young woman, Enriqueta Martí, aged 20, arrived at the city's railway station having travelled from her nearby town of birth, Sant Feliu de Llobregat. It was the first time she had been to Barcelona, and having heard of the great excitement about the exhibition and stories of the "The Pearl of the Mediterranean," as many called Barcelona, she had come with a fierce desire to seek a better life for herself.

Before leaving her father's house, she had answered an advertisement for a position as a domestic servant to a bourgeoisie family who lived in the l'Eixample area of the city. As Enriqueta entered the driveway of the magnificent house of her new employers, one can only imagine the awe she felt as she surveyed the gardens with their walls covered in vines, at fountains with cherubs spitting into a pond filled with colorful fish, and the imposing front porch with tall columns.

Inside the house, one would imagine, she would have been struck by the magnificent decor, velvet curtains, and marble floors. Enriqueta, as she laid in her narrow servant's bed that night in the eaves of the house, was determined that such luxury would one day be hers.

Enriqueta was an attractive, intelligent, slender young woman with dark hair, an angular face, and brown eyes with pupils as dark as wells. She was also acutely observant and a quick learner. She watched how the bourgeoisie behaved and

220

conducted themselves: their mannerisms and daily customs.

She listened to the conversations of the other servants and eavesdropped on her employers and their guests at every available opportunity. For Enriqueta, the drudgery, long hours, and low pay of the work were, for her, an education. She realized that she had to devise ways in which to provide services to placate those who had everything so that she might suckle at their many riches.

Enriqueta Marti

On her time off, which wasn't much, she took to roaming the streets of Barcelona City. During the time of the International Exhibition, the city was full of activity and public displays. Wealth was seemingly abundant around the exhibition areas of the city. Enriqueta would stand outside the Hotel Internacional, which had become the meeting point of national and international elite visitors, and dream of being a guest in the establishment.

The exhibition area of the city was in stark contrast to other areas of the city where acute poverty, overcrowding, and disease reigned supreme. Foul, fetid smells seeped from cracks and doorways in narrow cobbled streets; the air was unbreathable, and it was where pessimism and weariness weighed heavily down on the inhabitants.

In her wanderings around the city, Enriqueta realized there were plenty of opportunities in Barcelona for people with imagination and enterprise. Before long, she took to prostitution finding work in a high-class brothel in the center of the city and gave up her job as a domestic servant.

It was not an occupation she enjoyed, but for her, it was a means to an end. She quickly learned all the tricks of the trade and listened intently to the other girls' conversations, where she learned of many of the sick perversions of the high society gentlemen clients. Enriqueta filed all of this knowledge away for future use. Her numerous clients included many men of standing, men who would, in the future, come to her aid and indeed provide ready customers for her horrific product line to come.

In 1895, Enriqueta met and married an artist, Juan Pujaló. It was a stormy marriage, and they frequently broke up for months at a time and would then reconcile. They split for good in 1907. Juan later said it was because of her prostitution, her endless affairs, and her strange, unpredictable character.

In 1898, Spain went to war with the U.S. in which it lost not only its entire navy, but its last colonies of Cuba, Puerto Rico, Guam, and the Philippines. Barcelona, as a city, suffered the worst of the War. Not only was it the Spanish port that sent the most Spanish soldiers to fight, but the blow to Barcelona's trade from the loss of its colonies was enormous.

ENRIQUETA OPENS FOR BUSINESS

Sometime during the early 1900s, Enriqueta opened her own brothel, but this was not a normal one. She rented a smart apartment and began procuring her prostitutes. She roamed the poor areas and slums of Barcelona, mainly in el Chino, the Fifth District nowadays known as el Raval: an area full of illiterate and poor immigrants, unemployed and disfigured war veterans, and army deserters. Due to the area's close proximity to the port, boarding houses and hostels abounded.

According to the journalist, Josep Maria Huertas, "It was common for forty to fifty people to live in one house." Seedy taverns were transformed into bordellos or flophouses. Alcohol and morphine abuse was rampant in the area, as were diseases, such as typhus and tuberculosis.

Enriqueta, dressing herself in rags so she wouldn't stand out, kidnapped children between the ages of three to twelve-years-old. She would beg and join the bread queue in front of nuns' monasteries searching for the most abandoned, impoverished, looking children that might be found. These children, once she cleaned them up, she rented to her wealthy clientele for whatever depravity they desired.

At night, she would venture out, wearing her most expensive jewelry, dressed in silks and velvets as if she was a marquis. She would frequent the Casino de la Arrabassada, El Liceu (the Opera House in Barcelona), and attended the best parties held in luxurious homes where her ultimate customers, the high-society of Barcelona, mingled.

With her male clients well satisfied, Enriqueta set about expanding her business. She had, as a child in her hometown, learned of the various uses of herbs for medicinal and cosmetic purposes. She sent home for her notebooks of herb recipes and began to make various remedies and beauty products, which she began to sell to her male clients and their wives and mistresses.

Meanwhile, the Spanish were still struggling with controlling Morocco. In 1909, an army column was destroyed by the Berbers. Following this, the Spanish government attempted to raise an army of reservists from Catalonia to send to Morocco.

The Barcelona union, Solidaridad Obrera, which was led by a group of socialists and anarchists, called for a general strike on Monday the 26th of July in 1909, against the call-up of the reservists for an unwanted war in Morocco. By the following day, workers had taken over the city, stopping troop trains and overturning the city's trams. Within a couple of days, there was a general eruption of street fighting, strikes, riots, and the burning of monasteries and convents. A lot of the rioters thought the Catholic Church was part of the corrupt ruling class structure whose young men did not have to go to fight.

La setmana trágica

Security forces sent by the government in Madrid shot at demonstrators, causing the deaths of over a 100 people and injuring dozens more. This resulted in the building of barricades in the streets by the rioters. The government sent more national troops to the city to crush the revolt and a state of martial law was proclaimed. All suspected organizers of the revolt were executed. The weeklong civil unrest by the city proletariat became known as la setmana trágica.

With the Madrid government crackdown on law and order in Barcelona, Enriqueta's brothel on Minerva Street was uncovered. She was arrested and charged with managing a brothel, which offered children from the ages of three to fourteen for sexual services. A young man was arrested with her. He was supposedly from a wealthy family. The case never came to trial and was mysteriously dropped. It is thought that her rich, influential clients had a hand in this.

It was not long before Enriqueta's business took an even more extraordinarily sinister twist. Perhaps Enriqueta now felt protected and above the law. At this time, there was a superstition among upper class women that the blood of young children helped keep the bloom of youth and that young fat helped conserve a young skin. There was also TB raging through the city; at that time, it was a disease that was one hundred percent fatal, as in those years there was no penicillin, but there was a popular belief that ingested human blood soothed and healed tuberculosis.

Enriqueta now began kidnapping children of all ages, some for prostitution and some to be killed to create her healing tonics and "facial crèmes." Everything that she possibly could she used from these children: the blood, bones (that she pounded into powder), and the fat. Enriqueta offered creams, soaps, ointments, and potions to treat various diseases. Wealthy people would pay enormous amounts of money for Enriqueta's remedies.

Enriqueta rented several apartments: one in the exceedingly poor area of Ravel where she made up her potions. In another one, lived the children she prostituted. In another one, in Calle Ponent, she lived. And finally, the other one was a luxury apartment, out of which she ran her pedophile brothel.

In 1911, rumors began circulating through the Barcelona streets, plazas, markets, and neighborhood courtyards of missing children and babies. Most of the families who had children missing were too poor to investigate what had become of their children beyond reporting them missing, but the authorities did little to investigate. The stories of missing children became so widespread that the civil governor of Barcelona, Portela Valladares, late in 1911, made a statement saying the rumors were false and that children were not being kidnapped and murdered. He was desperate not to have another riot on his hands and again suffer interference from the Madrid government.

On February 10, 1912, a little girl named Teresita Guitart Congost went missing. This time, the poor people protested loudly. They were annoyed by the authorities' passive attitude to all the children that had been reported missing. A neighbor of Enriqueta in Calle Ponent, Claudia Elías, spotted a little girl peering out of Enriqueta's window. A little girl, she thought, that fit the description of the missing Teresita. Claudia told a friend, a carpenter, of her suspicions and together they went to the police.

ENRIQUETA´S ARREST

On February 27th, 1912, the police called on Enriqueta. When the police entered the apartment, they found two girls. One girl was named Angelita, who Enriqueta said was her daughter with her husband Joan Pujaló. The other was Teresita Guitart Congost who Enriqueta said she had found the day before lost, hungry, and wandering the streets. However, as Claudia Elias had spotted the girl five days previously, it was obviously a lie. Enriqueta was arrested, and the two little girls taken into care and questioned.

226

Marti at the time of her arrest

Teresita told how Enriqueta had befriended her with the promise of sweets. She also told the authorities that they were often left alone for hours and on one such occasion had gone into a room they were forbidden to enter. On looking around the room, Teresita said they had found a bag with clothes and a knife all covered in blood. After her statement, Teresita was returned to her distraught parents.

The little girl's statement was even more disturbing to the police than Teresita's. Angelita told the police that before Teresita arrived, there was a little boy of about five, named Pepito, staying with them. Claudia Elias had already told the police of seeing a little boy but that she had not seen him for a while. Angelita claimed that she had seen Enriqueta, who Angelita said she called "mama," stab him to death on the table in the kitchen. She said Enriqueta was unaware that she had seen this.

People chasing the car in which Enriqueta was driven off in

On learning of Enriqueta's arrest, Joan Pujaló went to the police and made a statement about his and Enriqueta's marriage. In his statement, he said they hadn't lived together for years and that they had no children together. Joan Pujaló said he had no idea who the little girl Angelita was. It later emerged that Enriqueta had stolen Angelita at birth from Maria Pujaló, Juan Pujaló's sister. She had helped her sister-in-law during her pregnancy and had convinced her that her baby had been stillborn.

228

One of the final photographs taken of Martí after her arrest. 1912

The police, under the direction of an investigative judge, began searching Enriqueta's properties. In the apartment where they had found Teresita and Angelita, the police found the bag containing the blood stained clothing and a knife. In another bag, they found dirty clothes and numerous small human bones. In a locked room, they discovered fifty jars, pitchers, and a washbasin with human remains that had been preserved: skeletons, greasy lard, powdered bones, blood, and pots containing potions, creams, and ointments packed and ready for sale.

The search of Enriqueta's properties

The police visited three more flats connected to Enriqueta. In them, they discovered fake walls and ceilings where human remains were hidden. They also found the remains of children in jars and vases, along with a book of remedies for almost every disease known. A book of recipes and potions written in Catalan in Enriqueta's handwriting, a box of letters and notes in code, and a long list of highly influential Catalan bourgeoisie were also found hidden. In one of the property's gardens, they dug up a skull belonging to a child of about three-years-old and numerous small bones of children around the ages of three, six, and eight-years-old.

The list of highly powerful people in Barcelona society was extremely controversial, as many people in Barcelona believed that it contained the names of Enriqueta's wealthy clients. The police did their utmost to prevent the names on

230

the list from being leaked, but rumors around the city claimed it contained the names of aristocrats, bankers, doctors, judges, politicians, and businessmen.

Overwhelming evidence and testimony by Angelita shattered Enriqueta's chance of much of a defense being offered. She was already known for, and confessed to, her services as a procurer for pedophiles. However, Enriqueta adamantly stated that her clients were the monsters, not her; it was just her business. In addition, she had been running her brothel for years, and it was because of whom her clients were that she was able to do so.

When questioned about all the corpses and body parts, Enriqueta confessed that she was a healer and used children as raw material for the production of her remedies. She claimed that the wealthy women who had bought her "face creams" knew what the products were made from, but a street child was little more than a piece of trash to them.

She was, she said, simply a businesswoman providing supplies for the demands.

"Child prostitutes for the gentlemen; elixirs and face creams for the ladies."

Enriqueta was imprisoned to await her trial in the "Reina Amàlia" jail.

THE MEDIA

The case made big news and little was talked about in the city except for the shocking revelations revealed in the media. The two little girls rescued from Enriqueta's apartment became darlings of the media, enjoying a certain celebrity status (albeit briefly).

Teresita Guitart with her parents and officers who rescued her

Angelita

Enriqueta herself attained a level of infamy (unwanted on her part) that put her face on the front pages of international newspapers and seedy tabloids alike. In the eyes of the press, she was a vampire preying on weak and vulnerable children. Barely mentioned in the media were Enriqueta's clients and their part in the crimes.

Anger and outrage began to take over the people of Barcelona, particularly in the poor and impoverished areas, such as Es Ravel from where most of the children had disappeared. The conservative press, to calm down the situation and possibly to prevent more riots, claimed that "the names and addresses contained in the list were people known for their love of charity, people who were also victims of Enriqueta's 'deception' who knew her from her having come to their homes to beg."

The public was highly suspicious of these claims; they wanted Enriqueta to face a public trial and be punished and executed along with any accomplices.

As Enriqueta languished in jail with her trial constantly postponed, and with no more gory details to print, the media moved on to other topics.

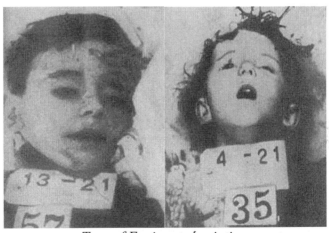

Two of Enriqueta's victims

THE END

On April 15th, the ocean liner Titanic sank after hitting an iceberg off the coast of Newfoundland, on her maiden voyage between Southampton, UK to New York City, US. The news of the sinking and the loss of more than 1,500 people aboard were greeted with worldwide shock and outrage. This news story eclipsed the story of the 'Vampire of Barcelona'.

Enriqueta never went to trial. She died at the age of 43 in the early morning of May 12, 1913, officially of a long illness. However, others believe that her fellow prisoners murdered her by hanging her in one of the prison yards after having being paid to do so by some of her wealthy ex-clients, who were terrified she would name them in her trial.

The death of Enriqueta Martí robbed the public and her victims' families of the chance to expose all of Enriqueta's secrets and gain information on her rich clients and conspirators. One can be sure, however, that those who were on the list, "so fond of charity" went to bed the night of her death and slept more peacefully than they had in the previous 13 months.

Enriqueta was secretly buried in a grave in the Cementerio del Sudoeste on the hillside of Montjuïc, in the city of Barcelona. Following her death, all her black books and client lists mysteriously disappeared.

Enriqueta operated for many years, but it will never be known how many murders she was actually responsible for or who her clients were.

CONCLUSION

We may look back at Enriqueta´s life and take comfort in the fact that the shocking story took place over a hundred years ago. We might think that in civilized modern western society the level of corruption and cover ups that took place then could never happen in this day and age.

Indeed, that might have been my conclusion, until I began to look into child sexual abuse in modern times and how wrong I would have been.

Enriqueta learned at a young age that pedophilia was an extremely lucrative business. She was prepared to supply the product (young children for sexual abuse) to customers who demanded the product. Her customers were the rich, privileged, and powerful who allowed her to operate with impunity for many years.

Today, pedophilia is a huge worldwide scourge, with pedophile rings operating in every corner of the globe. The trafficking of minors into prostitution is now the world's most profitable unlawful trade after arms and drugs.

In developing countries, intense poverty, the growing accessibility of fast internet connections, which allows real time webcam streaming of sexual acts with children, coupled with the existence of a huge and well-off overseas base of customers, has led criminals to mercilessly exploit children for enormous financial gain.

However, it is not only in developing countries that vulnerable children are being exploited. In recent years in Great Britain and other western countries, there has been a string of shocking child sexual abuse cases and murder, with many suspecting links and cover ups by people in power.

What I have discovered has deeply shocked me and will be the subject of a new book I am presently working on.

Chapter 14: Zebra! The Hunting Humans 'Ninja' Truck Driver Serial Killer

by Peter Vronsky

"When you hear hoofbeats, think of horses, not zebras."
- Dr. Theodore Woodward
Diagnostic Instruction to Medical Interns (1940s)

"The rite of confirmation, a revelational leap of lack of faith in humanity,
but also the onset of addiction to hedonistic nihilism.
The psychic abolition of redemption"[i]
- Serial killer Ian Brady on a serial killer's second murder

A serial killer can sometimes strike you like lightning at the most inconceivable moment and place in a most unexpected random way. Yes, some people by virtue of the stormy life they lead or by what they do to make a living, by choice or not, can increase their chance of becoming a victim of a serial killer—"victim facilitation" is the technical term. For example, street prostitutes, hitchhiking runaways, drug addicted homeless, inebriated college girls, runaway juveniles, trusting children, indigent poor, the helplessly aged and sick, the desperate online daters, graveyard shift convenience store workers, the restaurant hostess going to her car in a dark parking lot at the end of her shift [or stripper, night shift factory worker, office cleaner, night desk clerk, the legion of single mom wage earners, etc.]; they are all statistically preferred victims of serial killers for both logistical and pathological reasons. But for the rest of us, those of us snuggly secure in our nice Neighborhood Watch homes... it's all in the random chance of mathematics and the geometry of your turning right instead of left—just that one time—and the social and geographic lay of the God-given land you travel and the terrain on which you make your home.

With a poison-pill lottery-ticket winning odds of a chance, a serial killer can even come to you in daylight on a miserably cold January Tuesday morning in Kansas, as you are sleepily packing school lunches in the warm kitchen for your eleven-year-old girl and nine-year-old son finishing their breakfasts at the table, your husband nearby ready to drive the kids to school, the car warmed up ready to go, the family dog loping about on the kitchen floor for food scraps, when a serial killer bursts in through back yard door, overpowers you and your husband, puts the dog out into the yard, kills your husband, then kills you, then kills your nine-year-old son, and then walks your eleven-year-old girl into the basement, hangs her by her neck from a water pipe and molests her as she slowly strangles to death, the way Dennis Rader "The BTK Killer" did to the Otero family on a crisp winter's school day morning in their nice suburban bungalow that they had just moved into a few weeks earlier.

Or one can come to you on a hot and hazy July weekend afternoon at a crowded lakeside beach in a state park, looking all boyishly handsome, like a bright shining angel in his tennis whites, clean-cut, law school dashing and determined, but just so, so, cute and vulnerable with his arm in a cast, charmingly asking for help to unload his sailing boat. That was the way one came to twenty-three-year-old Janice Anne Ott, a big city probation caseworker, who should have known better when she was approached by Ted Bundy and left with him for a "short drive to help him launch his boat." As he beat and strangled her in the bush, biting and tearing at her with his well-cared for teeth, his fine college boy fingers thrusting into her violently and painfully, scratching and ripping her with his neatly trimmed kitten-sharp nails, the last thing she probably heard above his animal-like growling and panting was the playful splashing and laughter of bathers and lovers on the beach a short distance away. Just about the time that he was done with her and ready for more, eighteen-year-old Denise Naslund, on the beach for a picnic with her boyfriend and her dog, perhaps admiring the nearby beautiful tree line of death in her sight, began to feel the nagging urge to pee and started to scope out the public washroom at the edge of the beach parking lot. That is where she would last be seen and where her chance encounter with Bundy was awaiting her. Sometimes it's just a matter of when and where you choose to pee that determines whether you live tomorrow or die today. Both women's bodies were found two months later in a forest about four miles away, where Bundy squirreled them away so he could revisit them for necrophilic sex.

Or it could be on a spring day in April in Louisiana, and you are a recently divorced real estate agent behind in her monthly sales when a prospective customer phones you at your office, a doctor, you'd never met but says you were recommended and he urgently needs to find a house, and money is no object, and can you show him something today right away? You straighten the hem of your stylish power businesswoman red suit and skirt, make sure the buttons of your silky white blouse are neatly done up, as you freshen your makeup, don your business heels, and head out the door to meet your new potential client. When you don't come back at the end of the day, they find your car with your shoes tossed in the back, abandoned in the hotel parking lot where you said you were going to meet your client, and your body drenched in blood from two stab wounds in the chest a few miles away in a vacant house for sale, barefoot, hanging from the rafters of the attic on a strip of denim brought to the scene in his pocket by the killer, the way it happened to forty-year-old real estate agent Jean McPhaul at the hands of a suspected, but never convicted serial killer she had randomly encountered on an otherwise very ordinary working day. It can happen just like that; any time; anywhere; day or night.[ii]

For Darlene Ewalt in 2007, her serial killer came in the dark of a warm summer's night in a place where she felt the safest, in the bosom of her home and family. Ewalt was a forty-two-year-old mother and homemaker living in West Hanover Township, Pennsylvania, a typical suburban community nestled on Interstate I-81 between Harrisburg and Hershey. "Dar" as everyone called Darlene, was an attractive vivacious woman, tall and fit, with honey blond-brown hair. In some of her photos she resembles the movie star Susan Sarandon. She lived happily with her husband of twenty-one years, Todd, a carpenter, and their college-aged son Nick. Their daughter Nicole had recently moved out to a home of her own nearby, and both Dar and Todd, who'd first met when they were teens, were looking forward to a new "empty nest" life, as their son Nick was entering college on a football scholarship.

Todd Ewalt and Darlene Ewalt

Darlene and Todd's marriage, by all reports, was a happy and tranquil one. They supplemented the family income by hand tooling ultralight thoroughbred horse racing saddles, which Darlene would often personally deliver to customers. She handled the books and sales charm while Todd took care of the tooling work. Dar was a spirited and independent woman who periodically travelled by herself to her hometown in Nebraska to visit her family without her husband in tow. She loved to cook and bustle in the kitchen. She raised a Pomeranian puppy named Jag, bottle-feeding the pup, which she still sometimes carried around tucked into the pocket of her apron. She kept a pet bunny rabbit in a cage in the backyard.

West Hanover was a safe and cozy place to live and raise children. On a national violent crime (murder, robbery, rape, assault) index scale of a low 1 to a high 100, West Hanover recently rated 14.6 (the USA average being 41.4).[iii] The Ewalts' modest house on Manor Drive stood next to a T-intersection with Hershey Road (Highway 39), which passed behind their house and connected the nearby I-81 with the town of Hershey of the chocolate factory fame. If you drove slightly over the speed limit, the I-81 ramp was conveniently

241

just ten minutes straight up Hershey Road north of the Ewalts' house, a distance of two miles.

A sliding door from their kitchen led out onto a cozy patio with a BBQ at the back of their house, which they fitted out with typical comfortable patio furniture. The patio deck was sheltered by a copse of trees that screened their backyard from the adjacent busy Hershey Road. A suburban bicycle path on the other side of the trees paralleled Hershey Road as it weaved through the several quiet residential neighborhoods of single-family homes and some small condo complexes that stood between the Ewalts' house and the nearby I-81.

The night of July 12 was hot and humid, and Darlene was sitting out late on their backyard patio talking on a cordless phone. Their close friends Patty and Chet Gerhart had come into two extra tickets for a Caribbean cruise and invited Todd and Darlene to join them on the trip in October. Todd who coached junior football declined the offer, not wanting to take a week off at the height of football season, but he had no objections to Dar going with the Gerharts without him. That's the way they were. All day long Darlene was on the phone with the Gerharts and with her girlfriends looking for a companion to take the extra ticket her husband turned down.

At around 10 p.m. Darlene was still on the phone, excitedly chattering with Chet about the cruise when Todd slid open the patio door to tell her he was going to bed. Dar was a night owl, so it was not unusual for Todd, who kept early morning hours as a carpenter, to turn in before his wife did. Even though she told him she'd be up in a few minutes, Todd, accustomed to Dar's late night habits, knew better. He wasn't going to wait up for her. At 2:00 a.m., Darlene was still sitting on their patio in the sultry warm night, talking on the phone with Chet about the planned cruise. She felt completely safe and secure in the privacy of her backyard patio, two strong

242

and able men sleeping upstairs inside the house just a few yards away from her, the familiar voice of a friend on the other end of the phone, the nest-like comfort of home territory, the summer sound of crickets in her yard, warmly lit by the glow of the kitchen light, under a night sky canopy of stars.

As Darlene babbled and chuckled happily on the phone—as if in some slasher movie—a person suddenly came out of the dark of the bushes behind her, dressed entirely in ninja-like black clothing, face concealed in a balaclava hood. He was wielding a large serrated hunting survival knife in his gloved hand, with which he slit Darlene's throat from behind, almost from ear to ear, and then repeatedly stabbed her in the neck and chest.

On the other end of the phone Chet heard Darlene cry out, "Oh my God, Oh my God, Oh my God, Oh my..." and then nothing. The phone went dead.

It was as fast and as simple and as crazy as that.

It happened so fast that police would later note the killer probably got little or no blood splashed on him—there were no footprints in the gore or blood tracked from the scene. The only witness was the caged bunny rabbit in the backyard, a thought that crossed the mind of one of the perplexed investigators later that night at the scene.[iv]

Unable to get Darlene back on the phone, Chet and Patty quickly drove over to the Ewalts' house nearby to see what had happened. Chet rushed straight to the patio where he knew Darlene had been when they were talking. There he came upon a horrific scene: Darlene was still sitting in her patio chair, eyes open, a gaping gash across her throat, blood pooling at her feet as it drained from multiple stab wounds to her upper body and neck. Fleeing from the sight in shock and fear, Chet called 911 on his cell phone.

243

Pennsylvania State Police troopers arrived at the scene approximately twenty minutes after Darlene's murder. The killer might not have been far away. They entered the house cautiously with flashlights and weapons drawn, waking Todd and Nick who had both slept through the entire incident unaware of the horror that had just occurred on their patio. Still dazed from sleep, they were handcuffed. As Todd was led through the kitchen, he recalls seeing Darlene's purse and keys on the counter and wondering where his wife was. Only after Todd was separated from his son Nick and questioned was he told several hours later that Darlene was dead out back on their patio.

While in 2007 serial killers had been for decades a staple of popular culture and lore, for police arriving at the crime scene that July night there were no doubts as to who had killed Darlene. Their suspicions fell immediately on her husband Todd, not on some movie slasher of a serial killer in the bushes.

In American medical slang, rare exotic diseases are called "zebras" because of an aphorism coined in the 1940s by a University of Maryland Medical School professor, Dr. Theodore Woodward. He cautioned his interns studying in Maryland's horse country, when making a diagnosis to first look at the most common disease in their region, rather than the some rare exotic possibility, telling them, "When you hear hoofbeats, think of horses, not zebras." For police investigating a homicide, statistically rare serial killers are akin to Woodward's 'zebras.'

The more police went over the chronology of the evening and the relationship of the couple, the more they began bearing down on Todd as a suspect in his wife's murder. Darlene had been on the phone at 2:00 a.m. with *another man*, planning a trip *without her husband*. She took *long trips apart from him* including personally delivering products that could have been shipped by post. Was she having an affair? Had Todd overheard something on the extension phone that made him snap? In most unsolved murders of women, the husband or boyfriend is usually the first suspect and a knife is a frequent weapon of choice in these domestic type murders. Statistically speaking if you are going to be murdered, it is most likely your killer is going to be somebody close to you, somebody you know and love, and loves you (to death), not a random cold hearted stranger, let alone the rarest of all, a 'zebra' serial killer. The only place most police officers have seen a serial killer was on TV and in the movies, not in real life. In routine police experience and investigative strategy, there had to have been a motive for Darlene's murder; and the killer would *have known* that she was out on the patio that evening. Who but her husband, and maybe her son—police looked at the son too—knew that Darlene would be out alone on her patio that night?

As the Pennsylvania State police grilled Todd over the next day attempting to elicit a confession from him, Trooper Karl A. Schmidhamer told the press there was no need to warn neighbors of any possible danger, "We're treating it as a suspicious death," he said. "That's all I can say at this time."[v] Dauphin County District Attorney Edward M. Marsico Jr. who supervised the investigation would later admit, "The biggest mistake I think I said to the press was, 'We don't think this was a random act, neighbors don't have to be afraid.'"[vi]

***

Straight up Hershey Road from the Ewalts' house next to I-81, were three truck-stops the smallest and closest of which was only 1.4 miles away for a 'Ninja' serial killer on foot stalking across the woods, backyards and bicycle paths. After he was arrested, Darlene's killer, a long haul truck driver, would explain to police, that after parking his truck "I was walking around, monkeying around like I always do. I decided to go for a walk 'cause I was...I had lots of time. I got to where I'd walk five miles a night. ... I just walked down the street. ... Went and cut through some yards."[vii]

An FBI bulletin circulated to police just a month before, warned of a prevalence of murders associated with truck stops.[viii] Some 500 unsolved homicides of mostly female victims were clustered along the national interstate highway system, and the FBI had built a list of some two hundred truck drivers suspected in some of these murders, some of them serial killings.[ix]

The FBI announced in 2009 the Highway Serial Killings Initiative
after detecting an unusual pattern of unsolved homicides along
America's interstate highway system.

While the vast majority of truck drivers are hardworking honest citizens, nevertheless by 2007, a total of 22 truck drivers had been convicted of serial murder in the United States[x] (0.6 percent of the total 352 known male serial killers in the US since 1800 identified by one study, not an insignificant figure when you consider that the interstate and the prevalence of long-haul trucks only dawns in the 1950s.)[xi] Yet the Pennsylvania State Police did not survey the three truck stops near the crime scene on Manor Drive, they did not look at surveillance videos, they did not look at truck stop transaction records from the hours around the murder, they did not even look to see if the murderer might still be there, as unlikely as that would have been (yet actually it *was* likely in this case, as we will see from the next murder this offender perpetrates.)

For the District Attorney in charge of the murder investigation, *the only* logical explanation was that Todd had murdered his wife. Police did not search nearby or put up roadblocks for a possible suspect fleeing from a murder committed less than twenty minutes before their arrival at the scene. Instead, as the killer carrying his bloodied knife was still trudging on foot towards the truck stop where his tractor-trailer was parked, police focused on husband Todd, and even explored the possibility that their son Nick might have killed his own mother. Things like that, in police experience, were much more common and expected than random serial killers.

In many ways, the police were not at fault in their shortsightedness on the night of the murder. Firstly, serial killers are extraordinarily rare, again I repeat, between 1800 and 2013 in the United States, one study definitively identified only 352 known male and 64 female serial killers. (Using a broader methodology, including the new FBI parameter of two victims, the recently launched Radford University/FGCU Serial Killer Database contains 1,868 records of American serial killers, still a relatively small number of homicide offenders.)[xii] More individual fictional serial killers have been created in film, television episodes and books than actually ever existed in real life and only a minute fraction of homicides are perpetrated by serial killers. When police are confronted with a homicide scene, usually the *last* suspect that comes to mind is a serial killer.

Secondly, that night the police were not yet actually dealing with a serial killer. Darlene Ewalt, as far as we know today, was this killer's first victim. Every serial killer begins as an 'ordinary' killer with one first victim. It is a second victim that opens the gate into the hellish world of serial murder. (It used to be three victims minimum that defined a serial killer, until 2005 when the definition was rethought and fixed at two minimum separate incidents for "any motive" at the 2005 San Antonio Serial Murder Symposium sponsored by the FBI's

National Center for the Analysis of Violent Crime (NCAVC) Behavioral Sciences Unit (BSU).)[xiii] As British pseudointellectual serial killer Ian Brady, who raped and murdered five children and youths with his girlfriend accomplice Myra Hindley in the 1960s (The Moors Murderers), explained in his sophomoric book authored in prison, the second murder is the serial killer's transcendental metamorphosis:

> The first killing experience will not only hold the strongest element of existential novelty and curiosity, but also the greatest element of danger and trepidation conjured by the unknown. Usually the incipient serial killer is too immersed in the psychological and legal challenges of the initial homicide, not to mention immediate logistics—the physical labour that the killing and disposal involve. He is therefore not in a condition to form a detached appreciation of the traumatic complexities bombarding his senses. You could, in many instances, describe the experience as an effective state of shock. He is, after all, storming pell-mell the defensive social conditioning of a lifetime, as well as declaring war upon all the organized, regulatory forces of society. In extinguishing someone's life he is also committing his own, and has no time to stop and stare in the hazardous, psychological battlefield. In another very significant sense, he is killing his long-accepted self as well as the victim, and simultaneously giving birth to a new persona, decisively cutting the umbilical connection between himself and ordinary mankind. Having fought his former self and won, the fledgling serial killer flexes his newfound powers with more

confidence. The second killing will hold all the same disadvantages, distracting elements of the first, but to a lesser degree. This allows a more objective assimilation of the experience. It also fosters an expanding sense of omnipotence, a wide-angle view of the metaphysical chessboard. In many cases, the element of elevated aestheticism in the second murder will exert a more formative impression than the first and probably of any in the future. It not only represents the rite of confirmation, a revelational leap of lack of faith in humanity, but also the onset of addiction to hedonistic nihilism. The psychic abolition of redemption.[xiv]

**

Three days later and only twenty-five miles away from where Darlene Ewalt was murdered, thirty-seven-year-old Patricia Brooks was asleep on a couch on the first floor of her rural house on Bower Bridge Road in rural Conewago Township near Manchester, Pennsylvania, south of Harrisburg. Her mother and daughter were sleeping upstairs. Unlike Darlene Ewalt's home in its more crowded suburban setting, Patricia's house was one of several strung out on a lonely stretch of open country road. The house stood about a mile away from an exit off I-83. Not far from her house towards the interstate, on Locust Point Road was a small turn around on which a tractor-trailer truck could be easily parked.[xv] Typically of people residing in this safe rural area, Patricia did not bother locking her back door.

At around 2:00 a.m., Patricia was awakened by a stinging pain across her neck and shoulder. When she opened her eyes, at first she thought she was having a nightmare. Some kind of huge, foul smelling figure was looming over her, and again, as if in some Hollywood slasher film, she thought she saw the shape of a knife flaying at her throat and shoulder followed by fresh burning stings. When she began to feel a glycerin-like slippery warm liquid soaking her shoulders and back and saw sprays of her dark crimson blood on the white carpet, she realized this was not a dream. Blocking several more knife blows with her exposed arms and hands, Patricia rolled to the floor making enough of a commotion to wake her daughter and mother sleeping upstairs. As she heard their footsteps upstairs through the ceiling, Patricia played dead. She lay on the floor staring as if dead towards her attacker, who she would later describe to police as "dressed for the occasion," wearing all black, an outfit similar to a prison-guard uniform, she said. His face was unmasked, but he was wearing a dark cap and a wide, police-like utility belt strapped around his huge waist. She mentioned his bad smell and described him as a large man with a potbelly that had hung over his belt. He was white, with a stubbly beard and chubby face.[xvi] Her ruse worked. With the sound of footsteps upstairs, the intruder fled the house by the back door he came in through, leaving Patricia for dead. Rushed by ambulance to a hospital, she barely survived the several cuts to major veins and arteries in her neck, including nicks to both external jugulars and damage to her esophagus and trachea.

A witness driving to work toward the interstate on Locust Point Road early in the morning at around 4:00 a.m. later reported seeing a man walking alongside the road dressed oddly all in black. What struck the witness as strange was that it was summer, but the man was wearing gloves. Another witness reported a tractor-trailer unusually parked at a turn-around by the road just before the interstate.

251

Pennsylvanian Police would find in the area a pair of gloves, which later revealed DNA linked to the killer of Darlene Ewalt. But that would be much later.

Back in West Hanover, state police were still focused on breaking Darleen's suspected husband Todd as her killer. He was under tight surveillance and investigators put all sorts of pressure on him designed to unnerve a suspect. Some of the state troopers investigating Darleen's murder, when they got word of the second stabbing in the region, began speculating about a possible connection, but District Attorney Marsico dismissed the idea. He later admitted, "To their credit, state police were immediately concerned about that stabbing. Frankly, I was the one who said, 'You gotta be kidding me.' I, as the prosecutor, was saying, 'It just happened to be another stabbing.' I'm thinking, there's no chance two random women were going to get stabbed 20 miles apart."[xvii]

Marsico felt at the time that the crimes were too different from each other. Physically the two victims were dissimilar; moreover, one crime took place outdoors with the perpetrator leaving behind no traces, while the other was an indoor home invasion with lots of evidence left behind. Marsico believed it was a coincidence; the two crimes were just too dissimilar in his opinion to have been perpetrated by the same person.

***

Coincidences do happen and, in a strange way, often serial homicide is *all* about coincidences. For example, it happened to be a coincidence that the next truck stop at which the serial killer parked to foray from, the Pilot Travel Center on Interstate I-78 in Bloomsbury, New Jersey, just across the state line from Pennsylvania, was already the site of a previous trucker related serial murder. Back in February 1991, former truck driver John Fautenberry murdered another driver Gary Farmer who he had met in the diner of the truck stop. Fautenberry had given up driving and had taken to serial killing to make a living. In November 1990, he had killed his first victim, Donald Nutley, who he met at truck stop in Oregon and persuaded to go target shooting with him. Fautenberry shot Nutley dead, hid his body and stole his cash and credit cards. By February, Fautenberry was on the other side of the country, travelling through New Jersey when he ran out of money for food and gas. On February 1 he stopped at the Bloomsbury truck stop where in the diner he hit on a Springfield, Tennessee truck driver, 27-year-old Gary Farmer, who naively bought him breakfast. The two men returned to Farmer's truck cab where Fautenberry shot him dead with a .22 handgun and took his money and credit cards. The truck remained parked with its engine running at the truck stop for several days before anybody looked inside the cab and found Farmer's corpse. On February 17, while hitchhiking in Ohio, Fautenberry was picked up by Joseph Daron, who kindly drove him ten miles out of his way. Fautenberry shot him dead and took his cash and credit cards. On February 24, he returned to Oregon where he made a casual acquaintance with bank teller Christine Guthrie, who offered to give him a ride to Portland. On the way, Fautenberry persuaded her to pull off onto a logging road, where he shot her three times in the back of the head and took her bankcard. Fautenberry then made his way to Juneau, Alaska where, on March 13, 1991, he met Jefferson Diffee at a local bar. He accompanied Diffee back to his apartment where he handcuffed, beat, and stabbed him seventeen times. He was arrested three days later and confessed to all four murders. When the next serial killer arrived at the Pilot Travel Center truck stop at Bloomsbury, on the night of July 28, 2007, Fautenberry was on death row in Ohio awaiting execution by lethal injection (which was carried out in 2009.)[xviii]

Google Earth View of the truck stop in Bloomsbury, New Jersey, connected with at least two different serial killer cases.
©2014 Google

This new serial killing truck driver had departed with a load of plants from Donald Burcham's Tree Farm in Fancy Gap, Virginia, on Friday, July 27, at noon. After making a couple of stops in York, Pennsylvania in the vicinity of where he had attacked Patricia Brooks in her house as she slept on a couch several weeks earlier, he was headed to Uxbridge, Massachusetts, and then to Nashua, New Hampshire, north of Boston. Donald Burcham, who had hired the driver six months ago, would later tell police that the driver would make an average of four stops a week, all along the East Coast.

Bloomsbury is a small, quiet, friendly, bucolic, "quaint" little village tucked up beneath the belly of the busy I-78, which connects Pennsylvania through New Jersey to the New York City metropolitan area. Its 850 residents live in a five block wide strip of tree-lined streets, where everybody knows each other. As described by the victim before her murder on her MySpace page, living in Bloomsbury was like "living in a Norman Rockwell painting." It was a quiet little village of Colonial and Victorian-style houses with porches overlooking front yards and well-kept lawns, tree-lined streets carpeted in colored leaves in autumn, American flags fluttering from the houses, a village as pretty as the one in the movie *Halloween.* The village itself was and is almost crime free, yet statistically it has one of the highest crime rates in the United States: a rate of 38.5 crimes per 1,000 people in 2009. How could that be? The answer is found at the two truck stops skirting the east end of the village just off the I-78 exit. Of 33 crimes that occurred in Bloomsbury in 2009, 21 of them took place at the truck stops. Trooper John McGourty of Perryville State Police station recently explained to Bloomsbury's town council that the truck stop "works against you. That's where your big number comes from."[xix]

Whether 38-year-old Monica Lee Massaro knew about the serial killer history of the Pilot truck stop approximately 800 yards or a ten-minute walk directly up Main Street from her newly purchased house is not known. Massaro, a former mortgage and loan broker with shaggy blonde rock'n'roll tresses and big brown eyes was single and lived alone on the main floor of her modern Victorian style duplex with its welcoming porch.

Monica Massaro gave up the corporate life to "live in a Norman Rockwell painting" in Bloomsbury, New Jersey.

She had turned her back on the corporate rat race three years earlier and moved from Montgomery, New Jersey to Bloomsbury for a life as a free spirit, operating her own home-cleaning business from her house. It allowed her an independent schedule to pursue her passion for riding motorcycles, photography and attending rock concerts. Photos on her memorial Facebook Page reveal a pretty, 'rock chick' who avidly followed the band Aerosmith and was a fan of Kid Rock, Buckcherry and the Foo Fighters.[xx] She lived for concerts and music and hoped to publish a book of photos she took at concerts she had travelled to attend around the U.S. On her MySpace page she listed among her many passions, driving fast, reading, and wearing high heels and pink lip gloss. On an Aerosmith Fan Club message board, where her online handle was "NJragdoll", she once wrote, "I really like my lifestyle (being able to run around and go to shows, take off and do stuff...not have to get up to an alarm clock, etc...) so I decided to make my WORK fit my Life and not the other way around. I have very little stress anymore compared to when I was in Corporate America. I'm much happier." She had many friends in the area and frequently volunteered for events and programs in Bloomsbury where she lived happily and

256

described her newly adopted corner of New Jersey as "the last bastion of civilization."[xxi]

On Saturday night, July 28, Monica was planning to go out partying with friends as usual, but at the last minute inexplicably she changed her mind and decided to stay at home instead. It was a bad coincidence that this was the same night that serial death rolled into town in a tractor trailer truck, parked it at the convenient truck stop up the road from where Monica lived, put on its ninja black clothing, black running shoes, cloth hood, utility belt with assorted knives, a wire garrote, a Chinese throwing star and a tactical flashlight, and began walking into town, randomly trying doors, looking for the one left unlocked. Monica was so secure and so surrounded by friends in her "last bastion of civilization" that she hadn't even bothered to lock her front door. She rarely did, her friends would later say. After his arrest, her killer would confess to police, "I just walked down the street. ... Went and cut through some yards. I just picked one [house] at random, walking through the neighborhood... if I seen somebody in the house or I seen somebody awake, I'd pass it. I didn't want no confrontation. Couple of houses, they were locked. The door [to Massaro's house] was unlocked, and I went in."

In some ways serial killers can be like vampires...you have to invite them in. Dennis Rader, the murderer of the Otera family in Wichata Kansas, explained how his game of chance death worked with another one of his victims, a single woman he had chosen and stalked. He said, "I had many what I call them projects. They were different people in the town that I followed, watched. They're all over Wichita.... it just was basically a selection process, worked toward it. If it didn't work I'd just move on to something else, but my kind of person, stalking and trolling. You go through the trolling stage and

257

then a stalking stage. She was in the stalking stage when this happened."[xxii]

It was around 2:00 a.m., the preferred killing time for the trucker 'Ninja' killer. Monica was asleep in her first floor apartment bedroom. As he approached her house at random, the killer noted that there was only one car parked in the driveway. Peering inside the car he saw a woman's pocket book on the seat. As that was the only car parked at the house, it reassured him that the woman inside was probably alone. But would he want this woman? He needed to look inside the pocket book for her identification, but the car door was locked. He quietly walked up the steps of the front porch, tried the outer storm door; it was unlocked. Half way there. He then tried the inner front door of the house. It too was unlocked. Bingo. He went inside. The first thing he did was to immediately locate her car keys in whatever convenient place near the door she had left them. That's where most people leave their keys—near where they come in and go out. He then exited the house and returned to the car outside, unlocked the door and took the pocket book. Focusing the narrow beam of his small tactical flashlight he went through it, and finding photo identification he ascertained it belonged to a pretty, blonde female, exactly the target he was trolling for.

The killer now re-entered the house and began searching for her, randomly trying the doors of the hallway that ran its length. Opening one door, he discovered it was a closet. As he came around the corner of the closet door into Massaro's bedroom, she must have sensed or heard something moving in the dark of her doorway; she awoke and turned on the lights with a remote by her bedside.

"She sat straight up in bed and got out of bed when she seen me and started screaming," the killer later would confess.

***

When on Sunday, the next day, Monica did not pick up her phone, her friends assumed she was out. On Monday, employees at a business behind her house, found her identification in the parking lot trash bin, and knocked on her door to return it, but nobody came to the door. Monica also had an appointment with a client on Monday morning to which she did not show up. Accustomed to her dependability after failing to reach her, the client called the police. Sufficient calls came that Monday, for the New Jersey State Police entered Massaro's premises at around 5:00 p.m. that same day. They found Monica in her bedroom, face up on her blood-caked bed, her throat slashed at the jugular vein, her breasts, abdomen, thighs and genitals cut and stabbed multiple times. By then, her killer was already in police custody some 285 miles away for something else he had just done. But nobody knew that yet.

New Jersey State Police also began looking for 'horses not zebras' by attempting to untangle Monica's single New Jersey girl dating life. Not only was she dating but she was very active on social media and the list of actual local 'real time and place' and online virtual potential suspects, was almost infinitely long. With no signs of forced entry, it appeared as if Monica knew her assailant, let him in and might have been comfortable with having him in her house. The nature of the wounds inflicted upon her suggested to police a personal and passionate anger. The use of a knife suggested this was *very* personal. An ex-boyfriend? A jealously jilted lover? Perhaps even an obsessed stalker? It was easy for anybody to identify Monica and her home address from her online postings. A Facebook/MySpace frenemy? Monica, her many friends would say, would daily talk, text, e-mail, post to and online chat with

259

dozens of friends, acquaintances and clients. As in the case of Darlene Ewalt in Pennsylvania, investigators in New Jersey were first looking at 'suspect horses' nearby who were close to or in contact with her, people she knew, before police would even contemplate the possibility of a random stranger serial killer 'zebra'.

***

After having murdering Monica, the perpetrator was in no hurry to flee the area. He returned to the adjacent Bloomsbury Travel Center truck stop and lingered there over a hearty dinner and was still there at 5:00 a.m., a few hours after Monica's murder in a mood to shop, as indicated by the receipt for a radar detector he bought, before he finally got back into his vehicle and put some distance between himself and the scene of his latest murder before stopping again further along the interstate to get some sleep.

A serial killer's shopping receipt from the Bloomsbury truck stop on the night of Monica Massaro's murder.

The serial killer had a pick-up scheduled at a plant nursery in Nashua, New Hampshire on Monday morning, and when on Sunday night he arrived at the town of Chelmsford, Massachusetts, northwest of Boston, on the northbound I-495, he pulled into the roadside visitor information center and rest stop at Exit 33, the last place he could easily park his truck before his pick-up destination about eighteen miles further. Again this was going to be another one of those life-and-death coincidences.

The facility was a typical interstate rest stop without a gas station or restaurant, equipped only with picnic benches, washroom facilities, pay phones, vending machines and a kiosk with maps and tourist brochures that remained open daily until 8:00 p.m. Signs on the cinder block building reminded visitors, "NO URINATING AGAINST THE BUILDING. VIDEO SURVEILLANCE IN PROGRESS. THANK YOU FOR COMPLYING." There was rest parking for cars on one side and a section on the other side that could accommodate long tractor-trailer trucks. A recent tongue-in-cheek review posted on the internet of the rest stop, describes the facilities, "Inside, lovely crack den lighting gives an ambiance that suggests 'horror movie,' minus the buxom women running from a serial killer... Feeling refreshed from doing your business in the bathroom? Why not grab a snack? The mesh cage-like appearance [of the vending machines] offers all the comforts of Rikers Island without the potential of being shanked by a convict. Only MA [Massachusetts] public rest area for a while, especially on I-495. Nothing to see or do besides peeing or hoping for trucker/prostitute violence nearby."[xxiii]

The killer had not even showered after his previous murder, as he donned his black clothing, some of it perhaps still crusted in Monica Messaro's blood from the night before, still stinking damp with his own sweat and body fluids. He

261

must have been in a highly excited state as he began his foray much earlier than the previous times. It was only 10:00 p.m., a time when most people were still up and awake, when he began his usual path on foot through the dark of suburban bushes, forests and backyards, trying doors at random, looking for the one to find unlocked. The killer's route that night can be tracked by calls that came into the Chelmsford Police Department in the ensuing hours.

The first call came shortly before 11:00 p.m., from an apartment in a condominium complex just south of the rest stop on the other side of a small forest that screened it from I-495. A woman reported observing a "stocky built" figure dressed in all in black, prowling outside the ground floors of several buildings in the complex, trying different apartment doors. Chelmsford Police were on the scene by 11:09, but could not find anybody. The 'Ninja' had evaded them in the bush.

The next call came in at 2:00 a.m. and it was much more dramatic. This was about a mile further south in a large mobile home park. Three women lived in the trailer, a mother, her daughter and her fourteen-year-old granddaughter. The girl was on her computer surfing the internet when she saw a figure lurking outside their trailer picture window, peering inside. It appeared to her that the person was wearing some kind of hood over his head. The mother dashed outside to confront the prowler on the assumption it was a common Peeping Tom. She spotted him about two or three trailers away from her and shouted out. As the bear shaped man stopped and turned, she saw that he was masked and dressed completely in black and wearing a police-style utility belt. Instead of fleeing, he began to move towards her menacingly. Escaping back to her trailer, she locked the door behind her and cried out to her daughter to lock the windows. As they moved toward the kitchen where the phone was, they saw to their horror that the masked figure was peering in at them through the window. Reaching the phone, the mother attempted to call 911, but could not get through because their dial-up internet was still connected to the phone line. The black clad figure was now trying to get in through their door, pushing and pounding into it heavily. Then he smashed the porch light throwing the exterior of the trailer into darkness. The mother had it together enough to grab her cell phone and retreat with her daughter to their bedroom at the furthest end of the trailer. Wedging an ironing board against the door, she got a call into 911 from her cell. The call was logged at 2:09 a.m.[xxiv] Police rushed to the scene but were again unable to find the prowler. They searched the area for about an hour with no success, while the women packed their things and left the trailer to spend the night elsewhere, too frightened to remain there.

Later complicating the investigation was going to be another coincidence. As these calls streamed into Chelmsford Police, twenty miles away in Pelham, New Hampshire, a woman chose this exact moment to call police with a false report that she had been sexually assaulted by a mysterious intruder in her house.[xxv] What were the odds of that? It would later confuse police trying to link this serial killer's crimes.

As police were searching the trailer park, the killer was trudging in the dark through the fields and bushes along Hunt Road that turned northward and took him across a bridge over the interstate to the other side. At the intersection of Hunt Road and Pine Hill Road stood a large luxuriously restored historical farmhouse and barn with an in-ground pool and patio at the back. He came around the back patio and found the kitchen door open. He went inside and the first thing that caught his eye was an I-pod glowing in its speaker charge cradle. When he grabbed at the iPod he accidentally touched the play button sending music blaring through the house. One of the women living in the house recalled that it was 3:30 a.m. when she was awakened by the sound of her iPod in the kitchen and groggily went down to shut it off. Other than the unexplained activation of her iPod, she noticed nothing out of order, and immediately returned to bed and fell soundly asleep after her brief brush by a monster in the dark.

By then the killer was already back out on Pine Hill Road, headed next straight toward the home of Jeannie and Kevin McDonough and their two children, eighteen-year-old son, Ryan, and fifteen-year-old daughter, Shea. It was approximately 3:40 a.m. when he made his way up their driveway, past their dog Bosco, who for reasons never explained did not bark or stir that night when the 'Ninja' maniac walked up to the back door of their house.

***

Jeannie and Kevin McDonough lived in an idyllic, cozy four-bedroom New England Cape Cod style home about a half-mile by foot across the bush and fields from the I-485 rest stop. As Jeannie later wrote, "That June, *Money* magazine listed our town as the twenty-first best place to live in the country that year. It was a proud distinction, but to anyone living there, not surprising—it's a quiet, affluent suburb that boasted a very low crime rate. The type of community where you didn't have to worry too much if you happened to go to bed without locking the door."xxvi

In the days before that fateful weekend, Jeannie and Kevin were talking about a horrific home invasion that took place 125 miles south of them in Cheshire, Connecticut, where two men invaded the home of Dr. William Petit and his wife

264

and two daughters. After beating Petit into unconsciousness with a baseball bat, they raped the younger daughter and his wife, strangled her and then dousing the still living girls in gasoline as they lay bound on their beds, they set the house on fire. Petit managed to escape and was the only survivor. Jeannie wondered whether they should install a security system. Kevin replied correctly, "What are the odds of something like that happening here?"[xxvii] The odds were as slim as almost next to nothing; they always are when that rare serial killer comes to your door.

That Sunday night both their children, Ryan and Shea, were out as Jeannie and Kevin were preparing for bed. Shea came home shortly before midnight, but Ryan was going to spend the night at a friend's house, something Shea did not know when she deliberately left the back door unlocked because her brother sometimes forgot his house keys. Yes, serial killing often is all about odds and coincidences, and so far they had been favoring this killer. But now, they were going to turn against him.

Firstly, July 29 happened to be a particularly hot day, and secondly, the air conditioner in the McDonoughs' bedroom had broken down during the week and thirdly, they had not gotten around to repairing it. Fourthly, the kids' bedrooms were on the first floor, but it was so hot there that when Shea came home she decided to sleep in the guest bedroom upstairs where the air conditioner was working, next to the McDonoughs' bedroom. How is that for the algorithms of life and death chance?

Kevin was soundly asleep when Shea stuck her head into her parents' bedroom and told her mother she was going to sleep in the guest bedroom. Suffering in the stifling heat of their room, Jeannie asked Shea to leave their bedroom door open to allow for air circulation, but neglected to tell Shea her

265

brother would be sleeping over at a friend's house. The back door remained unlocked.

After watching television downstairs, Shea went to sleep in the air-conditioned guest room at about 2:00 a.m. Around 3:30 a.m., Jeannie thought she was awakened by the sound of their neighbor's dog barking. She got up and went downstairs to the kitchen for a drink of water and returned back to bed, her movements waking Kevin. Both were now drifting in and out of a restless disturbed sleep in their stiflingly hot room. They could not go back to sleeping soundly.

By now the killer had silently slipped into their house by the unlocked back door. As he did the night before at Monica Massaro's house, he collected purses and pocketbooks to identify the female occupants in the house. Taking the purses out back to a picnic table on their patio, the killer went through them under the pin-point beam of his small flashlight. He pocketed the money he found. Shea's purse and wallet would be later located on the picnic table in the backyard, with her identification sticking out. She was the target that the killer had selected.

The masked figure now slipped back into the house. After finding nobody on the ground floor, he crept up the stairs to the second floor in his black clothing, smelling of B.O., blood and death. A twelve-year veteran detective, who would later question the killer, noted that for the first time in his career he could not interrogate a suspect without keeping the door of the interview room open. The only words the detective could find to describe the smell was "decomposing" flesh.[xxviii] The foul smelling monster slipped by the open door of Kevin and Jeannie's bedroom as they tossed and turned restlessly and crept through the dark into the guest room, finding there who he was looking for.

Shea was fast asleep under a pile of blankets in the room cooled by the humming air conditioner. The killer quietly shut the door behind him. Hovering over the sleeping girl, he slowly pulled the blankets off her, inspecting "his catch" as she slept. He drew one of the two fifteen-inch fixed blade survival knives he was carrying: a SOG Specialty Knives &Tools manufactured "Jungle Primitive" model, a sword of a knife, with a partial fine serrated blade and coarse serrations along the spine meant for heavy sawing through wood or bone. Going with the ninja theme, the knife had a black TiNi (titanium nitride) finish, meant to camouflage the blade in the dark from glare and glint. A well-made but inexpensive product, the SOG Jungle Primitive retails for $66.25 and is advertised by SOG on its website as, "for the primitive in all of us. When the only thing that separates you from them is your equipment... does everything that you need it to do convincingly well."[xxix] Unless actually in a jungle or bush, it's the kind of knife only a psycho asshole would carry anywhere else.

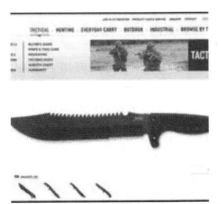

SOG Specialty Knives & Tools manufactured 'Jungle Primitive' model,
"for the primitive in all of us."
© 2014 SOG SPECIALTY KNIVES & TOOLS, LLC

Placing his gloved hand over her nose and mouth while pressing the cold razor edged steel of the Jungle Primitive against Shea's throat, he woke her, and said, "If you make any noise, I'll fucking kill you."

As Shea woke in sleepy confusion, her first thought was that her brother Ryan was playing a sick joke on her. But the huge shape of the figure looming over her and his horrific smell quickly told her this was not her brother. Next she thought, I must be dreaming. If so, the dream was the most subtly realistic one she ever had. Shea now had a life-and-death decision to instantly make: obey the intruder's instructions and be compliant in the hope he will not escalate his violence or disobey and resist in an attempt to escape. When the FBI interviewed serial killers in the 1980s in an attempt to map their mindset and behavior, they included questions on how the killers perceived their victims' behavior, compliant or resisting, and what their response was to that behavior.[xxx] Of the serial killers studied, 7.5 percent of their victims survived—not encouraging, but nonetheless a sliver of hope. The FBI then tried to pinpoint what it was in the victim's behavior that resulted in their survival. The question was whether to resist the attacker or comply. The FBI asked the serial killers, how did *they* perceive the behavior of their victims? In *the opinion of* the serial killers, 28 percent of all of their victims acquiesced or offered no resistance, 31 percent attempted to negotiate verbally, 7 percent verbally refused to obey the killer, 10 percent screamed, 5 percent attempted to escape, and 19 percent tried to fight back.

The serial killers said about themselves, that in the face of resistance from their victims, 34 percent had no reaction, 15 percent threatened the victim verbally, 25 percent escalated the level of their aggression, and 25 percent became outright violent. Thus, in more than two-thirds of the cases, the killer countered the resistance from the victim, and in half of the cases they countered it with increased force. In summary, resistance sparks force or increased levels of force. It should be pointed out, however, that of the victims in the survey who, in the serial killers' opinions acquiesced to their demands, *all were murdered without exception.* Of the twenty-eight victims who offered physical resistance in the form of screaming, running, or fighting, three survived. Thus, in conclusion: except for *a slight marginal advantage* in resistance, the bad news is that *both* resistance and acquiescence almost equally result in death.[xxxi] In other words, Shea had nothing to lose by resisting; it was the better choice, if only marginally by a sliver. But sometimes it's precisely that sliver margin that counts; it did for those three survivors, and it would for Shea that hot July night.

Instead of submitting to the intruder's demand, Shea began loudly whimpering under his gloved hand and kicking in her bed, causing the headboard to bang loudly against the bedroom wall of her parent's room next to the guest bedroom. Because their air conditioner was broken and switched off and their bedroom door was open, because it was a hot night and they slept restlessly, both Jennie and Kevin were awakened by the banging against their wall and the sound of their daughter whimpering in the next room. Their assumption immediately was that Shea was having a nightmare, and again, by a strange coincidence, instead of just one of them going, both of them together rose to check on her, something Jennie says had never happened before.

Now it was Kevin and Jeannie's turn to think they were in a nightmare when they opened the door of the guest room and found a huge, masked, fat circus bear-like figure dressed entirely in black with his back turned to them standing over their daughter with his hand over her face. Jeannie's first thought was the same as Shea's: her brother Ryan was playing a joke. The intruder had not seen them entering the room until Kevin shouted out to him, whereupon he spun around to face him, grazing Shea on the shoulder with the sharp knife blade. Seeing a masked man with a large knife in his hand, Kevin who was shorter and about eighty pounds lighter, but a former high school wrestler and now working in construction in much better shape than the six-foot overweight slob truck driver killer (who also had a serious back injury in a previous road accident), charged with the force of a parent's protective rage, tackled the intruder and brought him down in a wrestling lock. As they struggled, the masked man attempted to stab and slash Kevin. Jeannie leapt into the fray to try to disarm the intruder, but instinctively grabbed at the knife blade with her bare hands resulting in deep cuts to her palms, which would later require stiches. Despite the cuts, she would not let go.

The struggle was a protracted one, with Kevin holding down the killer in a choke hold from behind, eventually pinning him down between the bed and the wall. The killer kept a firm grip on his knife but Kevin kept a firmer one locked around his arm, immobilizing it. Kevin shouted to his daughter to call 911 and bring his gun. Shea, who knew that they had no gun in the house, had the presence of mind to affirm her father's call for the non-existent weapon and left the room calling 911.

The police were dispatched at 3:58 a.m. The 911 operator told Shea to go out in front of the house to flag down police cars when they came. Indeed, police would miss the house when they did arrive because its gold-colored brass address number hung on yellow-colored walls and was invisible at night under police spotlights. (The house is now painted a bluish grey.)

As Kevin kept the killer with the bad back immobilized

270

in a vice-like hold waiting for the police to arrive, he and Jeannie entered into a strange dialogue with him. Jeannie was still thinking that the intruder might have been some high school kid fixated on Shea, and was chiding him, "What were you thinking?" When the intruder responded in a thick middle-age man's southern accent that he was there only to burglarize the house, she realized this was no high school kid. The intruder began begging them to let him go, that he was "nobody" and only came looking for money to steal. He tried to persuade Jeannie to leave the room, "You're hurt. You should tend to your hands." Kevin and Jeannie would have none of it. The intruder made one last attempt to free his pinned arms in an attempt to rip his mask off, apparently knowing that being caught invading a home while masked carried a stiffer sentence. Kevin tightened his hold around the man's neck and growled, "Don't move a fucking muscle, you fat fuck!" Exhausted and firmly in the constrictor boa-like grip of the wiry-muscled Kevin, the intruder could no longer move or struggle. No doubt it felt like an eternity had passed when arriving police finally entered the house and after a brief struggle when he attempted to resist took the intruder into custody. That's how a fifteen-year-old girl and her parents captured a serial killer.[xxxii]

While there have been occasional cases where serial killers were apprehended when an intended victim escaped and caught the attention of police who arrested the perpetrator (Harvey Glatman, Jeffrey Dahmer), rarely has there been a case where civilians captured one themselves since the August 1985 morning, when a mob in Los Angeles chased down fugitive serial killer Richard Ramirez (The Night Stalker) on the street, and one of them took an iron bar to Ramirez's head. Police had to actually rescue him from the East LA neighborhood that was ready to beat him to death on

271

the spot. Sometimes serial killers might surrender to police on their own, but most serial killers are apprehended after long, difficult, and painstaking investigative work by police. In this case, nobody even knew that they had a killer in custody, let alone a serial one.

When the police officers ripped off the intruder's mask, they found an overweight, unshaven truck driver with sickly thinning hair who would later be identified at his booking as forty-two-year-old Adam Leroy Lane from Jonesville, North Carolina. He really was a 'nobody' with no past; not even a criminal record of the kind that almost every self-respecting serial killer accrues long before they begin their killing: voyeurism, panty stealing, petty thefts, maybe arson, maybe animal cruelty, maybe even more serious sexual offenses short of murder. But Lane's only brush with the law were speeding tickets, a minor conviction for passing bad checks, and only ominously with hindsight, a 1992 trespassing charge to which he pleaded guilty, paid a fine and was ordered to keep his distance from the complainant.[xxxiii]

Adam Leroy Lane booking photo shorty after resisting Chelmsford Police as they were arresting him in the bedroom of his teenage victim

***

This is where this serial killer story starts taking a different direction. Most serial killer accounts, including ones I authored, are written more or less the same way: there is a geographical setting of the crime scene—an ambience, as serial murder is often about geography as much as about compulsion and psychopathology (as geographic profilers will attest). This case certainly is an example of that. Then there are the biographies of the victims in an attempt to give them some semblance of humanity beyond merely "prop object" serial victims and a measure of the trajectory of their own lives that brought them to cross paths with a serial killer, often a very relevant component of every serial killer's choice of victim: the victimology. The focus then shifts on the details of the crime—the act the serial killer perpetrates—and of course, it is the apex of why these horrific narratives are recounted over and over. Finally, before or when we get to his (or her) apprehension and conviction, there is somewhere the biography of the serial killer, often going back to infancy, in an attempt to describe the process of how an innocent child grows up to become a compulsive, lethal killing machine. It is often a biography full of horror and abuse and frequently what the serial killer as a child experienced is as cruel and horrific as the acts they end up perpetrating as adults. I will have nothing like that for you here on Adam Leroy Lane.

Other than that he dropped out of high school, was married for a second time, and was the father of two step daughters and a daughter of his own, we know nothing about his background or his psychology or what triggered him to start killing at the age of 42 when the average age for serial killers when they start is 28 (unless he successfully concealed previous murders.) Police later went over his trucking routes across the United States as far as California, but could not flush out any positive links to unsolved murders. A few reporters looked up neighbors and fellow-workers in Jonesville, who described a cantankerous, controlling, difficult to get along with personality, rumors that he was accused of molesting one of his stepdaughters, but very little else. And we are going to see why little will come out about his past later when it reaches the court system.

Lane was even suspected in a 1996 murder of a police officer in Jonesville because he resembled police sketches of the suspect; but it wasn't him. In 2012, cold case detectives made an arrest and another suspect pleaded guilty to that murder. With no typical history of juvenile arrests and escalating crimes that most serial killers have before they commit their first murder, the forty-two-year-old truck driver weirdly started killing at a very late age for somebody with no history of bad behavior. Nor did Lane appear to have the intellect, discipline or skill to successfully cover-up previous murders. He just suddenly "went off"—"snapped"—without any obvious thing triggering him.

It is even a marginal question whether Lane is exactly a serial killer. Before the FBI San Antonio Symposium in 2005 fixed the number of killings defining serial murder at two separate events with a "cooling off" period in between, and the motive as "any reason," Lane would not have been even considered "officially" a serial killer, just the way Ed Gein, Albert Fish, and Wayne Williams were not, (even though they were) simply because each had been convicted of one or two killings (although suspected in more) and not the mandatory three threshold to garner a serial killer designation. We used to describe them as "suspected" serial killers; now we don't.

Moreover, Lane's two killings and attempted killings were so close together to each other, that he borders on a new debated category of rampage or spree serial killers, like

Paul John Knowles, Andrew Cunanan or the Washington Beltway Snipers, who once they began killing, never really returned back to their "normal" identities in the traditional sense of a prolonged "cooling off" period between killings, something which we still have not defined with any precision; what is exactly a "cooling off" period and how long is it? But the killings in these cases, extended beyond the usual single one day episode of mass killing often followed by a perpetrator's death at the hands of police or suicide that traditionally delineates mass murder from serial killing. These spree serial killers hover somewhere in between short period rampage killers and extended period serial killers and their classification is currently being debated.

Lane's sloppy rambling through people's back yards, rattling doors, pressing his face to the window, triggering calls to the police, is not the usual covert behavior of a typical serial killer stalking—at least not the cunning ones we are familiar with. And yet, there is no doubt, what Lane was doing, and how he was doing it, was what serial killers do, and that the only thing that separated him from the three-victim "traditional" definition of serial killer, was his previous two incompetent failures in killing victims he had targeted and his early arrest. There was an obvious irresistible pathological compulsivity to his actions typical of serial killer behavior. Lane just wasn't very good at it, but given time he would have gotten better; serial killing is a learning experience, as most profilers and serial killers will tell you. Unless they are in a final disintegrative phase of their killing 'career' (like Ed Kemper, after finally killing his mother, or Ted Bundy in Florida after escaping jail) most serial killers get better at what they do with time. I would argue, that given every serial killer begins as a murderer with one victim, we are beginning to sufficiently recognize their psychopathology to be fairly certain that even though caught after their first murder, these individuals would have committed a second and third and so on, had they not bungled their first killing. The case of Luka Magnotta in Canada, who murdered one victim and committed necrophiliac acts which he videotaped and posted to social media before dismembering his victim and mailing the body parts to Canadian politicians and a school, is an example of somebody who it is highly likely would have committed further homicides had he the opportunity. They are incipient serial killers in all sense of our understanding of their motives but for the fact that they were apprehended before they could commit a second homicide. Mark Twitchell ("Dexter Killer"), a fan of the TV show *Dexter* and a wannabe filmmaker who lured and murdered a male victim in his rented back lane "film studio" garage in Edmonton, Canada, is another recent example of an offender with a serial killing psychopathology who was aborted "at birth" after his first murder before he got a chance to kill again. No, statistically and semantically they are not serial killers; but yes, psychopathologically they actually are, they just did not have an opportunity to get the sufficient number of kills on their score card to be labeled as serial.

***

Before taking him away from the McDonoughs' home, police searched and disarmed Lane. In addition to the two fifteen-inch long hunting survival knives, Lane was carrying an assortment of weapons and tools in his "murder kit." From the ninja utility belt Lane was wearing, police removed a tactical flashlight, a Chinese martial art shuriken "throwing star" and a three foot steel cable improvised as a garrote with finger loops on each end. There was also a folded up leather-face hood

276

mask, in addition to the cloth military police style black balaclava "flash hood" he was wearing when he attacked Shea.

(Above Left) Lane's two knives tossed on the bedside table in the victim's bedroom shortly after he was disarmed. (Above Right) The 'Jungle Primitive' photographed by Chelmsford Police on the floor of the victim's bedroom.

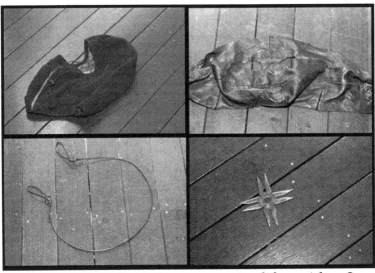

The assortment of masks and weapons seized from Adam Lane and photographed by Chelmsford Police at the scene.

As police put Lane into their cruiser, he whined about a cut lip he sustained when officers were forced to subdue him in the upstairs bedroom. Seeing an ambulance crew tending to

Jeannie's cut palms, his last words shouted from the back of the police car before he was driven away, were "She did that to herself!"[xxxiv]

At the police station when Lane was being booked he told police that his truck was parked at the rest stop on I-495. Police towed the dark blue tractor-trailer truck to a secure yard and filed for a search warrant before looking inside the cab. At this point, they still had no idea what they had on their hands. Once the warrant came in, the police began searching inside the truck driver's most private personal space, his truck cab and the spacious sleeping area in the back of it. There they pulled out a spotting scope, another flashlight, and knife after knife, all of which they lined up on the asphalt and photographed. Police also found a portable DVD player and some DVDs including mainstream titles like *Alien vs. Predator* and *Rambo*.[xxxv] At first glance it could be argued that the stalking and hunting humans theme of the DVDs was a coincidence, until they flipped open the portable player and saw the DVD Adam Leroy Lane was watching last: a 2002 independent low-budget film made in Maryland by Kevin Kangas, entitled *Hunting Humans*. Described by some as a "how-to" serial killing video or a *"Serial Killing for Dummies"*,[xxxvi] Kangas' film is loosely inspired by *American Psycho* and anticipates the noxious serial killer of serial killers, *Dexter*.

Lane's truck cab in police custody. Inside the cab police found an assortment of knives, a spotting scope and DVDs. The indie serial killer horror film Hunting Humans was cued up in his portable DVD player in the truck

The lead character in *Hunting Humans,* Aric Blue (portrayed by Rick Ganz) is an arrogant serial killer who narrates the film harping on his methodology on how not to get caught (don't have a motive, don't kill people you know, never hunt in the same place twice, etc.) until he finds himself being stalked by another serial killer. Here is how some reviewers who liked the film, wrote it up on Amazon:

Aric Blue (Ganz) narrates the film throughout his adventures as a loan telemarketer for a bank and his unique hobby after hours of, you guessed it, hunting humans. The serial killer is an arrogant, smug genius who thinks he's better than anybody else, and he's right. When

279

it comes to murder, he's the Albert Einstein of the community. This particular killer has a "code" he lives by to allow his slayings to remain hidden from the police.... He picks out his prey and then follows them around, jotting down their every move with an eye for choosing just the right moment to swoop in and stick the knife in. Or slip the rope around their neck. Or shoot them. His technique has worked wonders...[xxxvii]

Most of the victims of the fictional serial killer in *Hunting Humans* are males who are murdered in non-sexual thrill killings, but the first three minutes of the movie are as if from a completely different film. The movie opens with a female victim, an attractive woman in her mid-twenties who lives alone in one of those Cape Cod style suburban homes Lane was targeting. The serial killer's voiceover explains that people's identifiable patterns expose them to being victimized, and in this case, the fictional woman has a pattern of upon arriving home letting her dog out through a sliding back door that she then always leaves unlocked while she showers. The serial killer comments, how much more difficult it would be for him if she just "only sometimes" locked her door.

The scene is set using a typical slasher film technique: an ominous, voyeuristic, up-close point-of-view looking over her shoulder as she undresses slowly. As she takes off her blouse, she appears to be wearing a bra splattered with dark red blood. A second shot under a different shade of light reveals that shapes on the bra are actually decorative purple patterns that only appear dark blood-like under the other light. She strips off her bra, revealing her naked breasts to the camera. A long shot explores her body from the back dressed only in thong-panties as she prepares for her shower. The camera cuts-away to the bathroom door knob several times, suggesting that the serial killer is going to burst in through the door but as she draws the shower curtain back it reveals the serial killer standing nude in the shower with a big knife, which he thrusts into her midriff below and between her exposed breasts. Copious blood flows. The scene dissolves to the serial killer standing naked under a stream of water from the shower with a euphoric expression on his face. As the camera pans it reveals the dead victim, hanging nude from a hook in the shower. Looking over his shoulder, we see the naked serial killer moving toward the soaking wet corpse hanging in the shower, hovering over her. From the high camera from behind the killer we cannot quite tell how close he is to her naked body, to the wound in her abdomen, but it is suggestively close enough for him to penetrate her in a necrophilic act.

The film's director, Kevin Kangas insists that there was no sexual intent in that scene, "The first killing isn't meant to be sexual—it's not for Aric. He simply hangs her there out of convenience. It's a way to make sure the body stays clean and out of his way (and it seemed a very chilling way to show how cold he is—that it doesn't bother him at all to take a shower with a dead body."[xxxviii] Whatever Kangas' intentions were, the scene must have been the 'money shot' for the crazed Adam Leroy Lane.

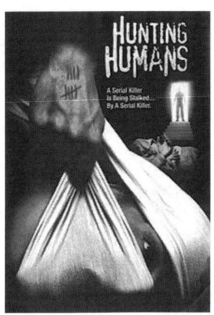

Adam Lane was obsessed with a scene in Hunting Humans, an indie film written, produced and directed by Kevin Kangas.
© 2009 Marauder Productions

Lane had rented the DVD in a store in his home town in North Carolina and never returned it. It is no surprise that Lane had this DVD loaded in his portable player. As the rest of *Hunting Humans* mostly depicts a psychological thriller cat-and-mouse game between serial killers murdering male victims, it is highly probable that Lane after perhaps having seen the film once, became obsessed with its three minute opening sequence. He probably masturbated to the scene repeatedly, which conveniently was located in the DVD's first three minutes; no need to cue it up with spermy sticky fingers to the "good parts."

Another DVD in Lane's cab was Canadian low-budget slasher film *Dead Stop*. Like *Hunting Humans,* this film too opens with a sequence in which a blonde body-painted stripper returns home, undresses to take a bath and is

282

strangled by a serial killer in her bathtub, who afterwards lays her naked body out and eviscerates her with a scalpel from a murder kit he carries.

From the choice of a female victim alone in her suburban house to his random entry through unlocked doors, roaming around the house with the victims inside unaware, to his use of a knife to kill, Lane was living out what he saw in his collection of DVDs. The doors left unlocked by his victims like the victim in *Hunting Humans* shifted the responsibility in Lane's thinking on the victim in a kind of reverse game of Russian roulette. By leaving their doors unlocked, the victims are inviting death, like a vampire, into their homes, "deserving" or "earning" it in a life-and-death game of chance where the serial killer makes all the rules. At one point the fictional serial killer in the movie declares, "I am a force of nature. Remorse is just not a part of me."

The fictional *Hunting Humans* serial killer possesses a variety of weapons, including big, heavy military style tactical knives, some of which look similar to the actual knives that were found in Lane's possession. One of the victims in *Hunting Humans* is killed by a garrote, something that was found in Lane's possession too. Three victims in the film are killed exactly the way Darlene Ewalt was murdered; their throats are slit from behind while they are seated. The movie serial killer is constantly entering his victims' homes as they sleep, moving about and exploring the house without waking them, just as Lane did in his acts, before killing them The only thing missing from Lane's arsenal that the fictional serial killer had in his was a handgun. Of course, there are dozens of serial killer and slasher movies that have elements of what *Hunting Humans* have, but it was in the end *Hunting Humans* that police found cued in Lane's portable DVD player in his truck. Very likely it was what he had been watching before he forayed out on his killing; or even after he came back, his clothes still soaked and damp with real blood. As no seminal fluids had been recovered from the crime scenes, it is typically likely that Lane would return to the security and privacy of his truck cab where he masturbated still dressed in the bloody wet clothing to the scene in *Hunting Humans*, achieving the climax he would have been unable to achieve under stress at the actual crime scene.

Did the *Hunting Humans* DVD *make* Adam Lane stalk victims and cut their throats with his Jungle Primitive? No. No more than SOG's advertising copy for the "primitive in all of us" made him kill. Did Adam Lane's choice of entertainment and weapons have anything to do with his brutal murders? Yes, everything. It was part of the 'killing for culture' psycho-social chemistry in which a serial killer like Adam Lane was steeped as he developed for reasons we do not understand but can only guess at, an irresistible compulsion to be a stalker of women, death from the shadows, ninja avenger of who knows what slights at the hands of women Lane felt needed avenging. While the movie, or any other one single thing, did not "make him" kill, it was in the language of forensic behavioral psychopathology, a "facilitator." It titillated, fed, inspired and nurtured his developing obsession; it comforted him, it excited him. He very likely masturbated to fictional scenes of stalking and murder, compulsively conditioning his sexual pleasure receptors, fusing them to fantasies and images of death, knives and mutilation, and somewhere along the road he began taking his sick fantasies out into the real world. We don't know the reasons why: it could have been behavioral, it could have been psychopathological, it could have been bio-chemical, neurological or pharmaceutical, could have been related to his road accident; we will probably never know for sure because Lane would plead guilty and after that nobody cared why, nor was it relevant to the sentencing that would be agreed in his plea deal. As one of the detectives investigating the case later commented, "There is no explanation. There is no 'why' with Adam Lane."

Once he committed his first murder and got away with it, he became drunk on the blood he spilled, buzzed on the transcendence of his dark angry fantasies into reality, high on the fact that it was actually happening so easily for him, so high that he probably lost touch with reality or just stupidly slipped into a mindless killing frenzy. His numerous failed attempts and the actual killings all took place in less than a month, and by the last twenty-four hours he was lumbering around like a dumb zombie, pressing his hooded face into windows and crashing and banging into doors, setting off police calls. He was either totally in a fantasy trance, or just an idiot, or a bit of both. What he wasn't was one of those mastermind serial killers he had watched on TV and in the movies, over and over. In fact, most serial killers turn out to be like him, of low or average intelligence, unless luck or coincidence is on their side, and for about a month, it was for Adam Leroy Lane. The mastermind serial killer is a myth.

***

It's also a myth that serial killers are caught in forty-six minutes plus commercials. Adam Leroy Lane was getting away with the two murders he had committed. Nobody had made the connection. Chelmsford Police found Monica Massaro's necklace inside Lane's truck, but other than bagging it as possible evidence, they did not pay much attention to it, as the McDonoughs did not report anything missing from their home. Monica's body, it must be remembered, was not discovered until Monday afternoon, and that would not have been widely known until Tuesday, nearly two days after Lane

285

had been arrested in Chelmsford. While the Chelmsford Police immediately speculated that this was probably not Lane's first crime of this type, they were focused on preparing evidence for the charges they had on hand for him, which were serious enough: masked home invasion, assault with intent to murder, and attempted rape of a child (based on Lane pulling back the bedcovers from Shea as she slept.) A police bureaucracy's first function is to assemble evidence for charges they have preferred, no easy task even in a routine case, and only later, investigate if additional charges might be pending for other crimes, and rarely if those crimes took place in other jurisdictions. For the time being, Monica Massaro's necklace held no significance, while the major crimes unit of the New Jersey State Police which was investigating her death, remained focused on her personal life and her online activities, just as convinced of a personal connection in her death as were the Pennsylvania State Police of a personal connection in Darlene Ewalt's death. It's a problem as old as the 1970s Ted Bundy case, and even older: "linkage failure" or "linkage blindness." How do police in different jurisdictions link similar cases to the same nomadic perpetrator? How do they know these cases even exist and how do they access data that may show similarities from a different jurisdiction or how can they even survey other police departments for similar cases? After being urged for twenty-five years by Los Angeles police detective Pierce Brooks, who in the late 1950s encountered multijurisdictional problems in investigating serial killer Harvey Glatman, the FBI finally in 1985 launched ViCAP—the Violent Criminal Apprehension Program.

The intention of ViCAP was to centralize in a database at the FBI facility in Quantico Virginia, details of homicides and rapes and other violent crimes committed by both convicted and unidentified perpetrators, so that various police agencies could submit detailed descriptions of unsolved murders in their own jurisdiction and hopefully make a computer match to a series of similar crimes in other jurisdictions linked to the perpetrator. The problem was that it required *a substantial amount of paperwork*. Need I say more? Overworked cops and paperwork don't mix well. The ViCAP form was fifteen pages long with 189 detailed questions, many of them multi-part.[xxxix] It was as painstaking as an income tax form, if not worse...and then it had to be put in the mail! To derive any benefit from ViCAP, a police agency not only had to fill out and file the form, but then had to make a formal request to the FBI to process it through their database and report back the results, if any. At that point it was a technological issue, computers were still a rare commodity and the postal service or courier were the only way to send a document as detailed as a ViCAP form. By 1990 things improved a little bit: police agencies were able to fax their forms rather than rely on snail-mail. By 1995 everybody had a PC and the FBI distributed ViCAP packages as computer software, where at least a police officer could digitally fill out the form rather than have to manually write or type it up on paper and could now e-mail it to the FBI as an attached electronic file. But again, to derive any result from ViCAP, a police agency had to file an official request for the FBI to search their massive database and report back on possible 'hits' in their system. There was no way for a police agency to log-on directly to query the FBI system and make a search of their own, without filing the long ViCAP form and request. And that's the way it was still, seven years ago from this writing, in the summer of 2007 when Chelmsford Police in Massachusetts, and state police in New Jersey and police in Pennsylvania, were all investigating crimes by the same perpetrator but did not know it. Classic case of linkage blindness that has plagued serial homicide even before the word 'serial killer' was coined.

The small Chelmsford Police Department which rarely dealt with homicides, let alone serial killers, had either never heard of ViCAP or did not understand that ViCAP also collected data on 'closed' cases in which a perpetrator had been identified. The Chelmsford police investigators were professional enough to realize it was very likely that Lane had committed similar crimes, and they put out a query for similar cases on the police 'teletype' communications system to other jurisdictions, and to make sure the system queries did not get lost in the routine communications every department is inundated in, they even made a series of phone calls to other jurisdictions along Lane's truck route, but because they already had identified their suspect, they did not think to file a ViCAP report.

After twenty-two years of being in operation, a lot of police departments like Chelmford's had lost touch with ViCAP's existence by the mid-2000s. Many police officers who were first introduced to ViCAP in the 1980s had retired, and police departments anywhere are constantly swamped with updates, bulletins, and info packages, in which the FBI's reminders of ViCAP were easily overlooked by a new generation of overworked officers on the force. Chelmsford police not immediately dealing with any urgent serial killer cases, would have put the ViCAP bulletins away in their "to be read when I have time" box. Nor did Pennsylvania State Police file a ViCAP report on Darlene Ewalt's murder because they were convinced that they already had their suspect in their sights, Darlene's husband Todd.

Once Chelmsford Police filed their charges against Lane related to the home invasion and entered the knives and masks into evidence, they chose not to hold the truck he was driving or his remaining personal belongings in it, including some of the black ninja-like clothing in the cab with bloodstains that were not immediately visible on the dark material. They felt it was all irrelevant to the pending charges against him for what Lane had done inside the McDonough house. Chelmsford Police phoned Lane's employer to come by and take his truck filled with Lane's belongings. Before leaving with the truck on August 17, its owner immediately cleaned out the cab on the spot and threw Lane's stuff into a nearby dumpster, including the blood stained black clothing. That's how close Adam Leroy Lane was coming to getting away with murder.

***

The break came from two Massachusetts State Police troopers who were not directly involved in the case, Kevin Burke and Mike Banks. They had by coincidence just attended a ViCAP seminar given by the FBI, precisely for the reasons I describe: to keep police departments aware of what resources are available to them from the Justice Department. Moreover, this particular seminar highlighted the FBI's current new focus in serial homicide: serial killing truck drivers. The FBI was getting ready to launch their Highway Serial Killings Initiative.[xl] Hearing about the Chelmsford case, the two troopers called the Chelmsford Police, advising them of ViCAP and the likelihood that the truck driving home invader they had in their custody, could have easily committed previously serial homicides as well. That got the ball rolling.[xli]

On August 10, ten days after Lane's arrest, Chelmsford Police filled out and sent the complex ViCAP form to the FBI. It was going to lead to a break in the case, but it just goes to show how after three decades of profiling and linkage issue solutions, a serial murder case could still sneak up on investigators. (The next year the FBI announced a major upgrade of ViCAP to a third generation version which would be accessible online. As of August 2008, its database of 150,000 closed and open cases, submitted over the years by some 3,000 agencies, including unsolved homicides going back as far as the 1950s, could now be queried online directly by authorized police agencies.)[xlii]

In the same way that Pennsylvania police had routinely begun investigating those who were closest to Darlene Ewalt, New Jersey police too were seeking a perpetrator among Massaro's friends and contacts. As New Jersey investigators over a period of two weeks began striking off possible suspects from Massaro's large circle of real world and online acquaintances, the presence of the truck stop up the road a few minutes' walk away from her house began to gradually nag at them. The prosecutor in charge of the case J. Patrick Barnes began searching for similar crimes along the interstate system and hit on a case that had recently occurred in Maryland. He contacted ViCAP for details of the case and was told by the FBI analyst there that the perpetrator in the Maryland case had been arrested on the day of Massaro's murder, but that there had been a home invasion with similar signatures just recently filed by Chelmsford Police.

The Chelmsford inquiry was assigned to Major Crimes Unit Detective Geoffrey Nobel, a twelve-year veteran of New Jersey State Police with a BA in Criminal Justice Studies and an MA in Education from Seaton Hall. He also had a sister living near Chelmsford and was therefore familiar with the home invasion and had been suspicious of the truck stop near Massaro's home. Again, the realities of overworked police departments are rarely portrayed in fictional accounts. When Nobel called the Chelmsford Police on August 20, he was one of many homicide officers calling in trying to tie their unsolved cases to the widely reported apprehension of the ninja truck driver by the McDonoughs. Chelmsford cops were busy and almost brushed off Nobel until Chelmsford detective George Tyros recognized the possible similarities between his case and the New Jersey case. It would take another day for Tyros to go through the evidence they collected from Lane to see if there was anything there to link him to the Massaro murder in Bloomsbury. There was! Tyros found a receipt for a radar detector purchased by Lane at the truck stop in Bloomsbury on the day of Massaro's murder! He immediately let Nobel know.

The next morning, August 22, New Jersey Detectives Nobel and Lieutenant Farneski were in Chelmsford. Upon their arrival there, they were horrified to discover that Lane's truck had been returned to its owner in Virginia while its contents were thrown in a dumpster that had been scheduled for removal the day before. Rushing to the site of the dumpster, they discovered that by some stroke of luck—another coincidence—the scheduled pickup had not occurred. Lane's property was still there and was immediately taken into custody by a "dumpster diving" detective in a biohazard suit. Some forty-five items belonging to Lane were removed from the dumpster and logged into evidence. A call to Virginia State Police resulted in them immediately seizing the truck and conducting a forensic re-examination of the cab from which an additional sixteen more items were logged into evidence.

The next day, August 23, Nobel and Farneski were ready to interview their suspect, held in the Middlesex County Jail in Cambridge on the home invasion and attempted sexual assault and attempted murder charges. While these charges were serious, Adam Lane with no serious criminal record in his past was in a position with luck to plea them down to lesser charges unless the detectives could implicate him in the murder of Monica Massaro in New Jersey the night before his arrest in Chelmsford.

The videotapes of Nobel's interview with Adam Leroy Lane reveal him as a sanctimonious fat-fuck of a good ol' boy redneck cracker. He drawls, "I got manners. I treat people the way I want to be treated... They took movies that I had in the truck, and I know this ain't got nothing to do with y'all, and made it seem like I was the worst mass murderer you ever seen in your life. Just because I like horror movies..."

Lane attempted to maintain control of the interview, firmly rejecting Nobel's attempts to establish a rapport with his suspect sitting adjacent to him at the table in the Chelmsford Police interview room.

Nobel: Tell me about your family. You have a wife, kids, children, daughters, something?

Lane: If I go into all that, y'all gonna be down there again.

[Puts his palms flatly down and leans into the table, commanding it].

Nobel: Okay, you'd rather not...

Lane: I'd rather not put them through none of this... I got arrested here for a week. My family couldn't go outdoor, my kids couldn't go outdoors and play in the yard because the media down there. Social Services went to my family, my wife down there, and wanted her to file a divorce against me because I got arrested and the charges I'm facing. I ain't been to trial yet, ain't been convicted of anything... I ain't putting them through that again. [Sweeping with his hand imaginary crumbs off the table].

Detective Nobel circled Lane, never bringing up the reason he, a New Jersey police officer, was there in

Massachusetts questioning Lane. They talked about baseball and football and the life of truck driving. Lane complained about his health, his bad back which he had injured in a road accident a few years earlier, his need for medication for his diabetes and for hallucinations that he claimed to have. This seemingly casual cat-and-mouse dialogue went for well over an hour. But for detective Nobel it was ringing an alarm: Lane had not asked him why a New Jersey cop was here to see him. Why? It could only be for one reason: Lane already knew exactly why Nobel was there.

Suddenly, Lane burst out, "Sir, if you drove all the way from New Jersey up here, then you have . . . have a reason other than just, I want to talk to Adam Lane."

Nobel now moved in on Lane, telling him that he was a suspect in the murder of Monica Massaro and that he had evidence that proved Lane was in Bloomsbury on the night she was murdered. Lane waved off the accusation, "See, the thing about this is, just like I told my wife, they're gonna hit me with everything they can find, that they can't solve. I didn't do it."

When Nobel attempted to put more questions to Lane, he refused to continue, "My lawyer can answer those questions. I'm done." Once a suspect refuses to speak and 'lawyers up', an investigator cannot continue questioning an accused further without the risk of violating a suspect's Miranda rights to have legal counsel present. It was a disappointing outcome and Nobel and Farneski began packing away their video equipment as Lane was cuffed to be taken away back to jail.

Suddenly just as they were about to leave Lane asked Nobel, "Trooper, could I ask you a question off-the-record? If you were me, would you talk?"

"Absolutely, I would talk," replied Nobel without hesitation.

"Do they have the needle in New Jersey?" asked Lane.

"The state hasn't executed anyone in years," Nobel offered.

"Well, how much time am I looking at then?"

"We're not attorneys and we're not authorized to answer those questions, but if there's something you want to tell us, we'll hear you out on it."

And that is how Lane returned to the table and confessed killing Monica Massaro.

Lane began babbling, "I know I'm driving the nails in my own coffin, but you wanted the truth. This is the best I know how to describe it. ... And I'm trying not to die. I'm trying to tell you it was an accident. ... I was looking for money. I was losing everything I had. I don't have much, didn't have much, and now I've lost everything, including my family. ... You all should get a big conviction off this."

According to Lane he was only burglarizing Massaro's house when "She sat straight up in bed and got out of bed when she seen me and started screaming. And I tried to get her to be quiet. ... And we started struggling. I didn't even have a knife out, I mean, you know I only had the knife there in case of a big dog."

"I tried to put my hand over her mouth to get her to be quiet. ... She bit my hand. ... Well, when I tried to get away, she wouldn't let me get away, *she* wouldn't let me leave. I tried to push her back on the bed so I could get out. I fell. I had two back surgeries, I ain't got no strength. I mean, I might look big and mean, but I'm not. I'm measly really when it comes to wrestling around with anybody. Ask the man that put a choke hold on me because he weighed 70 pounds less than I did."

"Well, I had pushed her down at that point. I was gonna show her the knife to scare her, maybe I thought she'd let me go. And I was leaning on the knife, next to the bed or on the bed, for support. And *she* rolled, and she rolled over to get away and got cut with it."

It is typical of serial killers to often lay blame on the victim for the circumstances of their "unintended" death. "I had the knife, it was on the bed...it was about that long [gesturing with a knife in fist motion]. She rolled against it and cut right here [gesturing with the edge of his hand across the side of his neck]. Best I could tell, and I'm no medic it cut this jugular vein right here... I thought maybe it was just a little scrape or something. God, there was so much blood. ... She bled to death. I couldn't do nothing about it. ... It didn't take very long. Less than 60 seconds." [Brings his hands to his face in a theatric show of simulated relived trauma and contrition.]

"I thought if I made it look like somebody murdered... went in and ravaged her and all that, it'd make it a little better, but they wouldn't look toward me. ... I wanted to make it look like somebody, like some maniac, sex crime. ... I cut here in a couple places. After she was dead. Between her legs, on her stomach... I didn't not have any relations with that woman, before, after or during."

Nobel asked, "Did you have any sexual attraction during any of this?"

"No!" Lane quickly shot back angrily. "Look I love my wife very much. I ain't out for sexual toys."

Serial killers, of course, lie. That's what they do and do it compulsively and strategically. Gainfully employed as a truck driver, he had no motive to commit such high-risk burglaries, entering houses with their owners inside them. It's not what burglars do. He entered the house with only one purpose: to kill a woman inside. After killing Monica, he lingered in her bedroom, inflicting post-mortem wounds on her body, not because as he said, he wanted to make it "look like a sex maniac" committed the murder, but because he *was* a raging sex maniac and now in the safety of the house, unlike the exposed patio on which he killed his previous victim, he finally had an opportunity to act out his sexual angry excitation compulsions, typically using a knife as a substitute for his flaccid penis, opening and penetrating the victim with its razor sharp edged steel (a dangerous compulsive paraphilic disorder called *picquerism*). [In addition to his confessed stabbing and slashing of Massaro's throat, stomach and "between her legs", Lane also stabbed her breasts.][xliii] Worst case scenario, Lane was sexually aroused by stabbing Massaro after her death; best case scenario, he stabbed at her breasts and genitals as symbols of her gender with which he was enraged. In that sense, he might not have felt he was committing a "sexual" murder in the context he understood it, even though he was. ("I didn't not have any relations with that woman, before, after or during.")

"See, this ain't making it better, this is making me look like a maniac. ... But I didn't mean to hurt nobody. I didn't want to go to jail for the rest of my life or get a needle stuck in my arm," blubbered the 'Ninja' serial killer.

Lane concluded, "I went out the back door beside the car and up through the yard and back to the truck stop. I took her pocketbook from the car and a necklace I found in one of the drawers... I threw the credit cards and license in, in the trash can. Threw the [pocketbook] on top of a building... I meant to throw [the necklace] away and never did. After that I went back to the truck and tried to eat, and I bought a radar detector and went somewhere else, laid down and tried to sleep."[xliv]

In the end it did not matter. Massaro was murdered and Lane confessed to having murdered her during the commission of several other felonies. Lane's serial killing career was ended in its first thirty days, if we accept the possibility that Lane had not committed other murders previously that he has not been linked to, (and so far, it looks like he did not.)

By now Pennsylvania Police were looking very hard at Lane as a possible suspect in the Darleen Ewalt murder and the attack on Patricia Brooks. Lane's DNA was found on the gloves recovered near the scene of the attack on Brooks while DNA from Darleen Ewalt was eventually found on another knife found among Lane's crazy arsenal of edged weapons in his truck.

***

Lane would face separate trials in three different states, Massachusetts, New Jersey and Pennsylvania, in that order. In each case, Lane would eventually agree to plead guilty in various deals. In Massachusetts based on the evidence that Lane had found money in the purses of the McDonough women but continued to go further into the house, on the extracted identification belonging to Shae found on the picnic table out back, and the fact that Lane pulled back her bed covers, he faced charges of attempted rape in addition to the other charges. Lane seemed to be fixated on clearing himself as a sex offender above all things. Partly because of his self-righteous shame and partly because he knew that convicted rapist sex offenders are often targeted by convicts in prison, he agreed to plead guilty to threat to commit a crime; assault and battery with a dangerous weapon; larceny of property over $250; resisting arrest; attempted murder; and possession of a dangerous weapon, if the rape charges were dropped. The McDonoughs agreed partly to spare Shea the trauma of having to testify in court. On December 11, 2007 Adam Lane was sentenced in Massachusetts to twenty-five to thirty-five years in prison on the said charges, but the attempted rape charge was dropped.

During the same month in 2007, New Jersey became the first state in the US in forty years to abolish the death penalty as a punishment "inconsistent with evolving standards of decency" and with no evidence that it served as deterrent, and that "the penological interest in executing a small number of persons guilty of murder is not sufficiently compelling to justify the risk of making an irreversible mistake." [xlv] New Jersey had the good sense to realize what the British learned centuries ago when public hangings of pickpockets attracted other pickpockets targeting the pockets of crowds watching the hangings. Hanging was no deterrent; it did not work. Considering that most homicides are committed in the 'heat of the moment' and that most murderers when they murder did not know they were about to kill, the death penalty is not a significant deterrent. It is certainly symbolic of our intolerance of murder but a lopsided comment on the 'sanctity of life' if the state takes it, no matter what. The only practical purpose is that it guarantees the offender will never offend again, but the price is high: $72,000 annual cost in New Jersey for keeping an inmate on death row through sometimes decades of appeals compared to the $40,000 annual cost of keeping one sentenced to life. And the risk of executing an innocent person, our society should indeed value infinitely more than the risk of not executing a guilty one. It's what separates the values of western civilization from all those other civilizations waging their cruel wars on us. Perhaps Monica was right, New Jersey is indeed the last bastion of civilization in the United States.

Adam Lane was now extradited to New Jersey to stand trial for first-degree murder of Monica Massaro. No longer facing a death penalty, Lane now plea bargained to avoid a life sentence. In exchange for a fifty-year sentence and the dropping of other charges against him in New Jersey, Lane pleaded guilty to first-degree murder and waived his right to further appeals. The judge noted that Lane would begin serving his fifty years only after he first served the minimum twenty-five for the Massachusetts conviction, and that under New Jersey's No Early Release Act he would be required to serve eighty-five percent of his fifty-year sentence. Lane would be one hundred eleven years old before he could be first eligible for parole. Considering his diabetic condition, this was as good as a life sentence. And Pennsylvania had not gotten their hands on him yet.

Lane was next shuffled off to Pennsylvania to stand trial for the murder of Darlene Ewalt and the attack on Patricia Brooks. In exchange for the state waiving 'aggravating circumstance' calling for a death penalty, Adam Lane pleaded guilty in June 2010. He was sentenced to life in prison for the murder of Darleen Ewalt and ten to twenty years for his attempted murder of Patricia Brooks, also to be served consecutively. Before Lane can begin serving his life sentence, he will have to serve the twenty to thirty-five years from Massachusetts, the fifty from New Jersey, and the twenty from Pennsylvania. We won't be seeing Adam Leroy Lane back on the interstate anytime soon, not until he gets driven down it, tits up on his back, in a box nailed shut.

***

For the families of Darlene Ewalt and Monica Massaro there was no real closure, no explanation. Todd Ewalt understands why he was suspected as a husband but it left him and his son bitter. Todd is convinced that he was on the brink of being indicted by a grand jury for the murder of his wife and might have been falsely convicted in Pennsylvania (where there still is a death penalty) had New Jersey police not made the connection between the murders. False convictions like that happen more frequently than we realize.[xlvi] Darlene's son Nick did not go to college that year and lost his scholarship. Jeannie McDonough in her book reports that her daughter Shea became a deeply troubled teen after Lane had victimized her. In her book, Jeannie describes concerns of alcohol abuse and fears that her daughter might be suicidal. When Shea turned twenty recently, it was reported by Chelmsford Police that she had been charged by them for failing to remain in her lane and driving under the influence one evening.[xlvii]

Bloomsbury, New Jersey was never the same Norman Rockwell painting town after Monica Massaro's murder. Its innocence was lost forever and the small town now sullenly regards the truck stops on its outskirts with suspicion and dread of what next will roll into them. On September 22, 2007, at a concert in Atlantic City, New Jersey, Steven Tyler and Aerosmith dedicated his power ballad "Dream On" to Monica Massaro.[xlviii] It was a touching tribute to a torch-bearing fan and would have thrilled the New Jersey 'rag doll,' had she been alive to see and hear it. But she wasn't.

The downside to Adam Lane's guilty plea bargains is that to this day we do not understand what he thought he was doing. Lane's lawyers did not offer any explanation in his various sentencing hearings because they did not have to. The sentencing was negotiated as part of Lane guilty plea deal. When he was customarily asked if he had anything to say to the court before his sentencing, Lane said nothing. If indeed Lane first began killing at the age of forty-two than he was statistically nearly twice the average twenty-eight year age most serial killers first begin murdering at, and that is confounding. His lack of a criminal record for the type of offenses serial killers typically accumulate beginning as juveniles—fetish burglaries, voyeurism and other sexual offenses—is unusual. Lane might be an indicator of future things to come. About the same time that Lane was being tried, in Canada, a highly successful and respected air force colonel, Russell Williams, a commander of a strategic air base in Trenton, Ontario, suddenly began inexplicably killing women when he was forty-six, an unusually mature age for a serial killer to begin killing. [See Kelly Banasky's chapter "Stripped of his medals and female panties" in this volume, on Russell Williams.] An intensive police investigation around the world in all the places that Williams had been stationed while serving in the air force, failed to link him to any unsolved homicides. Again, as in the case of Lane, Williams pleaded guilty and no psychiatric information was submitted into evidence by his defense.

The Adam Lane case, while the subject of several TV shows because of his unusual capture by a family, did not make big headlines and remained relatively obscure. In the pre-2005 San Antonio Conference era, Lane would not have even been "officially" labeled a serial killer with 'only' two victims in his body count. And even today, because the victims are so close to each other, and his behavior so erratic, one can argue that Lane is closer to being a 'spree' serial killer than the traditional, cunning, painstaking serial killer that cautiously stalks and kills his victims.

Again, while the vast majority of truck drivers are honest hard working people, the unusually high percentage of truck drivers among serial killers in many ways makes sense. Serial killers by their nature are loners and obsessively compulsive, which fits with the nature of the trucking profession. A trucker for hours on end finds himself alone in his cab, highly focused on a single task—steering a massive truck hurtling across thousands of miles of highway—it's the kind of work that the compulsively obsessed and lonely frequently find comforting and conducive to their personality. There in the solitude of a truck cab, as the miles click by, the serial killer can dwell and steep in his lonely dark fantasies.

The most recent FBI study on serial homicide indicates that one third of all the 480 serial killer victims in their study, were prostitutes.[xlix] Most of the murdered prostitutes are on the bottom scale of sex work—street walkers—not the online classified ad "escorts." And there is no more bottom scale than that of so-called "lot lizards" who desperately ply their trade in truck stops. The victimization of prostitutes has a double edge: firstly, street and truck stop prostitutes are easily lured by a stranger into an anonymous vehicle—it is the nature of how they do their business; secondly, many serial killers in general tend to target victims discounted by society, the kind of victim criminologist Steven Egger labeled as "the less dead": prostitutes, gays, runaways, homeless, poor, minorities, elderly. As Egger explained, "The victims of serial killers, viewed when alive as a devalued strata of humanity, become "less-dead" (since for many they were less-alive before their death and now they become the "never-were") and their demise becomes the elimination of sores or blemishes cleansed by those who dare to wash away these undesirable elements."[l] Hundreds of trucks on their way from hundreds of different destinations from hundreds of different origins pull into truck stops. Police files are full of cases where women were last seen wandering off between rows of anonymous parked trucks at a truck stop to never be seen again or found later somewhere at a remote part of the truck stop or along the highway. The FBI's Highway Serial Killings Initiative launched about the time that Lane was doing his killing, lists some five hundred unsolved murder cases of mostly women dumped on or near America's interstate system, with some two hundred potential truck driving serial killer suspects.[li]

The fact that truckers cover a great distance through multiple jurisdictions and routinely "belong" on the road, makes them formidable suspects when they are also serial killers. Unlike, say, a carpenter found cruising a known 'track' for prostitutes, the long haul driver suspect often has his truck route as both a vector and an alibi in a murder running through a truck stop with dozens of potential victim "lot lizards" which he does not need to explain.

The *Hunting Human* case as well, reminds us of the issue of facilitators. It had been long ago established that 'true detective' magazines in the pre-1990s, with the typical lurid portrayal on their covers of a victimized female, clothes often in a state of disarray, about to be raped and murdered, looking out at the reader as if he was the victimizer, were the preferred viewing material by so many serial killers that the genre was termed "serial killer porn" by some profilers.[lii] Today while true detective magazines eschew that kind of cover art, they also hardly exist anymore as a viable medium. DVDs and the internet is now the source of visual facilitators for serial killers, but again, as in the case of true detective magazines, there is no evidence that it "makes" serial killers kill, as there is no evidence that *Hunting Humans* or *Dead Stop* or the advertising copy for the SOG knife, "for the primitive in all of us" made Lane kill Darlene Ewalt and Monica Massaro. Yet at the same time, those products in Lane's possession, had *everything* to do with his pre-existing homicidal fantasies; they were a mirror to them.

Finally, the investigation of the 2007 murders of Darleen Ewalt and Monica Massaro at the hands of an emerging serial killer, shows just how difficult it still is as late as the twenty-first century to recognize serial killings for what

303

they are. It would be highly unfair to characterize the Pennsylvania and New Jersey initial police investigations as "bungled." In the murder of Darleen Ewalt and of Monica Massaro, it made perfect sense to suspect 'horses': the husband, the boyfriend, the online friend. Statistically that was the place to deploy scarce investigative resources and it shows that when a 'zebra' serial killer makes an appearance, it is very difficult, still today, to recognize. ViCAP going online in 2008, with police agencies now being able to directly query for results the massive database, without having to upload data and wait for an FBI analysis to come back to them, was a much needed step in alleviating some of the challenges still remaining in producing investigative 'linkage' in serial homicides. But serial killers are adaptive creatures, like a virus. They learn and they constantly mutate. The sad and frightening matter is that as we gaze into the future and catch its glimpse, we see it is all murder and murder.

✳✳✳

"Zebra! The Hunting Humans 'Ninja' Truck Driver Serial Killer" is a preview from Peter Vronsky's forthcoming book, *Serial Killer Chronicles: A New History of Serial Murder Today*, scheduled to be published in 2016 by Berkley Books at Penguin Random House.

Meet the Authors

Dr. Peter Vronsky

Peter Vronsky, Ph.D. is a criminal justice historian, filmmaker and the author of two bestselling histories of serial homicide, *Serial Killers: The Method and Madness of Monsters* and *Female Serial Killers: How and Why Women Become Monsters.*

"Serial Killer Zombie Apocalypse" is a preview from his forthcoming book for Berkley Books at Penguin Random House, on the history of serial killing since 2001, *Serial Killer Chronicles: A New History of Serial Murder Today.* Peter Vronsky teaches in the history department of Ryerson University in Toronto where he lectures on the history of terrorism and espionage in international relations.

Peter Vronsky books can be found at: www.petervronsky.com
Websites: www.petervronsky.org and
www.SerialKillerChronicles.com
Facebook: www.facebook.com/killersbypetervronsky

Sylvia Perrini

Sylvia Perrini is an author, historian, wife and mother to two sons and two daughters. Sylvia was born in Milan, Italy and moved to Staffordshire, UK when she was four. Her Italian father was a lawyer and her English mother a barrister.

Sylvia, studied history and law at Manchester University and developed a particular interest in women who live outside the common boundaries of society.

Sylvia lives with her husband and children in the New Forest, Hampshire, UK. Here she spends her time reading, writing and painting.

Author Page: www.amazon.com/SYLVIA-PERRINI/e/B007WRWEI0
Facebook: www.facebook.com/AuthorSylviaPerrini
Website: www.sylviaperrini.goldmineguides.com/

Michael Newton

Michael Newton has published 215 books under his own name and various pseudonyms since 1977. He began writing professionally as a "ghost" for author Don Pendleton on the best-selling Executioner series and continues his work on that series today. With 104 episodes published to date, Newton has nearly tripled the number of Mack Bolan novels completed by creator Pendleton himself. While 156 of Newton's published books have been novels-- including westerns, political thrillers and psychological suspense--he is best known for nonfiction, primarily true crime and reference books. He has written many books on serial killers including:

Silent Rage: Inside the Mind of a Serial Killer

The Encyclopedia of Serial Killers (Facts on File Crime Library)

Hunting Humans: An Encyclopedia of Modern Serial Killers

Daddy Was the Black Dahlia Killer: The Identity of America's Most Notorious Serial Murderer--Revealed at Last

Website: www.michaelnewton.homestead.com/
Author Page: www.amazon.com/Michael-Newton/e/B001IXMYNO
Facebook: www.facebook.com/MichaelNewtonAuthor

RJ Parker

RJ Parker, P.Mgr.,CIM, is an award-winning and bestselling true crime author and serial killer expert. He has written 16 true crime books, available in eBook, trade paperback, and audiobook editions, that have sold in over 100 countries. He holds Certifications in Serial Crime and Criminal Profiling. Parker publishes for several authors in True CRIME and CRIME Fiction under his company RJ Parker Publishing, Inc.

Born and raised in Newfoundland, he now resides in Oshawa and St. John's, Canada. To date, RJ has donated over 2,100 books to allied troops serving overseas and to our wounded warriors recovering in Naval and Army hospitals all over the world.

Facebook: www.facebook.com/RJParkerPublishing
Website: www.RJParkerPublishing.com

Dr. Katherine Ramsland

Katherine Ramsland Ph.D. is a bestselling author of books on serial murder and forensic psychology, is a professor of forensic psychology and criminal justice at DeSales University and currently directs the master's program in criminal justice. She holds master's degrees in clinical psychology, criminal justice, and forensic psychology, as well as a Ph.D. in philosophy. In addition, she has a certification in Medical Investigation (CMI-V) from the American College of Forensic Examiners International, and she is on the board of the Cyril Wecht Institute.

Ramsland has published 50 books, including The Ivy League Killer, The Sex Beast, Psychopath, The Devil's Dozen, The Forensic Psychology of Criminal Minds, The CSI Effect, The Forensic Science of CSI, The Science of Cold Case Files, The Devil's Dozen: How Cutting-edge Forensics Took Down Twelve Notorious Serial Killers, and Inside the Minds of Serial Killers.

Facebook: www.facebook.com/groups/57033499336/
Website: www.katherineramsland.com

310

Kelly Banaski

Kelly Banaski is a writer, mother of nine and an inmate liaison, living in rural Tennessee. Her blog, The Woman Condemned, details her insight to the lives of the women on death row through her letters, phone calls and visits over the past decade.

Kelly's ability to engage the criminal element and gain their trust was garnered in part by her unusual upbringing and progressed as she grew older allowing her a peek into the heads of infamous criminals nationwide. She uses these insights to aid inmates in restoring some of the good they took from the world and to help the public understand why some people kill.

Kelly entered a writing contest for the second annual Serial Killers True Crime Anthology, 2015, Volume II, and was selected over several other entries.

Blog: www.TheWomanCondemned.com
Website: www.KellyBanaski.com
Facebook: www.facebook.com/WomanCondemned

New True Crime Books by the Publisher

The following are a few true crime books that may interest you. A listing of all books can be found at:

www.RJParkerPublishing.com

Social Media Monsters: Internet Killers
by JJ Slate and RJ Parker
Rel. 09-18-2014

Who is really on the other end of that Facebook friend request, or behind that dating profile, or posting that item for sale on Craigslist? How can you be safe if you plan to meet up with a stranger you met online? What precautions should you take?

In this book, we have detailed more than thirty chilling true stories of killers that have used the internet to locate, stalk, lure, or exploit their victims. Facebook, Craigslist, MySpace, chat rooms, dating sites–it does not matter where you are online; killers are lurking in the shadows. They lurk in suicide chat rooms, search for escorts on Craigslist, and create fake social media profiles to fool and gain the trust of their victims. Someone you have been talking to for months or even years could be a completely different person from what you envisioned.

Missing Wives, Missing Lives
by JJ Slate

Rel. 06-16-2014

When a wife goes missing, her husband is often the prime suspect in her disappearance. But what happens when she is never found? In some of these cases, the husband was found guilty of murder, without a body.

Missing Wives, Missing Lives focuses on unique cases in which the wife has never been found and the undying efforts of her family as they continue the painful search to bring her home. The book covers decades old cases, such as Jeanette Zapata, who has been missing since 1976, to more recent and widely known cases, such as Stacy Peterson, who has been missing since 2007. Keeping these women's stories alive may be the key to solving the mystery and bringing them home to their family.

Parents Who Killed their Children: Filicide
by RJ Parker
Rel. 05-01-2014

What could possibly incite parents to kill their own children?

This collection of "Filicidal Killers" provides a gripping overview of how things can go horribly wrong in once loving families. Parents Who Killed their Children depicts ten of the most notorious and horrific cases of homicidal parental units out of control. People like--Andrea Yates, Diane Downs, Susan Smith, and Jeffrey MacDonald--who received a great deal of media attention. The author explores the reasons; from addiction to postpartum psychosis, insanity to altruism.

Each story is detailed with background information on the parents, the murder scenes, trials, sentencing and aftermath.

The Vampire Next Door: The True Story of the Vampire Rapist
by JT Hunter

Rel. 10-14-2014

John Crutchley seemed to be living the American Dream. Good-looking and blessed with a genius level IQ, he had a prestigious, white-collar job at a prominent government defense contractor, where he held top-secret security clearance and handled projects for NASA and the Pentagon. To all outward appearances, he was a hard-working, successful family man with a lavish new house, a devoted wife, and a healthy young son.

But, he concealed a hidden side of his personality, a dark secret tied to a hunger for blood and the overriding need to kill. As one of the most prolific serial killers in American history, Crutchley committed at least twelve murders, and possibly nearly three dozen. His IQ eclipsed that of Ted Bundy, and his body count may have as well. While he stalked the streets hunting his unsuspecting victims, the residents of a quiet Florida town slept soundly, oblivious to the dark creature in their midst, unaware of the vampire next door.

Serial Killers Abridged: An Encyclopedia of 100 Serial Killers
by RJ Parker
Rel. 05-31-2014

WARNING: There are dramatic crime scene photos in this book that some may find very disturbing.

The ultimate reference for anyone compelled by the pathologies and twisted minds behind the most disturbing of homicidal monsters. From A to Z, there are names you may not have heard of, but many of you are familiar with the notorious serial killers such as; John Wayne Gacy, Jeffrey Dahmer, Ted Bundy, Gary Ridgway, Aileen Wuornos, and Dennis Rader, just to name a few. This reference book will make a great collection for true crime enthusiasts. Each story is in a Reader's Digest short form.

Backseat Tragedies: Hot Car Deaths
by JJ Slate and RJ Parker
Rel. 04-15-2015

Picture this: A mother parks her car in the parking lot of a supermarket and hops out to grab a few items. She'll only be gone a few minutes, so she leaves her baby in the backseat and cracks the front window. The child, too small to protest, doesn't even know what is happening. In a matter of minutes, the car begins to act like an oven. The lack of ventilation inside causes the temperature to increase twenty degrees for each ten minutes she is gone, even with a window slightly open. The child s cries remain unheard and fall silent once his body temperature reaches 107°F. How many infants and young children die each year due to the negligence of their parents? The answer is too many. No child deserves to die this way.

Our first reaction when we hear of another hot car death is to instinctively blame the parents. We think they must not be fit to be parents in the first place. Many are too obsessed with themselves that they forget what a selfless act it is to care for a child, while others just think of themselves as being too busy in their own lives than to worry about a child. But many incidents of hot car deaths are tragic accidents. It is difficult for many of us to comprehend, but parents can become distracted by today's on-the-go lifestyles and simply forget their child is in the backseat of the car.

Backseat Tragedies: Hot Car Deaths explores the circumstances that led to the deaths of several children who died of hyperthermia, or suffered heatstroke in a car. We explain the facts about how quickly a car can heat to deadly temperatures and what steps you can take to prevent future tragedies. We hope to raise awareness about how a simple act of carelessness can result in the death of a beautiful child.

318

Serial Killer Groupies
by RJ Parker
Rel. 12-31-2014

Known as 'serial killer groupies' or even 'prison groupies', a great number of these women have shown a surprising desire to get connected to the serial killer of their choice. A large number of these women have become directly aligned with these killers, and some have even married, or gotten engaged with these criminals. It is believed that these women are living vicariously through these high profile criminals and enjoy the attention and notoriety in the media. Some SKG's are attracted to the celebrity status they acquire. They go on talk shows to announce their undying love for the serial killer and proclaim that he was not capable of these killings. Or, that he has changed. Some have taken credit for 'changing' the killer and that he's been regenerated.

Please feel free to check out more True CRIME and CRIME Fiction books, and authors by our friends at

www.WILDBLUEPRESS.com

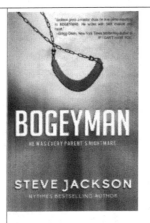

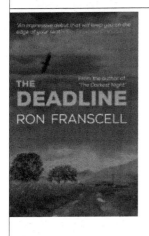

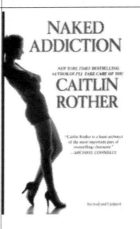

SIGN UP FOR

NEWSLETTER

AND UPCOMING RELEASES

References

The Babysitter

"Anonymous Source Claims More Victims in Oakland County Child Killer Case," WXYZ.com, May 16, 2012.

Ashenfelter, David, "In Oakland County Child Killings Shadowy Figure Offers his Theories," *Detroit Free Press*, May 12, 2012.

--"Informant Says He can Connect Oakland County Child Killings to Other Deaths," *Detroit Free Press*, May 14, 2012.

--"Decades after Oakland County Child Killings and No Peace for Victims' Families." *Detroit Free Press*. June 2012.

--"Did the Top Suspects in the Oakland County Child Killer Case Get Away With It? Evidence Shows They Might Have." *Detroit Free Press*. June 2012

Bob, Press Release. *Detroit Free Press*, October 16, 2013.

Catallo, Heather. "Family of Oakland County Child Killer Victim Takes Prosecutor, Police to Task for Unsolved Murders," WXYZ.com, September 12, 2013.

Connington, Bill. "Zombie" [play], 2010.

Cribari, M. *Portraits in the Snow: The Oakland County Child Killing.* Denver, CO: Outskirts Press, Inc., 2011.

"Detectives Revive Infamous Case; Citizens Encouraged to Come Forward with Tips About '70's Killings." *Michigan State Police Bulletin*, February 18, 2005.

Falcon, Gabriel, "Possible Leads Unearthed in Oakland County Child Killer Case," CNN.com, August 21, 2013.

"Is the Oakland County Child Killer Connected to John Wayne Gacy?" http://www.wxyz.com/news, Feb 1, 2013.

Keenan, Marney Rich, "Finding Timmy's Killer: Family Seeks Answers 32 Years after Son's Death," *The Detroit News*, October 26, 2009.

Martindale, Mike. "New DNA Evidence Surfaces in Oakland Child Killings," *The Detroit News*, August 24, 2007.

"Victim's Family in Oakland Child Killings Sues Molester over Death," *The*

Detroit News, October 19, 2007.

McIntyre, Tommy. *Wolf in Sheep's Clothing: The Search for a Child Killer.* Detroit, MI: Wayne State University Press, 1988.

"New Person Identified in Oakland Child Killer Case," Clickonit.com, November 2, 2011.

Oates, Joyce Carol, *Zombie*, New Hope, NJ: Ecco, 2009.

Phillips, Dave, "Prosecutor: DNA Presents First Link in Oakland County Child Killer Case; Person of Interest Named," *The News-Herald*, July 7, 2012.

Stables-Battaglia, Tammy, "Cops Comb Blue Gremlin near Grand Blanc for Ties to Oakland Child Killer," *Detroit Free Press*, August 20, 2013.

Michael Wayne McGray

Canadian Broadcasting Corp.
http://www.cbc.ca/news/canada/possible-serial-killer-in-custody-in-moncton-1.184325
MissingPeople.net
http://www.missingpeople.net/vpdprobe.htm
Court Case Queen vs. Michael Wayne McGray
http://caselaw.canada.globe24h.com/0/0/nova-scotia/supreme-court-of-nova-scotia/2001/05/29/r-v-mcgray-2001-nssc-75.shtml
Murderpedia
http://murderpedia.org/male.M/m/mcgray-michael-wayne.htm
Crimezzz
http://www.crimezzz.net/serialkillers/M/McGRAY_mich ael_wayne.php

Michael Swango

ABC News. "Poison Doctor Swango Indicted." July 11, 2000.
ABC News. "'Poison Doc' Pleads Guilty. Sept. 6, 2000.
Charlie LeDuff. "Man to Admit to Murdering 3 L.I. Patients." *New York Times,* Sept. 6, 2000.
Christopher P. Holstedge, Thomas Neer, and R. Brent Furbee. *Criminal Poisoning: Clinical and Forensic Perspectives.* Sudbury, Mass.: Jones & Bartlett Publishers, 2010.
James B. Stewart, *Blind Eye: The Terrifying Story Of A Doctor Who Got*

322

Away With Murder. New York: Simon & Schuster, 2000.

David Russell Williams

CBC News
http://www.cbc.ca/news/canada/biography-russell-williams-1.903318
NBC News
http://www.nbcnews.com/id/39556963/ns/world_news-
americas/#.U7CjXfldVvs
http://en.wikipedia.org/wiki/Russell_Williams
Transcript of Taped Interview with Russell Williams:
    http://murderpedia.org/male.W/images/williams_russell/edited-
    williams.pdf
Russell Williams video murder confession:
    https://www.youtube.com/watch?v=zLJzNpVrcGU
Colonel *Russell Williams: The making of a mystery man*, Greg McArthur
    and Colin Freeze - Saturday's Globe and Mail, October 18, 2010
The secret life of Col. Russell Williams expose, Jim Rankin and Sandro
    Contenta - TheStar.com, October 18, 2010
Crime Libary
http://www.crimelibrary.com/serial_killers/predators/david-russell-
    williams/the-dissappearance-of-jessica-lloyd.html
Ottawa Citizen
http://www.ottawacitizen.com/news/Williams+tearful+plea+forgiveness+
    falls+deaf+ears/3705505/story.html

Joanne Dennehy

http://murderpedia.org/female.D/d/dennehy-joanna.htm
http://www.dailymail.co.uk/news/article-2746674/Builder-James-Budd-
    reveals-hes-engaged-sadistic-triple-killer-Joanna-Dennehy.html
http://www.bbc.com/news/uk-england-26389479
http://www.mirror.co.uk/news/uk-news/joanna-dennehy-ex-boyfriend-
    tells-hell-2840683
http://www.independent.co.uk/news/uk/crime/joanna-dennehy-the-girl-
    from-a-loving-home-who-turned-into-a-serial-killer-9124128.html
http://www.theguardian.com/uk-news/2014/jan/28/murderer-joanna-
    dennehy-diagnosed-paraphilia-sadomasochism
http://www.troubleandstrife.org/new-articles/the-return-of-the-female-

serial-killer/

Donna Perry

Abrams, Stanley. "The Multiple Personality: A Legal Defense," *American Journal of Clinical Hypnosis*. Vol. 25, 1983.

Barker, Kim. "'Fear This': Robert Yates Sits in a Spokane Jail, Accused of one Woman's Death and a Suspect in as Many as 18," *The Vancouver Province*, April 23, 2000.

Clouse, Thomas. "Woman Linked to Prostitute Killings," *Spokesman-Review*. November 21, 2012.

Diagnostic and Statistical Manual of Mental Disorders-5. Washington, DC: American Psychiatric Association, 2013.

Gillespie, Kaitlin. "Charges Recommended in 1990 Spokane Prostitute Killings," *Spokesman-Review*, November 1, 2013.

Hill, Kip. "Perry Denies Her Role in 1990 Slayings," *Spokesman-Review*, March 18, 2014.

Saks, Elyn, with Stephen Behnke. *Jekyll on Trial: Multiple Personality Disorder and Criminal Law*. New York: New York University Press, 1997.

Harold Shipman

Clarkson, Wensley. *Evil Beyond Belief*. London: John Blake Publishing, 2005.

"Harold Shipman: full list of victims," *The Guardian*, July 19, 2002.

Kinnell H. G. "Serial homicide by doctors: Shipman in perspective". *BMJ* 321 (2000): 1594–7.

Peters, Carole. Harold Shipman: *Mind Set on Murder*. London: Andre Deutsch Ltd., 2006.

Sitford, Mikaela. *Addicted to Murder*. London: Virgin Books, 2000.

Whittle, Brian; and Jean Ritchie. *Prescription for Murder*. New York: Little, Brown and Co., 2000.

Lonnie Franklin, Jr.

The Grim Sleeper
http://thegrimsleeper.com/

Leonard, Jack (2010-07-15). "Authorities Missed A Chance to Catch Grim Sleeper Suspect". Los Angeles Times
LA Times
http://articles.latimes.com/2010/jul/15/local/la-me-grim-sleeper-dna-20100715

Rosemary West

www.crimelibrary.com/serial_killers/weird/west/index_1.html
http://www.biography.com/people/rosemary-west-230321
http://murderpedia.org/female.W/w/west-rosemary.htm
http://www.criminalminds.wikia.com/wiki/Fred_and_Rosemary_West
http://www.dailymail.co.uk/news/article-2565316/Avon-Monopoly-The-Archers-Why-Rose-West-loves-life-jail.html
http://www.theguardian.com/theobserver/1999/nov/21/featuresreview.review4

Don Harvey

Dirk Johnson. " Ex-Nurse's Aide Admits Murders Of 24 in 4 Years." *New York Times,* Aug. 19, 1987.
George Stimson, *The Cincinnati Crime Book*. Cincinnati: Peasenhall Press, 1988.
William Whalen and Bruce Martin, *Defending Donald Harvey: The Case of America's Most Notorious Angel-of-Death Serial Killer*. Covington, KY: Clerisy Press, 2005.

Brian Dugan

"A Timeline of the Nicarico-Dugan Case," *Daily Herald*, July 28, 2009.
Babwin, Don. "Brian Dugan Pleads Guilty to 1983 Rape and Murder of Jeanine Nicarico," *Huffington Post*, July 28, 2009.
"Brian Dugan Tries to Explain Murder," NBC, Sept 8, 2009.
Gregory, Ted. "Jeanine Nicarico Murder Case: Brian Dugan Sentencing to Focus on Psychopathy," *Chicago Tribune*, Nov. 8, 2009.

Kiehl, Kent. *The Psychopath Whisperer*, New York: Crown, 2014.

Possley, Maurice and Armstrong, Ken. "Prosecution on Trial in DuPage," *Chicago Tribune*, January 12, 1999.

"Rolando Cruz," The Innocence Project.

www.innocenceproject.org/Content/Rolando_Cruz.php

"The Trial of Brian Dugan," *Chicago Tribune*, December 1, 2005.

Enriqueta Marti

http://murderpedia.org/female.M/m/marti-enriqueta.htm
http://en.wikipedia.org/wiki/Enriqueta_Mart%C3%AD
http://themindofaserialkiller.tumblr.com/post/22930263966/enriqueta-marti
http://www.studybarcelona.com/history-of-barcelona.html
http://en.wikipedia.org/wiki/Tragic_Week_(Catalonia)
http://www.tourspain.org/barcelona/history.asp

---

i
      Ian Brady, *The Gates of Janus: Serial Killing and Its Analysis*, Los Angeles: Feral House, 2001, pp. 87–88
ii
      Stephen G. Michaud, (2007-06-26). *Beyond Cruel: The Chilling Story of America's Most Sadistic Killer* (St. Martin's True Crime Library) St. Martin's Press. Kindle Edition.
iii
      http://www.bestplaces.net/crime/city/pennsylvania/west_hanover_township
iv
      John Luciew, http://www.pennlive.com/specialprojects/index.ssf/2010/08/investigators_dig_into_victims.html [retrieved 5 October 2014]
v
      http://blog.pennlive.com/patriotnews/2007/07/state_police_investigating_sus.html [Retrieved 22/09/2014]
vi
      John Luciew,

http://www.pennlive.com/specialprojects/index.ssf/2010/08/law_enforc
ement_tells_the_publ.html

vii

   http://www.nj.com/news/index.ssf/2008/10/trucker_tells_how_h
e_killed_wo.html [Retrieved 20 August 2014]

viii

   John Luciew,
http://www.pennlive.com/specialprojects/index.ssf/2010/08/another_wo
man_is_killed_before.html

ix

   http://www.fbi.gov/news/stories/2009/april/highwayserial_0406

09

x

   Janet McClellan, "Delivery Drivers and Long-Haul Truckers:
Traveling Serial Murderers", *Journal of Applied Security Research,* Volume
3, Issue 2, (2008), p. 171

xi

   Eric W. Hickey, *Serial Murderers and Their Victims,* Sixth Edition,
Belmont, CA: Wadsworth, 2013. p. 224; 292

xii

   Aamodt, M. G. (2014, September 6). *Serial killer statistics.*
Retrieved (27 October 2014) from
http://maamodt.asp.radford.edu/Serial%20Killer%20Information%20Cent
er/Project%20Description.htm

xiii

   Federal Bureau of Investigation (FBI), *Serial Murder:
Multidisciplinary Perspectives for Investigators,* Behavioral Analysis Unit,
National Center for Analysis of Violent Crime (NCAVC), Department of
Justice, Washington DC: 2008. pp. 4-9

xiv

   Ian Brady, pp. 87–88

xv

   See Google Maps: https://goo.gl/maps/NvpU3

xvi

   Jeannie McDonough and Paul Lonardo, (2011-03-01). *Caught in
the Act: A Courageous Family's Fight to Save Their Daughter from a Serial
Killer* (Kindle Locations 427-430). Penguin Group US. Kindle Edition.

xvii

John Luciew, http://www.pennlive.com/specialprojects/index.ssf/2010/08/law_enforc ement_tells_the_publ.html [retrieved 20 August 2014]. One has to credit Marsico for acknowledging his mistake.

xviii
      www.drc.ohio.gov/public/clemency_fautenberry.pdf

xix
      http://www.nj.com/hunterdon-county-democrat/index.ssf/2010/11/bloomsbury_has_high_crime_rate.html

xx
      https://www.facebook.com/rememberingmonicamassaro

xxi
      http://www.pomc.com/mw_stories/monica_massaro.html [retrieved on 23/09/2014]

xxii
      State of Kansas vs. Dennis L. Rader, Transcript of Pleas of Guilty, June 27, 2005.

xxiii
      http://furiousflush.blogspot.ca/2010/02/massachusetts-i-495-south-rest-area.html

xxiv
      For a detailed description of the killer's movements that night, see Chapter 6 in Jeannie McDonough, & Paul Lonardo,(2011-03-01). *Caught in the Act: A Courageous Family's Fight to Save Their Daughter from a Serial Killer,* Penguin Group US. Kindle Edition.

xxv
      http://webcache.googleusercontent.com/search?q=cache:jHI8NF 9iFN8J:www.lowellsun.com/ci_6871894+&cd=4&hl=en&ct=clnk&gl=ca [Retrieved 03/10/2014 2:16:58 p.m.]

xxvi
      McDonough p. 23

xxvii
      McDonough, p. 39

xxviii
      McDonough, p. 72

xxix
      http://www.sogknives.com/jungle-primitive-hardcased-black-partially-serrated.html [retrieved 2 October 2014]

xxx

Robert K. Ressler, Ann W. Burgess, and John E. Douglas, *Sexual Homicide: Patterns and Motives*, Lexington, Mass.: Lexington Books, 1988

xxxi

Peter Vronsky, *Serial Killers: The Method and Madness of Monsters,* New York: Berkley-Penguin Group, 2004, pp. 371-372

xxxii

McDonough, p. 63

xxxiii

Allen G. Breed, "Trucker a suspect in several attacks", *Associated Press* in *Star News*, September 13, 2007 http://news.google.com/newspapers?nid=1454&dat=20070913&id=Qrkm AAAAIBAJ&sjid=BSAEAAAAIBAJ&pg=6895,3697525 [retrieved 2 October 2014]

xxxiv

McDonough, p. 65

xxxv

McDonough, p. 70

xxxvi

McDonough, p. 85

xxxvii

http://www.amazon.com/Hunting-Humans-Rick-Ganz/dp/B00009KUA0 [retrieved 3 October 2014]

xxxviii

Kevin Kangas, Facebook message to Peter Vronsky, October 15, 2014. See: www.kangaskahnfilms.com

xxxix

US Department of Justice, Federal Bureau of Investigation, *VICAP Crime Analysis Report* (FD-676 (Rev. 3-11-86) OMB No. 1110-0011, Quantico VA, 1986

xl

http://www.fbi.gov/news/stories/2009/april/highwayserial_0406 09

xli

McDonough, p. 92

xlii

http://www.fbi.gov/news/stories/2008/august/vicap_080408

xliii

McDonough, p. 218
xliv
http://www.nj.com/hunterdon/index.ssf/2008/10/trucker_tells_h
ow_he_killed_wo.html
xlv
New Jersey Death Penalty Study Commission Report, Trenton, NJ:
2007, p. 1
xlvi
For horror stories on false convictions and why it happens, see the
recent: Mark Geragos and Pat Harris, *Mistrial: An Inside Look at How the
Criminal Justice System Works...and Sometimes Doesn't*, New York:
Penguin Group, 2014.
xlvii
http://patch.com/massachusetts/chelmsford/juveniles-caught-
shrink-wrapping-car [accessed 23 Oct 2014]
xlviii
http://kickass.to/dream-on-aerosmith-live-in-japan-dolby-pro-
logicii-384kbs-2-mp4-t8451758.html [Accessed 10 October 2014]
xlix
Behavioral Analysis Unit, National Center for the Analysis of
Violent Crime, Federal Bureau of Investigation, *Serial Murder: Pathways
for Investigation,* Washington, DC: Department of Justice, 2014, p. 50
l
Steven A. Egger, *The Killers among Us: An Examination of Serial
Murder and Its Investigation*, Upper Saddle River, N.J.: Prentice-Hall, 1998,
pp. 74–75
li
http://www.fbi.gov/news/stories/2009/april/highwayserial_0406
09
lii
P. E. Dietz, B. Harry, R. R. Hazelwood, "Detective Magazines:
Pornography for the Sexual Sadist?" *Journal of Forensic Sciences*, Vol. 31,
Issue 1, January 1986, pp. 197-211

Made in the USA
Lexington, KY
30 August 2016